22.4.08

Stalin

European History in Perspective
General Editor: Jeremy Black

Benjamin Arnold *Medieval Germany*
Ronald Asch *The Thirty Years' War*
Nigel Aston *The French Revolution, 1789–1804*
Nicholas Atkin *The Fifth French Republic*
Christopher Bartlett *Peace, War and the European Powers, 1814–1914*
Robert Bireley *The Refashioning of Catholicism, 1450–1700*
Donna Bohanan *Crown and Nobility in Early Modern France*
Arden Bucholz *Moltke and the German Wars, 1864–1871*
Patricia Clavin *The Great Depression, 1929–1939*
Paula Sutter Fichtner *The Habsburg Monarchy, 1490–1848*
Mark Galeotti *Gorbachev and his Revolution*
David Gates *Warfare in the Nineteenth Century*
Alexander Grab *Napoleon and the Transformation of Europe*
Martin P. Johnson *The Dreyfus Affair*
Paul Douglas Lockhart *Sweden in the Seventeenth Century*
Kevin McDermott *Stalin*
Graeme Murdock *Beyond Calvin*
Peter Musgrave *The Early Modern European Economy*
J. L. Price *The Dutch Republic in the Seventeenth Century*
A. W. Purdue *The Second World War*
Christopher Read *The Making and Breaking of the Soviet System*
Francisco J. Romero-Salvado *Twentieth-Century Spain*
Matthew S. Seligmann and Roderick R. McLean
Germany from Reich to Republic, 1871–1918
David A. Shafer *The Paris Commune*
Brendan Simms *The Struggle for Mastery in Germany, 1779–1850*
David Sturdy *Louis XIV*
David J. Sturdy *Richelieu and Mazarin*
Hunt Tooley *The Western Front*
Peter Waldron *The End of Imperial Russia, 1855–1917*
Peter G. Wallace *The Long European Reformation*
James D. White *Lenin*
Patrick Williams *Philip II*
Peter H. Wilson *From Reich to Revolution*

**European History in Perspective
Series Standing Order
ISBN 0–333–65056–5 hardcover
ISBN 0–333–65057–3 paperback**
(*outside North America only*)

You can receive future titles in this series as they are published by
placing a standing order. Please contact your bookseller or, in the case
of difficulty, write to us at the address below with your name and
address, the title of the series and the ISBN quoted above.

Customer Services Department, Palgrave Ltd
Houndmills, Basingstoke, Hampshire RG21 6XS, England

Stalin

Revolutionary in an Era of War

KEVIN McDERMOTT

palgrave
macmillan

First published 2006 by
PALGRAVE MACMILLAN
Houndmills, Basingstoke, Hampshire RG21 6XS and
175 Fifth Avenue, New York, N. Y. 10010
Companies and representatives throughout the world

PALGRAVE MACMILLAN is the global academic imprint of the Palgrave Macmillan division of St. Martin's Press, LLC and of Palgrave Macmillan Ltd. Macmillan® is a registered trademark in the United States, United Kingdom and other countries. Palgrave is a registered trademark in the European Union and other countries.

ISBN-13: 978–0–333–71121–7   hardback
ISBN-10: 0–333–71121–1   hardback
ISBN-13: 978–0–333–71122–4   paperback
ISBN-10: 0–333–71122–X   paperback

This book is printed on paper suitable for recycling and made from fully managed and sustained forest sources.

A catalogue record for this book is available from the British Library.
A catalog record for this book is available from the Library of Congress.

10   9   8   7   6   5   4   3   2   1
15   14   13   12   11   10   09   08   07   06

Printed in China

Dedicated to Susie,
Frances Vera
and
Alexander Leo

Contents

Acknowledgements

I have accumulated numerous scholarly debts in the writing of this volume: hearty thanks to my friends and colleagues Jeremy Agnew (Sheffield College), David Mayall (Sheffield Hallam University), Barry McLoughlin (Vienna University), Professor Arfon Rees (European University Institute, Florence) and Matthew Stibbe (Sheffield Hallam University) for their insights, suggestions and companionship. I am particularly indebted to Professor J. Arch Getty (University of California at Los Angeles) and Professor Alfred Rieber (Central European University, Budapest) for reading draft chapters, making astute critical comments and supplying me with sources. The expert advice willingly offered by Professors Getty and Rieber has immeasurably improved the book, though, needless to say, all mistakes and oversights remain my own. Special thanks to James Harris and Sarah Davies for kindly sending me the proofs of their excellent edited volume *Stalin: A New History* and to John Morison for his ideas on the structure of the book. I am also grateful for the support of my colleagues in the History Department at Sheffield Hallam University, notably John Baxendale, Tony Taylor and Alison Twells.

Greatest thanks, however, go to Dr Aleksandr Vatlin (Moscow State University), who acted as a research assistant in the former Communist Party Archives, kept me up to date with Russian historiography and contributed to this volume in many other respects. His work was generously financed by a British Academy Small Research Grant, which also funded my own study trips to the Moscow archives. While there, Dr Gennadii Bordiugov facilitated access to various documentary collections. In addition, I wish to acknowledge financial assistance from my Department.

I would like to express my appreciation to the hardworking librarians and Inter-Library Loan staff of the Collegiate Crescent Learning Centre,

Sheffield Hallam University. Last, but by no means least, thanks to my extremely patient Palgrave editor, Terka Acton. Many others would have given up on the project, but Terka stuck with me.

Finally, this book would not have been completed without the constant support and encouragement of Susan Reid, whose comprehensive knowledge of Stalinist culture and openness to diverse methodologies have helped shape my thinking in more ways than one. Our wonderful children, Frances and Alex, have endured living with the looming shadow of Uncle Joe for nigh on a decade, which is more than any kids should bear. I dedicate this book to them in the hope that one day they will somehow find it within themselves to forgive their father! In the meantime, I look forward to writing a biography of Harry Potter or Dr Xargle.

Parts of the Introduction and Chapter Four were published in 'Archives, Power and the "Cultural Turn": Reflections on Stalin and Stalinism', *Totalitarian Movements and Political Religions*, vol. 5, no. 1 (2004), pp. 5–24 and in '"To the Final Destruction of All Enemies!": New Approaches to Stalinist Terror', *History Teaching Review Year Book*, Scottish Association of Teachers of History, vol. 17 (2003), pp. 17–23. I thank the publishers for permission to reprint them here.

Note on transliteration: I have used the Library of Congress transliteration system with the exception of well-known names such as Trotsky (Trotskii), Zinoviev (Zinov'ev) and Gorky (Gor'kii).

Kevin McDermott (k.f.mcdermott@shu.ac.uk)

List of Abbreviations and Glossary of Terms

apparat	bureaucratic machinery or staff of an organisation
apparatchik(i)	full-time official(s) of the party-state bureaucracy
Bolsheviks	revolutionary faction of the RSDWP (see below) formed by Lenin in 1903
cadre(s)	full-time official(s) of party, trade union, military and other mass organisations
CC	Central Committee (of the Communist Party)
Cheka	Extraordinary Commission; acronym of the Soviet secret police, 1917–22
Cominform	Communist Information Bureau
Comintern	Communist International
dacha	country residence
Duma	Tsarist national parliament
ECCI	Executive Committee of the Communist International
Ezhovshchina	'the time of Ezhov'; mass terror of 1937–8 named after the NKVD chief, Nikolai Ezhov
Gensek	General Secretary (of the Communist Party)
GKO	State Defence Committee
glasnost'	'openness'; a key slogan of Mikhail Gorbachev in the 1980s
Gosplan	State Planning Committee
Gulag	Main Administration of Camps
KGB	Committee of State Security (post-Stalinist secret police)
Koba	Stalin's early pseudonym
kolkhoz(y)	collective farm(s)
komitetchik	'committeeman'
Komsomol	Union of Communist Youth

korenizatsiia	'indigenisation'; Soviet nationality policy in the 1920s and early 1930s
kulak	better-off peasant despised by most Bolsheviks
Mensheviks	moderate Marxist faction of the RSDWP (see below)
mir	peasant commune
Narkomindel	People's Commissariat of Foreign Affairs
NEP	New Economic Policy
nepmen	private traders permitted under NEP
NKVD	People's Commissariat of Internal Affairs; incorporated secret police in 1934
nomenklatura	list of key administrative appointments approved by the party
OGPU	United Main Political Administration; title of the Soviet secret police, 1923–34
Okhrana	Tsarist secret police
Orgburo	Organisational Bureau (of the Communist Party)
Politburo	Political Bureau (of the Communist Party)
praktik	'practical worker'
Pravda	*Truth*, Bolshevik daily newspaper
Rabkrin	Workers' and Peasants' Inspectorate
RCP(b)	Russian Communist Party (Bolsheviks)
RSDWP	Russian Social Democratic Workers' Party
Secretariat	body responsible for the day-to-day work of the Central Committee of the Communist Party
semerka	'the seven', an informal grouping of anti-Trotsky Politburo members
smychka	worker-peasant 'alliance' under NEP
soviet	council (of workers, peasants or soldiers)
Sovnarkom	Council of People's Commissars (Soviet government)
SPD	German Social Democratic Party
Stavka	wartime Supreme Command
troika	three-man sentencing body
USSR	Union of Soviet Socialist Republics
Vesenkha	Supreme Council of the National Economy
vozhd'	'The Leader' (with connotations of strength and vision)
vydvizhentsy	lower-class promotees of the 1930s

Archival Abbreviations

RGASPI	Russian State Archive of Socio-Political History
f.	*fond* (collection)
op.	*opis'* (inventory)
d.	*delo* (file)
l. or ll.	*list(y)* (folio(s))

Introduction

Stalin: Interpretations, Models and Personality

31 March 2005: I have just heard on BBC Radio 4 news that a small town in Siberia has decided to erect a statue to Josef Stalin, the first new monument to the Soviet dictator in over fifty years. In Volgograd, he is to sit alongside effigies of Winston Churchill and Franklin D. Roosevelt. The same report informed me that in a recent poll in Vladimir Putin's Russia over 40 per cent of participants believed that Stalin was a positive historical figure. Hence, it would appear that surprising numbers of Russians and Georgians, yearning for a 'strong hand', regard the tyrant as a great statesman and state-builder. Even if many others react with revulsion, it is evident that Stalin continues to exert a very powerful attraction not only on 'ordinary' people, but also scholars, journalists, TV broadcasters and their ilk. Why is this?

Interpretations and Issues

Interpretations of Iosif Vissarionovich Dzhugashvili, better known to the world as Josef Stalin, range from the sycophantic and adulatory to the vitriolic and condemnatory. In the West and among many anti-communist Russians today his image is overwhelmingly negative: he is quite simply a mass murderer. But this pejorative stereotype has not always been dominant, even in the 'free world'. Stalin is still in many ways, to adapt Churchill's oft-repeated assessment of Russia, a 'riddle wrapped in a mystery inside an enigma'. How, then, should the historian evaluate a man who consciously shrouded himself in secrecy and fostered a mythic 'cult of personality', who created multiple identities for himself, who has many achievements to his

1

name, but also metaphorically oceans of blood on his hands? Even after the partial opening of former Soviet party and state archives, we can never be sure about the man, his mentalities, motivations, fears and aims.[1] There is, it seems, little point in posing the question: 'will the real Stalin please stand up?' His actions and legacies will always be filtered through the distorting prism of ever-changing political and academic agendas: how exactly did the beneficent 'Uncle Joe' of 1941–5 become the malevolent 'Red Devil' of 1947–53?

These are just a few of the pitfalls that await any intrepid voyager into the 'Stalin debate'. Other no less awkward dilemmas abound. First is the intractable problem of the role of individual agency in history: was Stalin able to impose his will and aims on Soviet state and society as an all-powerful dictator, or was he a hostage of specific historical conjunctures, whose actions were largely determined by harsh socio-economic, cultural and political realities? How far should we agree with E. H. Carr's famous judgement that 'more than almost any other great man in history, Stalin illustrates the thesis that circumstances make the man, not the man the circumstances'?[2] Or to put it another way: how to elucidate high politics and top-level decision-making, while remaining sensitive to deep-seated social, cultural and economic trends in both pre- and post-revolutionary Russia? The perplexing relationships between agency and structure, between the individual leader and society, are never far from the surface.[3]

A second, more practical, issue concerns the sources and mechanisms of Stalin's power, how they were exercised, how they changed over time and how he came to dominate key institutions, such as the Communist Party and the security apparatuses. Indeed, the concept of power, its acquisition, maintenance, use and abuse, is crucial to any understanding of the *vozhd'* (strong Leader). There can be no doubt that Stalin concentrated unprecedented political authority in his hands – by the mid-1930s he personally held the ultimate sanction of life and death over thousands of Soviet citizens and his word was gospel on any subject he chose to pronounce on. But the limitations of this power are equally deserving of attention: which factors constrained Stalin's dictatorial authority? How far was his control 'total'? For many years it was axiomatic that Stalin achieved and centralised power by means of organisational acumen, coercion and 'totalitarian' terror, by the manipulation of state propaganda and the creation of an almost deified 'cult of the personality', attributes that remain highly relevant. In the 1970s and 1980s, however, scholars began to move beyond these conventional categories of power by identifying beneficiaries of the Stalinist system: those upwardly mobile workers and peasants who gained positions of responsibility and thus formed a social base of support for the regime. What role did mass legitimacy play in Stalin's acquisition and consolidation of power? To what extent were his policies 'popular'? How far did Stalinist values and mentalities penetrate social consciousness?

Closely linked to this is a third vexed problem: the historiographical and conceptual question of how best to incorporate into what is ostensibly a political biographical genre the recent findings of socio-cultural historians, who by focusing on the production of knowledge, the construction and use of language, and the related notion of 'subjectivity' have undoubtedly enriched our understanding of the diverse methods of Stalinist social integration and discipline. Yet this new research and methodology present a major dilemma for the modern biographer of Stalin – how far does the 'cultural turn' help the political historian grapple with the question of Stalin's personal power as opposed to the disparate means by which the cultural authorities and propagandists sought to strengthen and legitimise Soviet rule? Is there any intersection between the role of the individual historical actor and the multiple dispersal and reception of power in society?

A fourth factor is the highly charged moral dimension: should scholars seek to historicise the horrors of Stalinism and thus appear to attenuate his personal responsibility and justify the unjustifiable? Or should they routinely condemn the mass murder in the name of humanitarianism and decency? The vast scale of Soviet repression and the targeting of social and ethnic 'aliens' have compelled historians to compare Stalinist and Hitlerite exterminatory policies. Some detect a close moral equivalence between communist and Nazi terror, estimating that the former destroyed far more people than the latter, as many as 100 million worldwide.[4] Others, while fully recognising the enormity of Stalinist mass coercion, continue to emphasise the uniqueness of the Nazi Holocaust.[5]

A further key consideration is an assessment of the roles and inputs of Stalin's top colleagues, men such as Viacheslav Molotov, Lazar Kaganovich, Anastas Mikoian, 'Sergo' Ordzhonikidze, Kliment Voroshilov, Nikolai Ezhov, Andrei Zhdanov, Georgii Malenkov, Nikita Khrushchev and others. Were these figures merely manipulable cronies, puppets of the 'Leader'? Or were they power brokers in their own right, capable of influencing decision-making and implementation? How on a day-to-day basis did Stalin and his immediate entourage actually work together, and how did this relationship change over time? How did they arrive at decisions and policies: Stalin spoke and the marionettes dutifully followed? Or were the Molotovs and Kaganoviches able to preserve a measure of autonomy, even criticality, in their relations with Stalin? To what extent did the 'boss' delegate authority

to his subordinates and how did they attempt to deflect criticism when
things went wrong?

Finally, but by no means least, it is essential to evaluate the relative weight
of ideology and *realpolitik* in Stalin's internal and external policy-making.
Did Marxist-Leninist theory underlay his actions and his rise to supremacy?
Or did cold practical solutions to hard questions take precedence over
Bolshevik 'political correctness'? Did Stalin use ideology cynically and
brazenly to revise aspects of Marxism-Leninism to suit his immediate
purposes, or should he be taken seriously as an ideologist whose beliefs
informed his entire worldview and many of his policies? Is it indeed necessary to consider ideology and *realpolitik* as mutually exclusive? I explore this
question by proposing an unstable synthesis between them, at some junc-
tures theory gaining the upper hand, at others practical considerations, but
at all times a shifting combination of both was present.

These are tantalising and difficult issues and I do not pretend to 'solve' or
'answer' them in this slim book, although I attempt to face them squarely.
My aims are more modest. I seek to introduce readers to the latest western
and Russian research on Stalin and Stalinism in order to explore the inter-
play between the motivations of Stalin's policies, their actual implementation and their impact on the Soviet people. It goes without saying that for
the historian, Stalin should not be seen as some super-natural demon or
God. He was a product of his times and to a large extent shared the concerns, preoccupations and dilemmas of any politician of his era. His 'solutions' to these problems were often highly unorthodox, it is true, but it
could be argued that much of his thought and even actions can be sub-
sumed in European-wide phenomena – the expanding role of the interventionist welfare state in economic and social affairs, the notion of 'managing
the people', the quest to conquer nature, even the belief in changing
human nature itself. This idea of a universal drive to 'modernity', or in
James C. Scott's words 'high modernism',[6] shared by all industrialising states
is a central issue for many contemporary comparative historians of Stalinist
Russia. But this approach should not be seen as an attempt to relativise, or
make mundane, the horrors of Stalinism, the terroristic essence of which
has long been accepted. Indeed, recent archival discoveries tend to confirm,
rather than challenge, the central organisation of the mass repressions indi-
cating, for example, that detailed quotas of arrests and executions were
defined by leading NKVD officials and ratified by the Politburo, that Stalin
personally ordered the destruction of many central and local party-state
functionaries, and that the carnage was eventually curtailed by Stalin's and
Molotov's direct intervention in November 1938. Although the input of

lower-ranking regional bureaucrats, even ordinary Soviet citizens, in the Great Terror should never be ignored, the signal organising role of the 'centre' – Stalin and his top party and secret police collaborators – is surely beyond doubt.

A further important focus of this book is the contradictory nature of the system Stalin did so much to create. This notion of contradiction, or paradox, is central to my argument. The paradoxes are legion: Stalin as 'Leader, Teacher, Friend' of the Soviet people, and yet the oppressor of millions; Stalin as convinced Bolshevik revolutionary and yet the enforcer of traditional conservative social and cultural values; Stalin, the egalitarian communist, presides over a hierarchically ordered party and society; the 'heroic' God-like figure of the cult compared to the human frailty of the fallible individual; Stalin as arch 'anti-bureaucrat', and yet bureaucratic red-tape mushroomed under his leadership; Stalin as 'omnipotent dictator', and yet dependent on provincial cliques and subordinates to carry out his will; Stalin, proclaimed the doyen of Marxist internationalism abroad, actively promotes Russian chauvinist nationalism at home; Stalin, the 'peace-loving' diplomat, does his utmost in the 1930s to prepare for 'inevitable' war; the image of material abundance in Stalinist culture and propaganda compared to the dire shortages, rationing and poverty experienced by millions of Soviet citizens; the 'most democratic' constitutional state in the world in 1936 descends into the bloodbath of the Great Terror in 1937–8; and the 'all-powerful' modernising communist state finds itself constrained and undermined by the political culture of a 'backward' peasant society. To what extent are these paradoxes 'real' or are they merely the product of comparing Stalinist images, myths and slogans with reality? Are they explicable not only by changing circumstances and priorities, but also by contradictory impulses in Stalin's own personality and persona: the tensions between his social and ethnic origins as a Georgian 'peasant' raised in a violent borderland of the Tsarist Empire and his self-fashioned identity as a Great Russian 'proletarian' steadfastly defending the integrity and unity of the Soviet state?[7]

This contradictory essence of Stalin and Stalinism, long established among the scholarly community, clashes head-on with the popular image of Stalin as an omnipotent, omniscient and omnipresent 'oriental' despot, who controlled all aspects of Soviet public and private life by means of a totalitarian grip on power and mass repression. Such an image (which is not inherently wrong) emerged forcibly in anti-Stalinist Soviet fictional works like Aleksandr Solzhenitsyn's *The First Circle*, Vasilii Grossman's massive tomes *Life and Fate* and *Forever Flowing*, and Anatolii Rybakov's epic trilogy *Children*

of the Arbat, Fear and *Dust and Ashes.* A sanitised version has been presented
in English literature too, notably Robert Harris' block-busting novel
Archangel and Mervyn Jones' *Joseph.* A similar vulgarisation has also featured
in ostensibly 'factual' productions, such as the BBC 2 programme appropri-
ately entitled 'Stalin – the Red God', the Channel 5 offering 'Stalin' in the
series 'The Most Evil Men in History', Martin Amis' controversial historical
'study', *Koba the Dread,* and most recently the *Timewatch* reconstruction of
the dictator's death, 'Who Killed Stalin?' Analogous representations filled
the British press on the fiftieth anniversary of Stalin's demise in March 2003
and in a BBC radio broadcast from June 2003 the celebrated commentator
Alistair Cooke described Stalin as 'the maddest and most criminal of
tyrants....the paranoiac of the century' compared to whom 'Hitler was a de-
mented boy scout.'[8] This unproblematised discourse continues to inform
the views of many students in British universities today. If this volume helps
to break down these over-simplistic stereotypes, it will have served its
purpose.

'War-Revolution Model'

While writing this book I pondered the value of several approaches to the
Stalin Question. The one I finally chose to prioritise – what I have termed
the 'war-revolution model' – is outlined below. But it might be instructive
for readers to have a glimpse of another interesting framework, which I
eventually discarded, but which still, I think, offers fruitful avenues for
future research. That is the notion that Stalin was a man who sat unsteadily
astride not only a geographical-cultural border (Georgia/Russia and
East/West), but also a temporal border, namely the cusp of 'pre-moder-
nity' and 'modernity'. It was David Hoffmann's and Yanni Kotsonis' path-
breaking edited collection *Russian Modernity*[9] that set me thinking about
Stalin as a 'product' of both the pre-modern and modern world. I asked
myself if this could in any way help to explain the perplexing combination
of modernising elements – the extension of state intervention, the appeal
to mass politics, the ordering, measuring and surveillance of society – and
the 'neo-traditional' features – the conservative social values and policies,
the primordial concept of the nation, the quasi-religious and cultic sym-
bolism – which is so characteristic of Stalinism. It seemed to me that the
uneasy triumph of the 'modernising' tendencies in Stalin's make-up suggested that he was driven not so much by an age-old autocratic urge for
personal power, but by the universal twentieth-century mission of mobilis-

ing whole populations for economic growth and national security, albeit in his case taken to grotesque extremes. But in pursuing this line of reasoning I came slap-bang up against the danger of relativising Stalin's crimes by implicitly comparing them to the policies of any 'modern' industrialised state and leader. In other words, what differentiated Stalin, born in the late 1870s, from say Churchill, born in 1874? Both could be said to be influenced by 'pre-modern' and 'modern' discourses, but only one turned out a mass murderer. Couldn't the idea be applied to any epoch and individual? Finally, I was stymied by the problem of how to demonstrate convincingly the impact of 'pre-modern' attitudes and concepts on Stalin, and how best to weave this strand into an essentially narrative biography.

Before discussing my own 'model', I must outline how other scholars have addressed the 'Stalin phenomenon'. The multiple competing interpretations of Stalin and Stalinism have been impressively analysed by Giuseppe Boffa,[10] and in the mid-1990s Lars Lih expounded the 'anti-bureaucratic scenario' as the most appropriate framework for comprehending Stalin's mentality and *modus operandi*.[11] Ronald Suny has identified a vital combination of terror with legitimised authority as the source of Stalin's power,[12] and Robert Tucker's 'imperial-communist' theory emphasises Stalin's statesmanship, Russian nationalist inclinations and the continuities with his Tsarist predecessors.[13] More recently, three major studies have done much to broaden our understanding of the nature of Stalin's ideas and Stalinism in general. David Brandenberger has controversially revised the notion of 'national Bolshevism' as the central plank of Stalinist mass culture and mobilisation,[14] Erik van Ree has coined the term 'revolutionary patriotism' to encapsulate Stalin's political thought,[15] and E. A. Rees stresses the affinities between Stalinism and 'revolutionary Machiavellism'.[16] These specialist accounts of the Stalin phenomenon have been enriched by Tim McDaniel's *longue durée* perspective, which locates the contradictions of Stalinism (and Soviet socialism in general) in the interpenetration of Russian messianism, Marxist ideology and modernisation theory.[17]

Given the originality and explanatory potency of these works, one wonders whether there is room for yet another 'master narrative'. I think there is and hence I offer a 'war-revolution model' as arguably the key to Stalin's beliefs and actions. This construct should in no way be artificially stretched to encompass all aspects and specifics of his words and deeds, nor should it neglect the plurality of sources, aside from Marxism, of his political ideas, nor yet blind us to his pragmatism and reluctance to be hamstrung by ideology. Indeed, it should be recognised that ideology was often used *post hoc* to justify and re-justify practical decisions. Rather, I see the model as a useful tool for placing Stalin in historical perspective, helping us move away from the more populist images of him as a brutal tyrant motivated solely by power lust, sickly paranoia and personal 'evilness'. In my opinion, such 'analyses' simply will not do. Furthermore, it facilitates an understanding of the mental landscape of Soviet leaders and of the constraints and pressures under which they operated. It also links Stalin's main theoretical principle – the revolutionary socialist transformation of society – and the actions he adopted to achieve this goal – a war-like assault on 'backward' social strata, class 'aliens' and diverse 'enemies of the people'.

As far as the war part of the equation is concerned, it would hardly be an exaggeration to contend that Stalin's entire worldview and many of his policies were filtered through the prism of war, actual and potential, civil and international, and the dangers, hopes, risks and opportunities associated with these periods of crisis.[18] War and revolution were inextricably inter-related in Marxist-Leninist theory (socialist revolution as a result of imperialist wars, the inevitability of inter-imperialist wars and of interventionist wars against socialist states), but for Stalin war became also a central tenet of his *domestic* policies – the idea of an internal 'class war' against ubiquitous 'enemies' seemed to take possession of him by the early 1930s. At the same time, international war posed a major threat to his authority and regime. It was certainly not lost on Stalin that the Soviet state itself was the product of 'total war' and the military collapse of Tsarist Russia in 1917. He was utterly determined that no such fate would befall his creation. His nightmare must have been an aggressive anti-Soviet coalition of European and Asian powers bolstered by internal opponents and discontents both within and outside the party. Hence, the absolute imperative for security and military strength; hence, the brutality and extreme urgency of the 'revolution from above'; and hence, the Great Terror as an assault on a perceived 'fifth column' both in the party-state apparatuses and in society at large (kulaks, social marginals, criminals, former Mensheviks and SRs, ex-White Guards, and suspect ethnic groups). For Stalin, the stability of the regime, and therefore of the entire Revolution and his place within it, was threatened by foreign wars of invasion and by an internal class war with the peasantry, 'bourgeois specialists', and 'anti-Soviet' criminal elements, all potentially allied with various party oppositions and insubordinate bureaucrats.

Wars, civil wars and the threat of war and social unrest formed a constant leitmotiv in the political careers and personal experiences of all top Bolsheviks. The brutalising effects of the First World War and especially the vicious Civil War (1918–21) were formative for Stalin. The era of 'Total War' between 1914–45 and the fierce ideological battles between Left and Right (and *within* the Left) epitomised the international context of Stalin's rise to power and the construction of the Soviet command economy.[19] Furthermore, as Peter Holquist has argued, World War One gave a great boost to the notion of 'managing the people', a new mode of governance based partly on surveillance of popular moods and the idea of social transformation. This was not simply a Bolshevik or 'totalitarian' tendency, but one which marked a general shift to 'modern' forms of state and social organisation.[20] Military aphorisms littered Stalinist rhetoric – 'the industrial front', 'the collectivisation campaign' – and the typical Stalinist style of dress was a military tunic, breeches and leather boots, symbolic of the aggressive male assertiveness of Bolshevik culture. Finally, victory in the Great Patriotic War (1941–5) was *the* major legitimising factor for the regime, while conversely the relative liberalisation associated with the war years must have been viewed with great apprehension after 1945, which in turn partially accounts for the rapid restoration of the more coercive methods of 'High Stalinism'.

The 'revolution' part of my equation is, admittedly, more problematic, given the conservative nature of much of Stalinist legislation during the so-called 'Great Retreat', the supra-class nationalist rhetoric from the second half of the 1930s and the regime's reliance on the Soviet 'middle class', especially after World War Two. But regardless of these contradictory tendencies, it seems to me that we should take Stalin seriously as a Marxist revolutionary dedicated to the construction of socialism, however grossly distorted his vision in practice. The recent work mentioned above by Erik van Ree has controversially restored the centrality of Marxist ideology to Stalin's thought and action.[21] He devoted his whole life to the cause of socialist revolution and suffered for it under the Tsars. His belief in the creation of a 'new Soviet person' and in a rapid socialist transformation of Soviet society should not be underestimated. Indeed, the 'second revolution' of 1928–32 irrevocably changed the lives of millions of Soviet people – a revolution *par excellence*, and even the Great Purge can in part be construed as an anti-bureaucratic revolution against 'Menshevik' inertia, routine and cliques in the name of Bolshevik activism and ideological commitment.

Neither can we continue to assume that Stalin was merely interested in 'socialism in one country', as customary wisdom would have it. He never eschewed the ultimate goal of international revolution, combining a tireless drive for socialist construction in the USSR with a firm belief in the Soviet Union as the embodiment of the revolutionary idea. As Lars Lih has observed, 'as first servant of the state, he was also first servant of world revolution.'[22] In this sense, war and revolution were central to Stalin's and the Bolsheviks' lived experience and had a crucial impact on their thinking, self-perceptions and actions. Indeed, it is possible to make a strong case that Stalin emerged as undisputed leader of the party in 1928–9 precisely because he was widely viewed as the chief exponent of ideological radicalisation and revolutionary upheaval in a crisis situation epitomised by war scares and civil war mentalities. Finally, it must be recognised that Marxist-Leninist ideology itself was not a static unchanging entity. It was a dynamic body of thought that included diverse currents, opinions and trends, some libertarian, others authoritarian; some inclined to nationalist proclivities, others staunchly internationalist; some socio-culturally 'progressive', others more traditional and 'reactionary'. Stalin's position within these currents also changed according to internal and external circumstances; he cannot be pigeonholed in one camp or another. But at all times he remained, in his private writings as much as in his public utterances, firmly committed to the broad Marxist-Leninist vision of socialist transformation.

It should be clearly stated that this 'war-revolution model' is largely implicit in the main discourse of the text, with the exception of the Conclusion. However, the attentive reader will detect its unifying presence in all the chapters: Stalin's early commitment to a 'class war' understanding of Marxism; the crucial impact of the Bolshevik Revolution and particularly the Civil War on his subsequent career and mentality; his ambivalent attitude to the moderate New Economic Policy of the 1920s; his recourse to 'War Scares' and belief in the 'inevitable war' between socialism and capitalism; his violent revolutionary onslaught on Soviet society after 1928; the Great Terror as a reflection of his fear of a domestic 'fifth column' linked to hostile foreign governments in an atmosphere of looming war threats; his ideologically-driven hatred of the imperialist Great Powers; and the immense significance of the 'Great Patriotic War' and the Cold War in his emergence as a world statesman spreading 'revolution' throughout Central and Eastern Europe.

Stalin's Personality

Although this book is not intended to be a conventional 'great man' biography, an essential variable which must be explored is Stalin's personality. Like Hitler, Stalin was able to stamp his character on the style and substance of state politics – personality and power cannot be separated. Indeed, in Moshe Lewin's view, 'Stalin actually *became the system* and his personality acquired therefore a "systemic" dimension.'[23] He has been variously described as a gangster and hoodlum, a latter-day Genghis Khan, a criminal paranoiac or psychopath, motivated solely by megalomania and intense vindictiveness,[24] but also as a cold faceless bureaucratic mediocrity, a mysterious 'grey blur' in the famous words of one of his Menshevik rivals, even a 'weak dictator'.[25] I am no psychiatrist and hesitate to pronounce on the mental state of the General Secretary (Gensek), but there can be little doubt that Stalin possessed a damaged brutalised psyche and was an unusually self-contained man, who increasingly rarely displayed 'normal' human traits, such as friendship and relational bonds. That said, the discovery of many of Stalin's letters and other personal documents and the marginal comments he made on memoranda, reports and books combined with the insights of those close to him have allowed historians to piece together a more detailed image of the dictator's physiological landscape, his private life and its impact on his politics.

Simon Sebag Montefiore adopts this approach in his massive *Stalin: The Court of the Red Tsar*, which seeks to inject a 'human' element into a character who appears to be the very embodiment of impersonal inscrutability. Sebag Montefiore offers a vivid picture of the intrigues that surrounded Stalin, his extended family and political entourage in the 1930s and beyond. The resultant image of the 'Boss' is arguably overdrawn and sensationalised, but none the less interesting and provocative:

> the real Stalin was an energetic and vainglorious melodramatist who was exceptional in every way....The man inside was a super-intelligent and gifted politician for whom his own historic role was paramount, a nervy intellectual who manically read history and literature, a fidgety hypochondriac suffering from chronic tonsillitis, psoriasis, rheumatic aches from his deformed arm and the iciness of his Siberian exile. Garrulous, sociable and a fine singer, this lonely and unhappy man ruined every love relationship and friendship in his life by sacrificing happiness to political necessity and cannibalistic paranoia.[26]

The Stalin who emerges is no less monstrous than the traditional portraits, far from it; but by plumbing the depths of his familial and working relationships Sebag Montefiore has added an extra, though not unproblematic, dimension to our understanding of Stalin's motivations and *modus operandi*.

Robert Service in his recent biography summarises Stalin's complex character and conduct thus:

> Stalin in many ways behaved as a 'normal human being'. In fact he was very far from being 'normal'. He had a vast desire to dominate, punish and butcher. Often he also comported himself with oafish menace in private. But he could also be charming; he could attract passion and

admiration both from close comrades and an immense public audience. On occasion he could be modest. He was hard-working. He was capable of kindliness to relatives. He thought a lot about the good of the communist cause. Before he started killing them, most communists in the USSR and in the Comintern judged him to be functioning within the acceptable bounds of political conduct....He was also an intellectual, an administrator, a statesman and a party leader; he was a writer [and] editor....Privately he was, in his own way, a dedicated as well as bad-tempered husband and father. But he was unhealthy in mind and body. He had many talents, and used his intelligence to act out the roles he thought suited to his interests at any given time. He baffled, appalled, enraged, attracted and entranced his contemporaries. Most men and women of his lifetime, however, under-estimated him.[27]

While Service's account of Stalin is balanced and careful, I find more convincing Richard Overy's insistence that ultimately it was not Stalin's profound personality defects – envy, jealousy, petty ambitions, vainglory, vindictiveness, sadism, the search for fame – which adequately explain his brutal actions, relevant though they are. Rightly in my opinion, Overy emphasises that:

the one consistent strand in all his activity was the survival of the revolution and the defence of the first socialist state. Power with Stalin seems to have been power to preserve and enlarge the revolution and the state that represented it, not power simply for its own sake. The ambition to save the revolution became for Stalin a personal ambition, for at some point in the 1920s....Stalin came to see himself as the one Bolshevik leader who could steer the way with sufficient ruthlessness and singleness of purpose. His instinct for survival, his unfeeling destruction of thousands of his party comrades, his Machiavellian politics, point not to a personality warped by self-centred sadism, but to a man who used the weapons he understood to achieve the central purpose to which his life had been devoted since he was a teenager....[the] overriding historical imperative to construct communism.[28]

Thus, it was Stalin's warlike commitment to the Marxist revolutionary ideal (or at least his understanding of it) that better accounts for the terroristic methods he employed in the struggle for the communist utopia.

A final key insight is that Stalin was a *litsedei*, a man of many faces. It has been argued by a leading American scholar that there were 'several Stalins':

'Stalin the harsh schoolmaster' severely chastising his pupil-colleagues, 'Stalin the wise padrone' patiently soothing relations with visiting western statesmen, and 'Stalin the grand editor' scrupulously reviewing and editing all major documents of state. What emerges is a contradictory figure whose characteristics and comportment are constantly changing, whose personality shifts from one month to the next, and whose policies result in one crisis after another.[29] This interpretation reiterates Kaganovich's assessment of his boss. 'There were various Stalins', Kaganovich said shortly before his death in 1991. 'Post-war was one Stalin, the pre-war was another. Between 1932 and the 1940s was yet another. Before 1932 he was entirely different. He changed. I saw at least five or six different Stalins.'[30] Noteworthy here is Kaganovich's emphasis on the turning point of 1932. The 'boss' seems to have altered irrevocably after the traumatic suicide of his second wife, Nadezhda Allilueva, in November of that year. Hitherto capable of Georgian-style hospitality, sociability and geniality at his country *dacha* at Zubalovo, which was regularly a party haunt for his extended family and members of his political 'clan', from then on Stalin began to withdraw into himself, his kinship structure shattered and his private stability ruined.[31]

This notion of 'several Stalins' is a useful corrective against over-simplification and cosy monocausal explanations of his actions and attitudes. It helps us appreciate the dynamic nature of his power from *primus inter pares* in, say, 1928–9 to unassailable dictator a decade later. It suggests that, de-pending on the situation and his interlocutor, Stalin, like all successful politi-cians, could be a consummate actor, tailoring his remarks to fit the audience, and a master of deception, feigning moderation, even amiability. Finally, it is a salient reminder that Stalin was prey to vacillations, inconsistencies and *ad hoc* responses to unforeseen circumstances. 'My' Stalin is, thus, a more human figure, not in the sense of emphasising his private life and relation-ships or indulging in fantasies about his positive characteristics and achieve-ments, but in recognising in him aspects of a 'normal' politician. Like Churchill or Roosevelt, Stalin frequently faced profound crises to which there were no self-evident solutions, had to deal with incompetent and possi-bly insubordinate officials and a recalcitrant society, at times must have felt overwhelmed with the complexity of domestic and foreign situations, and therefore may have experienced a measure of powerlessness. Surely even the 'omnipotent' Stalin may on occasion have felt unable to cope and may have had cause to doubt his abilities and policy preferences? The dreadful days after 22 June 1941 are a case in point. None of this seeks to diminish his overall control of Soviet decision-making, or attenuate his cruelty, brutality and overweening self-confidence. But it does complicate the over-simplified

stereotypical image of the self-possessed arrogant dictator in whom all power
and knowledge is vested.

* * * * * * *

The book is structured broadly chronologically, the main focus being on the
period 1917–53, the years of Stalin's rise to power and undisputed rule over
the Soviet party and state. Relatively little is known for sure about his
Georgian childhood, youth and exiles in Tsarist Russia. Although speculation about the psychological impact of his abusive father, loving mother,
and seminary education is interesting, it lies largely outside the framework
of this text, because, while I do not totally ignore the psycho-analytical
approach, I find more persuasive those interpretations that place the young
Stalin in the socio-cultural and political context of a modernising Georgian
borderland. Stalin's Marxism, his gradual rise to prominence in the pre-revolutionary Bolshevik Party, and his actions during the massive upheavals of
1917–21 are discussed in chapter 1, 'Revolutionary'.

We know much more about Stalin's activities in the inner-party power
struggles of the 1920s, and recent writings and archival sources have not substantially altered our knowledge. Stalin's vicious, and ultimately successful,
factional struggles against first Trotsky, then against the United Opposition
(Trotsky-Zinoviev-Kamenev), and finally against the Bukharinite 'Right' left
him by 1929 as *primus inter pares* in the Politburo and recognised leader of
the Soviet state. In chapter 2, entitled 'Oligarch', I trace these mercurial
battles through the prism of the domestic and foreign policy clashes of the
NEP era, Stalin's building of a collegial clan of devoted followers, and his
undoubted abilities as a party organiser and 'workaholic' leader.

In the third chapter, 'Moderniser', I examine Stalin's 'solution' to the
economic crises of NEP in the late 1920s and early 1930s. The prime focus is
on his 'revolution from above', that intensely rapid state-led socio-economic
transformation of the Soviet Union based on the forced collectivisation of
agriculture, the 'elimination of the kulaks as a class', and unheard-of tempos
of industrial growth, all in the name of 'constructing socialism' and drag-
ging Russia into the twentieth century. The result was a drastic reduction in
the urban standard of living, the unprecedented growth of the Gulag system
of labour camps, and most horrifically the Great Famine of 1932–3, which
claimed the lives of at least five to six million peasants. How to judge Stalin
as a 'necessary' moderniser against the backdrop of this unspeakable human
suffering? Other important themes such as the nationality question, social
and cultural policy will be discussed in an attempt to gauge the 'modernity'
or 'neo-traditionalism' of the Stalinist polity.

The momentous transition from *primus inter pares* to unassailable tyrant forms the basis of chapter 4, 'Dictator'. The emphasis is on the Terror and recent historical explanations of this phenomenon. In the course of the 1930s, the nature of Stalin's power substantially changed. If in the early years of the decade he often sought his colleagues' advice, operated generally through the formal channels of the Politburo as a collective decision-making body, and maintained comradely relations with his associates, then by the Great Terror (1936–8) Stalin had proved himself capable of physically destroying colleagues, 'friends', even close relatives, making any survivor totally dependent on him. He brooked no opposition, by-passed the Politburo, and ruled through informal sub-committees and often drunken gatherings at his country residence (*dacha*). His capriciousness became even more pronounced after the war, when politics in his entourage appeared to degenerate into an almost Byzantine complex of intrigue, back-stabbing and currying of the tyrant's favour. And yet no individual can attain 'total' power and mastery over complex political and socio-economic processes, particularly in a state as vast as the Soviet Union. What, then, were the limits and constraints on Stalin's apparent omnipotence and how did he attempt to free himself from them?

In chapter 5, 'Warlord', I back track a little to evaluate Stalin's impact on military strategy in the 1920s and 1930s and assess his record as the 'Generalissimo' of the Soviet armed forces. The Second World War, or Great Patriotic War (1941–5) as it is known in Russia, represented the supreme test of the leader and the system he had created. In many ways, these years were the lowest and highest in his career: the ignominy of Hitler's Operation Barbarossa, the timing of which Stalin had obstinately refused to accept, and the resultant destruction of large portions of the Red Army and air force contrast markedly with such turning-points as the Battle of Stalingrad and the ultimate triumph over the Nazis. Stalin had emerged victorious from the 'war of the century' and the USSR was soon to become the second superpower in the world. How much credit does Stalin deserve for this truly historic achievement? How did he mature as a military strategist during the war? Did the Soviet Union win the life-and-death struggle with Nazism because of, or despite, Uncle Joe's policies?

The final chapter, 'Statesman', begins with an appraisal of the impact of World War II on the USSR and an assessment of Stalin's power under 'High Stalinism'. The prime focus, however, is on his performance in the field of international relations and diplomacy, concentrating on the early Cold War period. It is commonly assumed that until the war Stalin took scant interest in foreign affairs, preferring to concentrate on building 'socialism in one country'. Archival materials have proven this assumption to be woefully wide of the mark. Throughout the interwar period, Stalin devoted a substantial amount of his time to the international position of the USSR and regularly intervened in policy and decision-making, not only in official Soviet diplomacy but also in the affairs of the Communist International (Comintern), the worldwide organisation of communist parties set up by Lenin in 1919. Indeed, the signing of the Nazi-Soviet Pact of August 1939 was largely his doing, as was the 'Sovietisation' of Central and Eastern Europe after 1945. Which principles drove his foreign policy? Was he a far-sighted diplomat, or a self-deluded dilettante? How successfully did the dictator defend the national and security interests of the Soviet Union? The chapter concludes with an overview of Stalin's still mysterious end, locating it in a broader 'paradigm of death' that, arguably, haunted him for many years.

Needless to say, there are no definitive answers to the 'Stalin phenomenon'. Scholars will never reach a consensus on his motivations, achievements, crimes and legacy, and nor should they. The continuing declassification of hitherto top secret Russian archival documents will no doubt add nuance to our understanding of this elusive tyrant. What follows is my contribution to the on-going Stalin debate. I can only hope my efforts have not been in vain.

Chapter 1: Revolutionary

What made an ordinary bright Georgian lad a dedicated Marxist revolutionary and one of the leaders of the Bolshevik Party? How, if at all, did Stalin's
formative years impact on his subsequent beliefs and actions? What aspects
of his personality, upbringing, education and environment shed light on the
mature adult? Although much of Stalin's boyhood, adolescence and early
manhood are still shrouded in mystery and myth, we know enough to trace
his development from Orthodox seminarist to revolutionary activist to
Bolshevik oligarch. This elusive task of reconstruction can best be undertaken if we eschew monocausal explanations for Stalin's unusual odyssey and
accept that multi-faceted approaches – psycho-historical, socio-cultural and
politico-ideological – are required to grasp the complex forging of any individual's identity. The historian's work is made all the harder in Stalin's case
in that he took great pains to conceal evidence about his early life and deliberately fashioned and re-fashioned his own biography and identity for political purposes helped by a legion of propagandists and sycophants. Archival
sources made accessible since the collapse of the Soviet Union have added a
few new 'facts' and nuances, but still obfuscation all too often reigns. Hence,
the following pages, which contain their fair share of 'might haves' and
'it appears', should not be seen as a definitive account of Stalin's pre-
revolutionary pilgrimage, but rather as a brief narrative of his early life and a
critical survey of existing historiography.

The Young Dzhugashvili

Born the only surviving child to poor parents on 6 December 1878[1] in
the small Georgian town of Gori, Iosif Dzhugashvili (transcribed from the

Georgian as Ioseb Jughashvili) endured a tough childhood characterised, so
it is always alleged, by harsh beatings, especially from his drunken father, ill
health and an incongruous keen sense of humour, fine singing voice and
love of poetry and nature.[2] Much has been made of the violent abuse meted
out by his father, but such treatment was relatively common at this time,
even in 'civilised' Victorian Britain, and we cannot adduce a direct causal relationship between the young Iosif's sufferings and the later actions of the
General Secretary of the Communist Party. There was nothing in Stalin's
early family life that suggested a mass murderer was in the making.
Physically, he was rather unprepossessing – his face was pock-marked, the
second and third toes of his left foot were joined, he suffered from a chroni-
cally stiff left arm, probably as a result of a serious childhood accident, and
grew to be no taller than five feet five inches. Nevertheless, he was a preco-
cious, gifted, energetic and by all accounts strong boy, quite capable of
looking after himself. His father, Vissarion, was a cobbler and his mother,
Ekaterina, a devoutly religious woman from an aspiring peasant family.
Sometime around 1884, Vissarion found work in a large shoe factory in the
capital city Tiflis (Tbilisi), returning home now and again. Ekaterina remained in Gori to support her young son by eking out a meagre living as a
washerwoman and seamstress. The parents clashed deeply over Iosif's
future. Vissarion attempted to make a cobbler of him, at one point drag-
ging the lad off to Tiflis to work in the shoe factory, Stalin's only first-hand,
but none the less significant, experience of the degradation of manual
labour. Vissarion died in Tiflis, probably in 1909. Ekaterina had loftier aims
and was utterly determined that Iosif should become an Orthodox priest.

Consequently, regardless of his impoverished upbringing, Dzhugashvili
gained a better formal education than many of his contemporaries. He attended the Gori Church School, where he was a true believer and an excellent pupil, and became proficient in the Russian language, though always
spoke it with a thick Georgian accent laced with the occasional grammatical
error. From 1894 to 1899, at his mother's insistence he trained to be a priest
at the Orthodox Seminary in Tiflis. In these years the seminary was the seat
of high learning in Georgia with a richly deserved reputation for student
radicalism and fierce anti-Russian sentiment, an atmosphere which undoubtedly impacted on the budding priest. It is here, in the stiflingly oppressive environment of the seminary, that we can begin to trace for the first
time Iosif's pilgrimage from solid conformist to militant Marxist. There was
nothing unusual about his entry into the clandestine world of the student
revolutionary movement. Although initially he continued to be a most dili-
gent scholar earning top marks, even for theological studies, by 1896–7 he

was coming under the sway of radical activists, eagerly devouring proscribed literary and historical works and throwing himself into the role of autodidact. He continued to be a voracious reader for the rest of his life. He claimed to get through as many as five hundred pages a day and his library contained approximately 20,000 volumes.[3] Stalin may have lacked the oratorical and intellectual prowess of a Lenin, Trotsky or Bukharin, but he was certainly no fool.

It was in these years, 1897–8, that Dzhugashvili came into contact for the first time with Marxist ideas and study circles, but it should be emphasised that his conversion was cautious and gradual, including a flirtation with Georgian nationalism and possibly with peasant based Populism. He was influenced by local Marxists, notably Lado Ketskhoveli, under whose guidance he conducted propaganda among small groups of Tiflis railway workers. Contrary to the myths later peddled by Stalinist apologists, he was not a Marxist by 1894–5 and he played no leading role in establishing Marxist study circles in the seminary. As a pupil he had become acutely resentful of the repressive nature of both the religious institution and the Tsarist regime – the state-imposed 'Russification' campaigns and the insistence on teaching in the Russian language, the 'outrageous regime' of the monk-tutors, most of whom were Russians and despised Georgian culture, the 'jesuitical methods' of their 'spying [and] prying' on students[4] and the harsh social realities of a steadily modernising Tiflis. By the time he was dismissed in May 1899 – not as he would claim for disseminating Marxist propaganda, but for absenting himself from examinations without good reason – Dzhugashvili was on the verge of becoming a committed revolutionary-agitator spurred by a deep hatred of the Russian governing classes and an awareness of the crass social inequities he saw around him.

But he was not yet a fully paid up member of the Marxist movement. For over a year, it seems, he was employed at the Tiflis Observatory taking meteorological readings, some of which survive to this day. However, he continued his activities among the local workforce, hence attracting the attention of the police. In March 1901, following a raid on the Observatory, he took the momentous decision to go underground. From now on, ill nourished, clad in the dirty black shirt, red tie and unpolished shoes considered *de rigueur* for the socialist militant, and presumably surviving on paltry financial resources, Dzhugashvili was to devote his life, whether he knew it or not then, to the cause of the professional revolutionary. Symbolically, by this time he had adopted the fantasy nickname of his boyhood, Koba (meaning, apparently, 'The Indomitable' in Turkish vernacular), as his underground pseudonym, although he first published under this name only in 1906. Koba was the Georgian literary hero-outlaw, who in the popular novel *The Patricide* led the people against Tsarist oppression. We can surmise that the young Stalin's self-image was of a noble vengeful rebel resisting injustice in the name of the downtrodden masses. The name Koba stuck and friends and enemies alike, particularly Georgians, used it well into the 1930s.

How far Stalin's family background, social and ethnic position, and religious education help to explain his development as a revolutionary is open to question, but one scholar has argued that:

> Stalin was undoubtedly a compound social victim: a member of a humiliated minority in the Russian Empire; a boy whose father was a failure by most measures and whose mother did domestic work; a dutiful and gifted child subjected to the stultifying regime of a claustrophobic seminary; a romantic youth looking to the past for his values who was forced, ultimately, to choose the future.[5]

Stalin's future in 1900 lay in the revolutionary Marxist underground movement, a milieu which shaped his intellectual evolution and social identity and eventually gave him the opportunity to break out from the parochial Caucasian environment to the wider Russian national scene.

The Revolutionary Underground

The Georgian revolutionary movement to which Koba had committed himself was dominated in the early years of the twentieth century by Menshevism, a relatively moderate form of Marxism broadly analogous to mainstream European Social Democracy, or more accurately its left wing. By contrast, he was attracted to Bolshevism, the radical wing of Russian socialism led by the charismatic Vladimir Ilich Lenin, and it is safe to assume that by the end of 1904 at the latest Koba had become a convinced 'Leninist' and ardent adherent of the Bolsheviks in their doctrinal and organisational disputes with the Mensheviks. Formally, the Bolsheviks and Mensheviks were unified in the Russian Social Democratic Workers' Party (RSDWP, founded in 1898), but after 1903 the organisation split into two factions following Lenin's insistence, bluntly argued in his major piece *What is to be Done?* (1902), that the party should be a small conspiratorial body composed of totally dedicated professional revolutionaries whose aim was to bring socialist consciousness to the working masses from without. Left to their own devices – the 'spontaneous' movement, as the Leninists disparagingly termed it –

proletarians would only achieve a 'trade union consciousness' based on material and economic needs, not political and ideological convictions.[6] In many ways, the Mensheviks shared the Bolsheviks' revolutionary credentials, both factions being overtly Marxist in orientation and both fundamentally opposed to the repressive Tsarist state. Nevertheless, the Mensheviks were prepared to accept that the party should be open to all who supported its platform, tended to adopt a more conciliatory stance towards non-party organisations and the non-proletarian classes, and after the abortive Revolution of 1905–06 were more willing to participate in electoral and parliamentary activities.

To be a revolutionary of whatever hue was a dangerous 'profession' in Russia. Forever on the run from the *Okhrana*, the Tsarist secret police, the threat of arrest and internal or external exile hung over every anti-state rebel. Physical injury, sometimes the ultimate sacrifice, was not infrequent. In this atmosphere, class-based hatred, internecine intrigue and clandestine conspiracy became second nature to many subterranean militants, particularly Bolsheviks. It was as a member of the revolutionary underground in the early 1900s that Koba proved himself a capable organiser and party stalwart among the emergent working classes of Transcaucasia. But what exactly did it mean to be an illegal 'undergrounder'? Above all, Koba's was a highly itinerant existence. He operated in several towns – Tiflis, Batumi, Kutaisi and Baku – flitting from one 'safe-house' to another and endlessly dodging the police. Together with his co-revolutionaries he established secret printing presses, wrote numerous anti-Tsarist articles, leaflets and manifestoes, gave lectures to groups of workers on the virtues of Marxism, helped to organise strikes and protest marches and engaged in interminable debates with his colleagues and enemies over 'correct' strategies and tactics. Most importantly, while deep in the underground Koba struggled constantly and sometimes successfully to create Bolshevik-dominated party committees, a tough job in most parts of the Caucasus. Koba's anti-Menshevik factional activities in the Social Democratic Party became almost legendary and he was not averse to using strong-arm methods: one leading local Menshevik famously described him as a 'disorganiser' and 'madman'. More positively, Koba must have possessed a certain charisma as he was highly adept at gathering a tight-knit loyal band of followers, an essential attribute that would figure prominently throughout his life. 'Sergo' Ordzhonikidze, Avel Enukidze and Kliment Voroshilov were among those early friends and co-workers who would later become firm 'Stalinists'.

Among his co-revolutionaries in the Caucasus, Koba soon acquired a reputation for being coarse, vindictive, frequently rude; he made enemies fast and his political foes noted portentously a tendency to despotic behaviour. By all accounts, he developed an aloofness and a contempt for 'wavering intellectuals', preferring practical work among ordinary labourers, though even here he appears to have functioned best in small groups and harboured a superior attitude to proletarians. In the harsh world of inter-factional sectarian struggles, Koba was a fiery, objectionable and resolute protagonist. 'He spoke with cruelty and hostility', remembered one adversary. 'His words were imbued with raw power and determination. He was often sarcastic or ironical....Sometimes he would....curse obscenely.' Upbraided by his listeners, he would apologise 'explaining that he was speaking the language of the proletariat'.[7] He was deeply intolerant of opposing viewpoints and something of a loner. He also displayed anti-semitic proclivities, as in his commentary on the national composition of the delegates to the London congress of the RSDWP in May 1907. Koba wrote: 'one of the Bolsheviks....observed in jest that the Mensheviks constituted a Jewish group while the Bolsheviks constituted a true-Russian group and, therefore, it wouldn't be a bad idea for us Bolsheviks to organise a pogrom in the Party.'[8] According to one memoirist, in 1905 Koba in a speech to unimpressed Georgian workers had referred to several leading Mensheviks as 'circumcised Yids'.[9] Whether such outbursts reflected a genuine anti-semitic streak or were tactical devices to lambaste the hated Mensheviks is not clear, but they provide an unpleasant foretaste of Stalin's post-war assault on Soviet Jewry. In general, the image these disagreeable traits conjure of the young revolutionary is that of a hard-headed self-confident, but vulgar man who was prepared to engage in subterfuge, slander and personal malice. That said, Stalin, who had a sharp logical mind, was able to attenuate these urges when deemed necessary and we should be wary of a strictly teleological interpretation of them.

In addition to focusing on the many negative aspects of his personality and *modus operandi*, scholars have also speculated that Koba was a Tsarist secret police spy and that he was directly or indirectly involved in violent bank 'expropriations' (robberies) with the aim of filling empty Bolshevik coffers. Evidence exists for both claims, but hard proof is still lacking. In a recent volume Ronald Brackman insists that Stalin was indeed an Okhrana *agent provocateur* and that this 'fact' explains the hidden motives behind the Great Purges of the 1930s.[10] In my opinion, Brackman's evidence for both assertions is neither convincing nor adequately referenced. It is possible that the young revolutionary on occasion anonymously tipped off the Okhrana as to the whereabouts of his political rivals, but this does not mean that Stalin was a paid agent of the police or sought to undermine the party and movement. As for Koba 'the robber-bandit', Miklos Kun, citing archival sources, has concluded that from late 1904 or early 1905 '*Stalin took part in drawing up plans for expropriations*, including the most notorious attack in Erevan Square, Tiflis in June 1907 in which several people were killed. Kun argues that as a result he was in all likelihood temporarily expelled from the party, an act Stalin fervently denied as late as 1918.[11] Whatever the case, it is more or less certain that Koba never personally participated in armed hold-ups, his involvement being restricted to a logistical level. Lenin reportedly valued Koba's 'technical' work and Stalin himself, even when asked directly by an interviewer in the 1930s, refused to comment on this controversial aspect of his underground life, perhaps a tacit sign of his complicity.

By the turn of the century Koba-Dzhugashvili had already come to the attention of the authorities and he was arrested, imprisoned and exiled to Siberia on several occasions in the 1900s and 1910s. Among his temporary homes in the chilling climes of the north and east were Novaia Uda, Solvychegodsk, Vologda, Monastyrskoe, Kureika and Achinsk. His longest term of banishment was from February 1913 to February 1917, a full four years in which, apparently, he improved his hunting and fishing skills. It is ru-moured that he fathered at least one child on his Siberian sojourns. In general, Stalin's private life was subordinated to his professional revolutionary activities in line with Bolshevik political culture. A good example is his rela-tionship with his first wife and his attitude to parental duties. Yet here for a rare moment we also gain a glimpse of Stalin the sentient human being. As ever, details are scanty and there is much confusion over precise dates, but it appears that sometime in 1905 (possibly 1904 or 1906!) he married Ekaterina Svanidze, a Georgian whose father and brother were active in the Marxist movement. The couple lived together sporadically and in difficult conditions in Tiflis, Stalin travelling to various destinations on party business. In March 1907 (some say 1908) a son, Iakov, was born, but tragically within a few months Ekaterina died either from tuberculosis or post-childbirth complica-tions. Although some accounts dramatise the effects of her untimely demise on Stalin – 'she is dead and with her my last warm feelings for human beings have died'[12] – it is probable that for a while he was devastated by his loss. The infant Iakov was brought up by Ekaterina's sisters. Stalin rejected him, scarcely saw him before he was twenty and paid him little attention after that. There was no time or inclination to be a model father.

Sources of Stalin's Marxism and Social Identity

The underground Koba was not only skilled as a political intriguer and in-fighter. He was also a propagandist with more than a passing interest in basic Marxist theory. Even a cursory glance at his early writings, which were all composed in Georgian, shows a fascination with the class struggle, the proletariat's bloody revenge on their persecutors and the revolutionary efficacy of 'the street' – mass demonstrations, violent strikes, the historic value of confrontations with the Tsarist 'bullet and whip'. For instance, in March 1902 he bemoaned the position of 'us' workers in stark terms: 'Others live off our labour; they drink our blood; our oppressors quench their thirst with the tears of our wives, children and relatives....Blood to such a government, may it be cursed!' In January 1905 at the start of the abortive revolution, he incited the proletariat to 'take revenge' for the 'valiant comrades who were murdered' by the police: 'It is time to *destroy* the tsarist government! And we *will destroy* it.' In June of the same year he wrote: 'When the enemy sheds tears, is killed, moans and writhes with pain, then we must beat the drums and be happy.' Again in August he demands: 'Blood for blood and death for death – that is how we will answer! To arms, on to revenge, long live the insurrection!'[13] These sentiments could be dismissed as the melodramatic ramblings of a young hothead and indeed Koba would soon enough adopt more moderate positions, but Erik van Ree, an expert on Stalin's political thought, has recently concluded that he was and remained 'a convinced adherent of the Bolshevik ideology of murderous class war.'[14]

Similarly, one of Stalin's leading biographers, Robert C. Tucker, argued over thirty years ago that what drew the rebellious Dzhugashvili to Marxism, and later to Lenin's militant interpretation of it, was 'the grand theme of class war....[its] vision of past and present society as a great battleground where-on two hostile forces – bourgeoisie and proletariat – are locked in mortal combat.' In this Manichean universe, one or other – 'us' or 'them' – must definitively win the historic struggle. Early in his underground activities, it appears Koba had become convinced that armed revolution was the decisive means of crushing Tsarism. This underlying belief in a messianic class war can be traced throughout Stalin's subsequent career and, though undoubtedly co-existing with more pragmatic inclinations, it is a constant leitmotiv of both his thought and actions. Tucker's emphasis on Koba's interest in, and firm grasp of, basic Marxist theory is well-placed, helping us to comprehend his growth and relative success as a Bolshevik propagandist. Indeed, 'a knowledge of the fundamentals of Marxism and the ability to explain them to ordinary workers were Djugashvili's chief stock-in-trade as a professional revolutionary'. As such, they were one of his greatest strengths. In short, Stalin took ideas seriously, albeit at an unsophisticated level, so much so that he composed a lengthy theoretical tract in late 1906 and early

1907 entitled 'Anarchism or Socialism?' in which he expounded crudely on the 'dialectical method'. For him, Marxist ideology was a means of understanding the world around him and of transforming that world along socialist lines. Tucker also speculates that in Bolshevism's 'hard' revolutionary essence Stalin found a spiritual and psychological home that fitted easily with the needs of his militant rebel personality.[15]

Tucker's 'psycho-historical' approach to Stalin's intellectual development proved highly influential, but to a large extent has been superseded by a more socio-cultural interpretation associated with two American academics, Alfred J. Rieber and Ronald Grigor Suny. It is in the diverse and rapidly shifting socio-cultural and multi-ethnic conditions of an imperial periphery, Georgia and the Caucasus as a whole, that these two scholars locate Stalin's odyssey from aspirant priest to Marxist revolutionary. Although concentrating on different factors, both Rieber and Suny emphasise the broader social contexts that had a seminal effect on Stalin's evolving mentality and outlook: the 'cult of violence' and traditions of resistance, rebellion and socially sanctioned 'blood revenge' embedded in the Caucasian consciousness; the 'warrior' and 'honour and shame' society in which the reliance on personal trust and the constant fear of betrayal were intimately interwoven; and the multiple channels of cultural and intellectual currents including Georgian nationalism, Populism and various adapted forms of 'western' Marxism. Rieber weaves a complex argument in which he seeks to integrate Stalin's personal and political development. Most significantly, he maintains that in the first two decades of the twentieth century Stalin, as a man of the imperial borderlands, forged a social identity combining Georgian, Russian and proletarian components in order to promote specific longer-term political goals including his vision of a centralised multi-cultural Soviet state and society. The historic salience of this is that by 'constructing and disseminating a multiple identity, he could appeal in the 1920s and 1930s to all sections of the party: the Great Russian centralizers, the supporters of cultural autonomy among the nationalities and the lower strata, all of whom....came to trust him'.[16] In an era of mass politics, Stalin could claim to be a 'man of the people' from humble origins espousing broadly popular policies. Thus, Rieber's innovative interpretation enriches our understanding of important sources of Stalin's power and authority.

Suny likewise insists that Stalin's evolution can best be reconstructed by placing the young Dzhugashvili-Koba firmly in his cultural milieu and by tracing his formative experiences in the Caucasian labour movement.[17] Suny's early Stalin is a product of successive 'cultural' influences – the Georgian context, the 'seminary', the 'intelligentsia', the 'movement' and finally the 'party'. Examining Stalin's operations in the oil-rich city of Baku from June 1907 to May 1908, Suny argues that it was here that Koba became involved in the everyday struggles of the working class. He was drawn into trade union activities, particularly among the unskilled Muslim oil workers, and began to advocate more pragmatic policies in light of the Tsarist 'reaction' after the failure of the Revolution in 1905–07. At the same time, he prioritised tireless underground organisational work and played a leading role in securing Bolshevik dominance of the local Baku Social Democratic bodies, an important triumph. In short, Koba not only consolidated his skills as a consummate underground 'committeeman' (*komitetchik*), actively pursuing anti-Menshevik manoeuvres and strengthening the Bolshevik faction, but he also emerged as a capable practical worker (*praktik*), seeking to defend the material interests of local proletarians.

According to his own later testimony, it was in Baku that Stalin became a 'journeyman in the art of revolution'.[18] He was by no means the colossus depicted by the myth-makers of the 1930s and beyond, but he had undoubtedly become one of the leading Bolsheviks in the region. As such, his actions and writings, now in the Russian language, began to be noticed by the exiled Bolshevik leaders, Lenin included. In the longer term, this was probably the most significant outcome of Stalin's time in Baku. As noted by Isaac Deutscher, 'in going from Tiflis to the oil city on the Persian border, Koba was really moving from his native backwater into the main stream of national politics.'[19] For Rieber, Baku represented a 'halfway house' on Stalin's pilgrimage from the 'stifling atmosphere' of Georgia to his final Russian destination: 'The key to his growing success as a professional revolutionary was his closer association with things Russian.' This meant that Koba was gradually 'shifting from his primary aim of being a Bolshevik in Georgia to becoming a Georgian in Russian Bolshevism.'[20] A crucial figure in this transition was Vladimir Lenin.

Stalin and Lenin

As we have seen, there is much in Stalin's early life that is extremely difficult for the historian to reconstruct; hard facts are few, confusion and myth, often deliberately engineered for political reasons, proliferate. One thing is for sure, however. That is the significance of Stalin's complex and contradictory relationship with Lenin, which some historians, notably Robert Tucker, place at the core of their interpretation of Stalin's evolution as a 'Russian' Bolshevik leader. Tucker maintains that 'as a very young man Stalin had formed a hero-identification with Lenin….had dreamed of becoming the leader's alter ego and closest companion-in-arms.' In short, Stalin was motivated by a craving to be the 'second Lenin' and it was this psychological need that drove his long-standing quest for glory and power.[21] We do not have to subscribe to such a subjective evaluation to appreciate that Lenin's patronage, though never unequivocal, was to prove vital to Stalin's rise up the party ladder both before and after the Revolution.

Stalin first met Lenin at a Bolshevik faction conference in Tammerfors (Tampere) in Finland in December 1905. It is possible that they had communicated by letter once or twice before this time and it is certain that Stalin was aware and highly approving of Lenin's seminal composition *What is to be Done?* He called this controversial tract 'a splendid book' and defended its Marxist credentials against its Georgian Menshevik critics. He was attracted by the 'proletarian firmness' of Lenin's position, his denigration of 'spontaneity' in the working-class movement, and his emphasis on the vital role of the intelligentsia in instilling socialist consciousness in the workers.[22] Stalin doubtless considered himself one of those socialist intellectuals on whose shoulders lay the burdensome task of preparing the workers for the revolutionary battles ahead. Lenin's vision of a militant united party energetically pursuing the class struggle must have appealed to Koba, who by 1901–02 had experience of organising strikes, demonstrations and other direct actions. It gave coherence and immediate purpose to his dangerous work and, it might be speculated, provided the isolated Dzhugashvili with a sense of community and belonging. Koba was so closely identified with Lenin's ideas that his Georgian opponents reportedly referred to him as 'Lenin's left foot'.

According to his own testament, however, Stalin was initially taken aback by Lenin's less-than-imposing stature and demeanour at the Tammerfors gathering. In late January 1924 a few days after Lenin's death, he reminisced about his first impressions of the Bolshevik leader:

> I was hoping to see the mountain eagle of our Party, the great man, great not only politically, but, if you will, physically….What, then, was my disappointment to see a most ordinary-looking man, below average height, in no way, literally in no way, distinguishable from ordinary mortals….It is accepted as the usual thing for a 'great man' to come late to meetings….[but] Lenin had arrived at the conference before the delegates, had settled himself somewhere in a corner, and was unassumedly carrying on a conversation, a most ordinary conversation with the most ordinary delegates.

Only later did Stalin realise that this 'simplicity' and 'modesty' was one of Lenin's main strengths 'as the new leader of the new masses'.[23] Everything about this passage suggests that Stalin was talking about *himself*, not Lenin, in a sophistic attempt to stake his claim to be the 'new leader'. But it also implies a certain criticality towards the 'mountain eagle', a measured autonomy and suppressed tension that would characterise the two men's relations right up to Lenin's death.

On several occasions after their opening encounter Koba was to demonstrate that, though he greatly admired Lenin, he was by no means his puppet. For example, at the RSDWP's Stockholm Congress in April 1906, his first trip beyond the confines of the Russian Empire, Koba in his maiden address to a party convention spoke assuredly against Lenin's agrarian policy, declaring that the peasants did not want the land nationalised, but divided among themselves. Only then would they back a workers' revolution. In the following year, while operating in Baku, he initially opposed Lenin's policy of participating in the work of the State Duma (parliament), supporting instead a hard-line boycott of Bolshevik delegates. It is true that by 1908 Koba rather reluctantly shifted towards Lenin's stance, but in July of that year he vented his exasperation with the Bolshevik foreign émigrés, calling Lenin's philosophical disputes with his critics 'a storm in a teacup'. Moreover, he repeated the accusation in January 1911, adding that although the workers tend to favour Lenin's position, 'in general [they] start to look at the situation abroad with contempt....I think they are right.'[24] This outburst, which reflected the distrust and resentment of the Russian-based Bolshevik *praktiki* towards their out-of-touch exiled leaders, came to the attention of Lenin, who allegedly asserted that these 'nihilistic little jokes....reveal Koba's immaturity as a Marxist.'[25] Notwithstanding these muted long-distance altercations, Lenin had begun to take note of the young Caucasian activist. In the summer of 1907 he commented positively for the first time on one of Koba's sharply anti-Menshevik polemics and in 1910 he praised another of Stalin's writings, *Letters from the Caucasus*. It can be surmised that Koba had won a measure of respect from Lenin, who in a missive to the renowned Russian author Maxim Gorky in February 1913 famously called him 'a marvellous Georgian'.[26]

In January 1912 came a crucial breakthrough for Stalin: Lenin co-opted him onto the leading Bolshevik body, the Central Committee, a clear sign that he valued Koba's total loyalty as a battle-hardened party organiser, resolute anti-Menshevik crusader and, perhaps, as a counterweight to the troublesome Bolshevik 'intellectuals' whom Lenin had a tough time controlling. It is also likely that Stalin's non-Russian background went in his favour at a time when Lenin wished to broaden the national base of the party leadership. For Stalin, this promotion represented the longed-for elevation to the centre of revolutionary politics, a major step in realising his struggle to transcend the Caucasian peripheries and penetrate the national Russian mainstream. It is surely not coincidental that in the course of 1912 and early 1913 Koba, having experimented with various aliases and initials, adopted for the first time a new highly symbolic pseudonym, 'Stalin'. It was not uncommon for Bolsheviks to give themselves what would be called today 'macho' names – Molotov comes from the Russian word for 'hammer' and Kamenev from 'stone'. But 'Stalin' signified more than just a hard proletarian image (*stal* being Russian for steel). It was also indicative of his growing identification with Russia and concomitant attenuation of his 'Georgianness', and, arguably, a subconscious recognition of his admiration for Lenin by using the same Russianised suffix 'in'.

The first lengthy text to bear the signature 'K. Stalin' was his theoretical work *The National Question and Social Democracy* (later famously known as *Marxism and the National and Colonial Question*) published between March and May 1913. The piece, written largely in Vienna, was commissioned and edited by Lenin and was rather unoriginal, borrowing unacknowledged many ideas from contemporary Marxist thinkers, particularly Karl Kautsky. But it did go a long way in establishing the author as the Bolshevik expert on the complex nationality issue, a truly sensitive one in the multi-ethnic Tsarist Empire. Stalin's treatise on the national question is worth examining not only because it was commended by Lenin and thus helped to cement relations between the two men, but also because it expounded Stalin's principal tenets on this key problem, some of which he was to implement while in power. He began by defining the nation in orthodox Marxist terms as 'a historically constituted, stable community of people, formed on the basis of a common language, territory, economic life, and psychological make-up manifested in a common culture.' Stalin's main aim was to attack the emerging trend in central European Marxism, associated with the Austrian Social Democrats Otto Bauer and Karl Renner, of the 'national cultural autonomy' of peoples. As far as Lenin and Stalin were concerned, Bauer's and Renner's notions were a very dangerous disguised form of nationalism, which if applied in the Tsarist Empire could strengthen separatist sentiment and weaken both the centralised Russian state and the unified Social Democratic Party. National inclinations were already manifesting themselves among Jewish and Caucasian components of the RSDWP and Lenin was deeply anxious to maintain party unity across national lines by developing a comprehensive nationalities policy that would combat what he termed 'Great Russian

chauvinism'. Stalin countered the Austrians by emphasising that nationalism was a temporary phase of the human condition that would wither
away with the abolition of capitalism and the advent of socialism. In the
meantime, 'the only correct solution is *regional* autonomy, autonomy for
such crystallized units as Poland, Lithuania, the Ukraine, [and] the
Caucasus' within the confines of a democratised, but still centralised state.
This regional autonomy would guarantee ethnic minorities the right to
use their own languages, possess their own schools and enjoy civil and religious liberties.[27] It is instructive to note that, contrary to received
wisdom, the first two provisions were generally upheld under Stalin's dictatorship as we shall see in chapter three.

Stalin learnt much from Lenin's style of leadership, organisational principles and ideological prescriptions: a profound assurance in the veracity of
one's convictions, a resolute rejection and subversion of opposing viewpoints, and a semi-militarised conception of the party as an army of proletarian soldiers. But Stalin also gleaned more positive attributes from Lenin:
the recognition that on occasion tactical compromises and retreats were
necessary, the ability to find and enunciate direct, simple and clear solutions to difficult problems, and an attention to detail on all matters, especially personnel issues. For Lenin, Stalin had proved himself a staunch
Bolshevik stalwart, but evidently he had not made an indelible impression
on the 'great man'. In November 1915 Lenin wrote to a comrade request-
ing him to 'find out...the surname of "Koba" (Iosif Dzh....?? We have forgotten).'[28] Neither was Stalin well-known outside a relatively small circle of
Bolshevik operatives and Caucasian Social Democrats. This situation was to
change as a result firstly of his actions during the Revolution and more
notably the Civil War, when he made himself indispensable to the new
leader of the Soviet republic.

Stalin in 1917

The February Revolution of 1917 swept away the discredited Romanov
dynasty. At the time Stalin was languishing in exile in north central Siberia,
where he had lived for the previous four years. Under a general amnesty announced by the liberal Provisional Government, which had assumed power
following the abdication of Tsar Nicholas II, he and other Bolshevik exiles
hurried back to Petrograd, the cauldron of revolutionary activity. Stalin was
to play a significant, but by no means glorious, role in the Bolshevik seizure
of power. Historians differ on this question. One has argued, mistakenly in

my opinion, that Stalin 'missed the revolution' and forever thereafter
attempted to distort the record.[29] His hesitancy and inability to adapt to
rapidly changing situations have been emphasised by Trotsky among others.
He even made several important practical and theoretical blunders and took
no direct part in the revolutionary coup in late October 1917. For other
scholars, Stalin's views throughout 1917 were solidly orthodox Bolshevik, he
contributed valuable behind-the-scenes organisational work to the party, he
was one of Lenin's trusted servants, and, although by no means a charismatic figure, he nevertheless proved his mettle in the course of the revolutionary events.[30] This latter view may be exaggerated, but it is surely
incontestable that Stalin emerged from 1917 as one of the leading lights in
the new ruling party and government of Soviet Russia. As his confidence
grew, he was to use this position to further his own power and authority.
Later still, he was able to rewrite history and propagate the myth that he
was, with Lenin, co-leader of the Revolution.

Following his return to Petrograd in March 1917, Stalin was initially
denied full membership of the 'Russian Bureau of the Central Committee',
the *de facto* highest ranking Bolshevik Party body, 'in view of certain personal
characteristics', doubtless an oblique reference to his domineering style.[31]
This proved a temporary setback and soon he joined the Bureau and, together with Lev Kamenev, took control of the editorial board of *Pravda*
(*Truth*, the Bolshevik daily organ). For the rest of March and into April
Stalin, convinced that socialist revolution was not on the immediate horizon,
espoused a relatively moderate stance of 'conditional support' for the
Provisional Government, essentially accepting the notion of 'dual power' to
be shared between the middle-class executive and the newly-created
Petrograd Soviet (Workers' Council). As for the on-going hostilities, Stalin
rejected the slogan 'Down with the War!' as impractical and called on belligerent governments to begin peace negotiations. He even associated
himself with the idea of unification with the Mensheviks, though probably in
the belief that many on the left of the Menshevik Party would defect to the
Bolsheviks. More damaging for Stalin's longer-term reputation was that in
maintaining this 'wait-and-see' position he found himself distinctly at odds
with an impatient Lenin, who had arrived in Petrograd from foreign exile in
early April 1917 determined that the Bolsheviks should adopt more strident
policies. Like many leading Bolsheviks, Stalin reacted coolly to Lenin's
radical *April Theses*, which called for no truck with the 'bourgeois'
Provisional Government, a transfer of power to the Soviets and a revolutionary end to the war. The incredibly bold, but tacit, implication of the *Theses*
was that the Bolsheviks should aim to seize power on their own. Few in a

party of approximately 30,000 members could readily accede to this conclusion. It is not surprising, then, that for about three weeks after Lenin's
return Stalin kept up his semi-opposition to the *Theses*, yet another indica-
tion of a certain intellectual independence from the party's recognised
leader. This was, however, a dubious quality later erased from the Stalinist
history books.

In any case Stalin's recalcitrance was short-lived. In the months before the
October Revolution he collaborated closely with Lenin, often acting as his
spokesman in the party. This did not mean that Stalin lost all his critical fac-
ulties and was a mere mouthpiece for the leader. Indeed, on one or two occasions he displayed his customary degree of autonomy. But his image as a
firm adjutant of Lenin was surely consolidated. In addition, he gained valuable experience and confidence as a political leader. In July and August
1917 when Lenin was forced to go into hiding, he was able to influence
party strategy and tactics and together with Iakov Sverdlov he co-organised
the Sixth Party Congress at which he delivered the main report and was
elected to the Central Committee and its 'Inner Committee' of eleven.
Stalin subsequently became heavily involved with editing and writing for the
party press. Moreover, as a member of the Petrograd Soviet's Executive
Committee for five months he kept the Bolsheviks abreast of developments
in this crucial organisation. On the day the seizure of power began,
24 October, Stalin delivered a report to Bolshevik Soviet delegates in which
he showed familiarity with both the political and military preparations for
the insurrection. It cannot be denied that he played no direct or heroic role
in the October coup, but Stalin contributed valuable behind-the-scenes work
and emerged as an important figure in the party hierarchy. Tucker's overall
assessment of Stalin's strengths and weaknesses in the revolutionary year is
judicious:

> Stalin was not really in his element in the turbulent mass politics of
> 1917....In no way did he show himself as a colorful personality. Lacking
> oratorical gifts, he did not make it a regular practice to address mass
> meetings....Above all, he failed to show the distinctive qualities of out-
> standing revolutionary leadership in a time of crisis and fluidity: quick
> adaptability, innovative thinking, sensitive insight into mass feeling and
> response, and decisiveness.

However, regardless of these limitations, the year 1917 'was a milestone
on the path of Stalin's rise. Being at the center of revolutionary events,
taking part in the deliberations of the Bolshevik Central Committee, acting

as one of the party's leading organizers, he greatly matured as a man of politics. It was then....that he achieved the status of a recognized member of the Bolshevik general staff.' This lofty position was affirmed in late November when he was appointed to an informal 'foursome', together with Lenin, Trotsky and Sverdlov, to decide on all urgent questions of the day. According to Tucker, 'Stalin at this time functioned more than ever in his now-familiar role as Lenin's right-hand man for special assignments', a role he was to pursue with alacrity during the Civil War.[32] At absolutely critical moments, such as the vehement debates on the Treaty of Brest-Litovsk which in March 1918 ended the war with Germany on the eastern front and which even Lenin described as humiliating for Russia, Stalin stood solidly behind the Bolshevik leader. There can be no doubt that Lenin highly valued this loyalty and support.

On the day after the seizure of power in Petrograd, Lenin had designated Stalin as Commissar of Nationalities in the new fifteen-member revolutionary government, the Council of People's Commissars (Sovnarkom). At first sight, the position appeared less than pivotal. Indeed, Stalin's was the last name on the list of government ministers and, in a situation symptomatic of the chaos and confusion of the early post-revolutionary period, his Commissariat initially had no premises, scarce funds and hardly any officials. It was no more than a desk with a cardboard sign bearing the title of the department. But the 'nationality question' struck at the heart of *the* crucial issue: the very survival and consolidation of the infant Bolshevik regime. How should the new central Russian power react to the ever-growing demands and aspirations of the non-Russian peoples? How best to attract the numerous ethnic minorities and regions to the revolutionary socialist Soviet state? How to implement Lenin's contentious notion of 'national self-determination' up to and including secession without overseeing the collapse of centralised authority and hence of the revolution itself? The stakes were exceedingly high and the Bolshevik leaders had no agreed coherent set of policies up their sleeves. On the contrary, Stalin had a tough time defending the actions of his Commissariat against those 'left' Bolsheviks who denied the centrality of nationalism and asserted the primacy of the internationalist revolutionary agenda.[33]

Among Stalin's first acts as Commissar was to formalise the independence of Finland, hitherto a province of the Tsarist Empire, but his main job was not to encourage separatism, far from it. He was most reluctant to accept an autonomous 'bourgeois' Finland and certainly an independent Ukraine was out of the question unless under a 'proletarian government'. In general, his invidious task was to find ways of securing the territorial integrity of a

centralised socialist Soviet state while satisfying the legitimate goals of oppressed minorities. Broadly in line with Lenin's prognoses, Stalin's controversial formula for this delicate balancing act was 'Soviet federalism', a
concept of a polyethnic state that he would later dub as 'national in form,
socialist in content'. Harking back to ideas outlined in his *Marxism and the
National and Colonial Question*, Stalin sought to disarm 'bourgeois' nationalism and win over the lower classes of the 'culturally backward' peripheries by
promoting the 'forms' of nationhood within a federative socialist state. This
could only be achieved, he argued in April 1918, if 'these regions are autonomous, that is, have their own schools, courts, administrations, organs of
power and social, political and cultural institutions, and unless the labouring
masses of these regions are fully guaranteed the right to use their own language in all spheres of social and political activity.' These concessions, so
Stalin and Lenin believed, would accelerate the process of class differentia-
tion in the borderlands, thus isolating the 'bourgeois nationalist' oppressors, recruit local workers and peasants to the Bolsheviks' socialist cause, and
bring about the 'sovietisation' of these regions, that is 'their conversion into
real Soviet countries closely bound with central Russia in one integral
state'.[34] This 'sovietisation' of the under-developed peripheries was vital for
Stalin as it provided the best means, together with conventional military
might, of safeguarding the beleaguered Soviet regime from its numerous
domestic and foreign enemies. It is precisely here, in these formulations of
1918–20, that we glean the first intimations of Stalin's later theory of 'socialism in one country', a theory which emphasised the internal sources of
Soviet survival and downplayed the necessity of workers' revolution in the
advanced capitalist countries. Indeed, Stalin had made his position on international revolution abundantly clear in January 1918: 'There is no revolutionary movement in the West, nothing existing, only a potential and we
cannot count on a potential.'[35]

Stalin in the Civil War

The new Commissar of Nationalities had little enough time to devote to his
governmental duties. From mid-1918 to early 1921, Russia was embroiled in
a savage Civil War that pitted the 'Reds', the Bolsheviks and their leftist
allies, against the 'Whites', pro-Tsarist forces supported by several anti-
communist foreign powers, with the amorphous 'Greens', roving armed
peasant bands, resisting Red and White exploitation equally. The Civil War
engendered a vicious class-based Red and White Terror that took countless

victims, it ended in a famine of immense proportions, it necessitated the creation of hypertrophied party and state bureaucracies, it saw the voluntary and forced exile of thousands of educated and experienced specialists, and it bolstered a militaristic 'command-order' and siege mentality among the communist leadership and party as a whole, a tendency that Stalin found highly conducive and was to use to his advantage in subsequent years. The overall policies enacted by the Bolshevik government during these critical years became known as 'War Communism': the creation of a one-party dictatorship, the large-scale nationalisation of industry, services and trade, and the forcible requisitioning of grain from the peasantry. These repressive measures, combined with an Allied blockade of the country and military exigencies, resulted in economic breakdown, widespread hunger, the depopulation of urban areas, and met with stiff resistance, particularly in the villages. Together with the entire party, Stalin became accustomed to the notion that 'might is right'. In Moshe Lewin's words, it was here that 'Stalin learned the secret of victorious politics in the most daunting situations: State coercion was the secret of success; mobilization, propaganda, military might, and terror were the ingredients of power.'[36] The Civil War, thus, had a brutalising and truly seminal impact on the evolution of Soviet society, state and politics; it was in many ways the crucible of Stalinism.

In this ruthless often barbaric struggle, Stalin was to play a highly significant and not uncontroversial role in securing a Red victory, an outcome that was by no means inevitable. Indeed, it would hardly be an exaggeration to claim that it was the Civil War far more than the Revolution itself that 'made' Stalin and propelled him to the top ranks of the Bolshevik Party and Soviet state. He revelled in the violent atmosphere, presenting himself on his expeditions to various battle fronts as a crusading man of action who, above all, got things done no matter what the cost. Unsurprisingly, this abrasive attitude sparked friction with many of his colleagues, notably Trotsky, the founder and commander of the Red Army and 'hero' of the revolution. The bitter personal and power struggle between the two men that was to culminate in August 1940 with a Stalinist axe in Trotsky's head had its origins largely in the acrimonious disputes of the Civil War. However, Stalin not only gained enemies in these years. He also assiduously cultivated a proto-clan of influential loyal followers, some of whom remained convinced devotees until well after his death. Even more important in the shorter term, he earned the trust of his greatest patron, Lenin, who relied on Stalin's energy, boundless capacity for work and ability to cut through Gordian knots. This trust was never unequivocal and on more than one occasion Lenin had to diplomatically rein in his headstrong emissary.

Nevertheless, Stalin emerged from the Civil War as an authoritative figure with a keen understanding of power, its uses and abuses.

Before outlining Stalin's political and military activities during this period, a happy event in his private life should be mentioned. In 1918, possibly 1919, he married for a second time. His wife, Nadezhda Allilueva, was over twenty years his junior, the daughter of pro-Bolshevik parents whom Stalin had known since his underground days in Tiflis. For a few months in 1917 he had lived in the Alliluevs' spacious apartment in Petrograd and he must have been taken with the young woman of the house and she with the 'experienced revolutionary'. Theirs was to be a turbulent relationship, though not without reciprocal affection. Two children were born, Vasilii in 1921 and Svetlana in 1926. The former turned out to be a glaringly incompetent alcoholic airman, the latter, on whom Stalin doted in her early years, a Soviet émigré who wrote two compelling books about her father.[37] Nadezhda was a committed independent-minded party member, who wished to expand her education and who at times took issue with her husband's policies. She was also given to bouts of depression and illness, a state Stalin's inveterate roughness, inattentiveness and boorishness probably exacerbated and certainly did nothing to alleviate. Add in Stalin's aversion to female emancipation and the reasons for conjugal tensions are not hard to find. The troubled marriage ended tragically in November 1932 when, after an unpleasant public wrangle with a semi-inebriated Stalin, Nadezhda shot herself in her Kremlin bedroom.[38] Her suicide, obviously the result of a deep-seated *angst*, profoundly affected Stalin's mental landscape – 'the children forgot her in a few days, but me she crippled for life', he later remarked self-pityingly.[39] According to his daughter, he became depressed and muttered 'I can't go on living after this'; he felt betrayed and even considered resigning as Party General Secretary.[40] It can be speculated that the psychological damage suffered at this time contributed to his increasing insularity, suspiciousness and vindictiveness.

But these calamities lay in the future. When Stalin, accompanied by Nadezhda in her capacity as personal secretary, embarked on his first Civil War venture to the Volga city of Tsaritsyn (later Stalingrad) in the early summer of 1918, he had a pivotal job to do for the endangered Soviet state: secure supplies of grain from the fertile south to the hungry towns in the centre and north of Russia. For the first time in his career he was granted emergency powers and he used them mercilessly, executing numerous anti-Bolshevik 'plotters' and class enemies. Clearly indicative of Stalin's mentality at this time is a telegram he sent from Tsaritsyn in response to the unsuccessful assassination attempt on Lenin's life in late August 1918: 'open and systematic mass terror against the bourgeoisie and its agents' is being instituted in the region, he wrote. His insubordinate handling of the military and his undisguised resentment and distrust of the ex-Tsarist officers now commanding the Red forces – 'I can only deplore [their] so-called science'[41] – brought him into overt conflict with Trotsky, the Commissar of War, and cost thousands of lives. Robert Conquest's verdict on Stalin's Tsaritsyn campaigns is damning: 'He had acted with an almost unbelievable lack of discretion. He had grossly exceeded his powers. He had disobeyed orders, and refused to implement the Soviet policy on military experts.' His later communications to Lenin exhibited 'a manic, even on the face of it self-defeating, egotism.'[42] By contrast, Robert McNeal's assessment is more sober. Initially, Stalin 'seems to have made some progress' in 'unsnarling food transport'; he enjoyed at least the partial support of Lenin, who 'was far from quick in acceding to [Trotsky's] demand for Stalin's dismissal'; what is more, the Bolshevik supremo regarded 'the measures decided on by Stalin' at Tsaritsyn 'as a model' to be emulated, and in January and May 1919 despatched him on important expeditions to Viatka and Petrograd, cities threatened by the Whites. Operating with his customary zeal, 'Stalin overcame the crisis in Petrograd'[43] and he continued to perform sterling work on many fronts throughout the Civil War. As a result of the remorseless pressure his health suffered and in April 1921 the Politburo authorised a three-month recuperation period at a spa in the North Caucasus.

The low point of Stalin's military career came during the Russo-Polish War in the spring and summer of 1920. In April the Poles had invaded the Ukraine and captured Kiev, but were repulsed by the Red Army. An exultant Lenin, desperate to extend the socialist revolution to the heartlands of Europe, ignored the advice of Trotsky and other top Bolsheviks and in July exhorted his forces, commanded by a young former Tsarist officer Mikhail Tukhachevskii, to march on to Warsaw and beyond. Stalin, who in late May had been appointed political commissar of the southwestern front, in effect refused to comply with orders from the High Command to assist Tukhachevskii's initially triumphant thrust towards the Polish capital, supporting instead an attack on the city of Lvov. The outcome was a rout of the over-extended Red Army at Warsaw and a rapid retreat into Soviet territory. To be sure, the situation was complicated and Stalin's insubordination was far from the sole cause of the Polish debacle. But he gained a somewhat tarnished image and began, possibly, to nurse a deep grudge against Tukhachevskii, whose grim fate will be outlined in chapter four.

In sum, many historians draw a distinction between Stalin's crisis man-agement behind the front lines, which was crudely effective, and his martial exploits, which were modest. Tucker's judgement is representative:

> Although Stalin acquired valuable military experience in the Civil War, he did not emerge from it with a party reputation for having a first-class military mind. He was not one of the principal organizers of the Red Army, nor did he show the qualities of an outstanding military leader....[Yet] whatever his military failings, he recommended himself by his wartime services as a forceful leader with an ability to size up complex situations quickly and take decisive action.[44]

The main dissenter to this consensus is McNeal, who argues more posi-tively that Stalin became 'a political-military chief whose contribution to the Red victory was second only to Trotsky's....If his reputation as a hero was far below Trotsky's, this had less to do with objective merit than with Stalin's lack of flair, at this stage of his career, for self-advertisement.' The results of his relentless efforts 'were not necessarily ideal, but on balance they were successful, sometimes brilliantly so'.[45] This assessment may be slightly gener-ous, but it can be concluded that Lenin, while regretting Stalin's excesses and mindful of his overweening vanity, was to a large extent dependent on the Georgian's decisiveness and resourcefulness, qualities that not all leading Bolsheviks displayed during the desperate Civil War years.

It is in this period, 1918–21, that two inter-related developments of great significance become discernible – the evolution of an embryonic 'Stalinist clan' and the gradual accretion of Stalin's political authority. Stalin assidu-ously sought to strengthen his personal power by cultivating a group of dedi-cated followers in the central party *apparat*, the military and the provinces. He was not unique in this among Bolsheviks and was assisted by a political culture and Civil War conditions that laid great store on the patron-client relationship. As the Australian scholar T. H. Rigby has pointed out 'the prevalence of clientelist norms and practices among provincial party and government officialdom made it easier for Stalin to use the personnel-assignment powers of the Central Committee apparatus to build a nation-wide "machine" personally loyal to him.'[46] Stalin's 'clan' was created from three main sources: the 'Caucasian circle' that included Ordzhonikidze, Enukidze, Sergei Kirov, Anastas Mikoian and the Svanidze family; the so-called 'Tsaritsyn mafia', dating from the summer of 1918, comprised another old associate from the Caucasian days, Voroshilov, now an officer in the Red Army, and rising military dignitaries, such as Semen Budenny,

Georgii Zhukov and Semen Timoshenko; and a group of leading Ukrainian communists, notably Vlas Chubar, Grigorii Petrovskii and Emanuel Kviring. In the central party bodies, Stalin formed tight working and factional relationships with Valerian Kuibyshev and Viacheslav Molotov, who as a secretary of the party from 1921 was a person of considerable influence. Later, the clique was joined by Lazar Kaganovich, who in 1922 Stalin appointed head of an important Central Committee bureau. All these men became leading Stalinists of the 1920s and 1930s, paradoxically not a few of them his victims.

While constructing a personal following of some clout, Stalin also consolidated his authority in the state and party edifices. From the earliest post-revolutionary days, he acted, as we have seen, as Commissar of Nationalities, and in March 1919 he was assigned a new portfolio, the post of People's Commissar of State Control, a department that soon became known as the Workers' and Peasants' Inspectorate (Rabkrin). His task was to oversee and improve the performance of state officials; in essence, to create a centralised network of efficient rule-abiding administrators, one of Lenin's pet schemes. As boss of two government agencies, Stalin was automatically a member of the Soviet 'cabinet', Sovnarkom, and also of its influential 'Little Council'. In addition, he was deputy head of the Council of Labour and Defence that provided economic and logistical support to the armed forces. However, Stalin's authority grew not only in state commissions and institutions, but portentously also in the Communist Party. Two months after his appointment to Rabkrin, in May 1919, the Eighth Party Congress elected Stalin to the first Political Bureau (Politburo), at that time a rudimentary five-member executive of the Central Committee, but an organ that would rapidly become the supreme power locus in the Soviet system. He was simultaneously voted onto the party's Organisational Bureau (Orgburo), an important administrative body that *inter alia* was responsible for the deployment of key personnel within and outside the party. Through his contacts with Molotov, Stalin was also peripherally involved in the activities of the Secretariat, the organisational hub of the Communist Party. Moreover, he had established close links with the Cheka, the Soviet secret police apparatus led by Feliks Dzerzhinskii, a relationship that was to prove vital in the political battles that lay ahead.

It is true that Stalin's governmental posts were not regarded as highly influential and that he devoted relatively little time to them, particularly Rabkrin, which achieved little under his stewardship. It is likewise certainly the case that Lenin was *the* recognised leader of the party and that other Bolsheviks, Trotsky, Zinoviev, Kamenev and Bukharin for instance, were

more in the public spotlight than Stalin, who preferred to operate behind
the scenes. But accumulatively, his positions in the Central Committee, its
Politburo and Orgburo, his membership of Sovnarkom and its inner
bureau, his leadership of two state commissariats and his contacts in key institutions, such as the military and Cheka, meant that Stalin was placing
himself, consciously or otherwise, at the apex of power in the party and state
hierarchies. Indeed, some historians have maintained that as early as 1920–1
Stalin was dominant in the party upper reaches and had created a spring-
board for his subsequent conquest of the party in its entirety. I would hesitate to assert that Stalin set himself the goal of becoming supreme party
'boss' in this period. It seems more likely that he came to the realisation of
his own power potential over time, probably in the course of Lenin's prolonged incapacitation in 1922–3 which occasioned the first overt inner-party
struggles. At a minimum, it can be concluded that by 1921 Stalin had proved
himself an indispensable and loyal 'Lenin man', had emerged as an ambitious, artful and self-confident politician and had carefully constructed an
influential political clientele. He was about to become a leading contender
for Lenin's mantle – a Bolshevik oligarch.

Chapter 2: Oligarch

The turbulent political history of the years 1922–9 has not been a favourite theme in recent historiography of the Soviet Union. There have been few archival 'sensations' on Stalin's rise to power and most historians, particularly of the younger generation, have either preferred to re-evaluate the traumatic events of the 1930s and 1940s or increasingly have turned to socio-cultural explorations associated with post-modernist methodology. In many ways, then, this chapter presents more difficulties than any other. On the one hand, I do not wish to simply rehash older accounts of Stalin's fierce battles with his arch-rivals Trotsky, Zinoviev, Kamenev and Bukharin, but on the other there is relatively little new research to assess and critique. In terms of published archival evidence, we do now have Stalin's letters to Molotov and other correspondence between Bolshevik leaders, plus several other important sources,[1] but this constitutes a rather thin documentary base for such a pivotal subject. In this chapter I aim to synthesise the various approaches to Stalin's ascendancy, incorporating new evidence where appropriate.

There is certainly more to the 1920s than the various inner-party power struggles, but for our purposes the overriding question, and the one that has exercised participants, scholars and interested lay people ever since his triumph, is: why Stalin? How was a comparatively ill-educated man with few oratorical skills and intellectual pretensions able to defeat the 'giants' of Bolshevism and gain mastery over the Communist Party and Soviet state by the end of the decade? Was his ascent primarily the result of behind-the-scenes manipulation, callous back-stabbing and political intrigue? Was he simply more ruthless, determined and brazen than his opponents? Was he just plain lucky that his adversaries under-estimated him and ultimately capitulated without putting up much of a fight, regardless of Lenin's warnings about Stalin? Or did the Georgian possess hidden reserves and

strengths, both organisational and ideological, which account for his unlikely victory? How far was Stalin able to project himself to the bulk of party
activists as the kind of leader who would defend their interests and those of
the Soviet Union? In the final analysis, was he a more adroit politician than
Trotsky, Zinoviev or Bukharin? Or from a structural less personalised approach, were there longer-term social, economic and cultural processes at
play in the party and country at large which worked to Stalin's advantage?
To what extent was he merely the mouthpiece of an emergent aggressive
bureaucracy untrained in the intricacies of Marxist-Leninist theory? What
impact did international affairs and the continued isolation of the USSR
have on the inner-party disputes? These are the main themes to be discussed in this chapter, beginning with a broadly chronological narrative of
Stalin's struggles against his various opponents in the years 1923–9 and
then adopting a more analytical approach to the issues that divided the
party.

    First, however, a brief assessment of the wider historical context of the in-
ternecine struggles is necessary. After the devastating Civil War had been
won, Lenin decided that the policies collectively known as 'War Communism' could not continue. Economic ruin, workers' strikes and unrest,
peasant rebellions, rampant disease, internal party dissent and, most ominously, the Kronstadt naval base revolt in March 1921, which had to be mercilessly put down, convinced the Bolshevik leader that more conciliatory
policies were required to rebuild the shattered economy, heal social divisions and bolster the popular legitimacy of the Soviet state. The outcome
was the New Economic Policy (NEP), which sought economic reconstruction by a retreat to 'semi-capitalism' and by forging an 'alliance' (*smychka*)
between the workers and the peasantry, between town and country. Largely
as a result of these concessions, by the mid-1920s industrial production in
most sectors of the economy had returned to 1913 levels, which was no
mean achievement. Culturally and socially, NEP Russia was relatively diverse,
intellectual and artistic monolithicism was not yet a feature of life, academics enjoyed a measure of autonomy and various citizens' initiatives existed
outside of direct state control. For this reason several scholars have suggested that an embryonic civil society was emerging in NEP Russia and the
years 1921–8 have often been regarded with some justification as a 'golden
era', a 'liberal' interlude between the twin horrors of the Civil War and
Stalinism.

    But this rosy picture needs to be qualified. Profound social tensions
bubbled just below the surface, the gap between a 'modernising' urbanising
socialist state and a 'traditional' peasant society was still dangerously wide,

party control over large swathes of the country was not deeply rooted, 'enemies' at home and abroad were still perceived as ubiquitous, not all branches of the economy prospered, unemployment grew, censorship existed and, above all, the USSR remained a one-party repressive state.[2] It was in these circumstances and with these mentalities that the inner-party battles took place, the burning question being none other than the future direction of the entire revolution. Initially, from 1923 the main disagreements were broadly between the Zinoviev-Kamenev-Stalin 'troika' and Trotsky and his adherents, the so-called 'Left Opposition'. By 1925–6, however, with Stalin moving closer to Bukharin's moderate pro-NEP formulations, a fragile 'United Opposition' of Trotskyists and Zinovievists challenged the 'party majority' on a wide range of domestic and foreign policy issues. By the end of 1927 this ill-assorted coalition had been crushed and in the first months of 1928 bitter divisions began to emerge between the Bukharinist 'right-wing' of the party and the Stalinist dominated Politburo and Central Committee. By late 1929 Bukharin and his chief supporters, Aleksei Rykov and Mikhail Tomskii, were definitively defeated. Stalin, whose 'cult of personality' dates from precisely this time, was now firmly chief oligarch – *primus inter pares* – and the recognised leader of the party.

Stalin as General Secretary

All accounts of Stalin's rise to pre-eminence emphasise his accumulation of a vital organisational power base in the upper reaches of the burgeoning party-state structures. As we saw in the previous chapter, already by 1919 he held several highly influential positions: People's Commissar of Nationalities, head of the Workers' and Peasants' Inspectorate (Rabkrin), member of the party's five-man Politburo, and a leading figure in the Central Committee and Orgburo with personal links to the Secretariat and Cheka, the fearsome secret police. He had also gained serviceable military and administrative experience during the Civil War and gone some way in establishing his own 'clan' of devoted followers. This was impressive enough, but Stalin's key promotion came immediately after the Eleventh Party Congress in April 1922 when he was appointed, with Lenin's active backing, General Secretary of the Communist Party. The post was newly created and was by no means perceived as a stepping stone to absolute power. Indeed, most Bolshevik luminaries apparently regarded the job as a humdrum bureaucratic chore, far below the acumen of a Trotsky, Zinoviev or Bukharin. That's not how Stalin saw it. He had no intention of becoming a mere administrator. Lenin, too, appears to have pushed for Stalin's appointment not so much because he valued Stalin's organisational capacities but more his political support for 'Leninist' policies. At this time, Stalin was to a large extent 'a Lenin man' and the party boss desperately needed loyal adherents in positions of authority.[3]

Stalin's commitment to Lenin and the Bolshevik leader's fundamental policies was to prove of inestimable worth in the struggles for power that wracked the party from 1923 onwards. Regardless of the two men's differences, some of which were profound as we shall see, Stalin could plausibly claim that the personnel of the party's Central Committee, Politburo and Secretariat had been elected with Lenin's approval, that the New Economic Policy at home and the moderate foreign diplomacy and Comintern[4] strategy abroad were Lenin's creation, and that, above all, the 'ban on factions', which was ratified at the Tenth Party Congress in March 1921 to ensure strict party unity and which Stalin was to use assiduously in future against all his opponents, was Lenin's brainchild.[5] Hence, the organisational structures, personnel and policies of the party over which Stalin formally presided could be persuasively construed as genuinely 'Leninist', while the carping criticisms and alternative strategies of his Trotskyist rivals were relatively easily rebuffed as 'un-Leninist', ultimately 'anti-Leninist', manifestations. It is hardly surprising, then, that Stalin was to play an influential role in forging the 'Lenin cult' after the leader's death in January 1924. Even more fundamentally, as a respected Russian historian has recently reasserted, a key factor in the making of the 'Boss' was the one-party political system inherent in which was the principle of 'Leadership' (*vozhdizm*) and the establishment of a party-state apparatus headed by the *nomenklatura*, responsible officials appointed by the party.[6] The basis of this system had been firmly laid under Lenin.

What is more, Stalin's position as party General Secretary was pivotal in the all-important fields of organisation and personnel matters. Graeme Gill, a renowned expert on the Stalinist political system, has identified three main bases of power of the General Secretary. Firstly, Stalin 'had a significant influence on the course of information flow to the Politburo, the structuring of its agenda and the whole course of its operations'. This was a vital attribute given the Politburo's status as the hub of decision-making in the Soviet hierarchy. Secondly, Stalin's personal secretariat spread its 'tentacles into all areas of Soviet life' and established very close relations with the Secret Department of the Central Committee Secretariat, a powerful body that appears to have conducted the bulk of the preparatory work for the Politburo, Orgburo and Secretariat. Finally, and most relevantly for our purposes, Stalin 'had access to the appointment process. As the only full member of the Politburo, Orgburo and Secretariat, he was strategically placed to monitor personnel issues in all fora.' In the opinion of many experts, what this meant in practice was that by the mid-1920s Stalin was able to promote his supporters into the Politburo, stack party congresses and the Central Committee with regional officials who were generally nominated by Stalin's apparatus and thus largely loyal to him, and, conversely, restrict the election of opposition delegates to party plena. The formal 'party majority', that is the 'Stalinist majority', would then vote to demote or expel Stalin's successive 'minority' rivals, Trotsky, Zinoviev, Kamenev and Bukharin, a process Gill terms 'the emergence of monolithism' in party congresses. Similarly, local Oppositionist strongholds, such as Zinoviev's in Leningrad, were smashed in short order by the sustained pressure of the central party apparatus.[7]

The latest archival research, however, has cast some doubt on Stalin's clientelist powers. According to James Harris, they appear less fail proof or perversely manipulative than many scholars have surmised:

> There is no evidence to suggest that the fact of appointment was the basis for a special relationship between senior officials and Stalin. Stalin could not automatically command the support of officials in leading Party and state organs....Stalin won the support of [regional] secretaries by attacking intra-Party democracy and reinforcing their power within their organisations....[and because he] remained attentive to the needs and desires of Party officialdom....Many Party secretaries voted for Stalin at Party Congresses. They helped him defeat his rivals in the Politburo because they had a common interest in it, not because they felt personally beholden to Stalin.[8]

Regardless of the nuances of the debate, no historian would dispute Gill's conclusion that the 'position of General Secretary was clearly of crucial importance organisationally, and it was one which an ambitious man could use to further that ambition, as Stalin showed.'[9]

Before this could happen though, Stalin had to survive some very awkward moments that potentially threatened his leadership aspirations, even his entire career. In 1922–3 he and Lenin clashed over the complex and highly contentious nationalities issue and the related question of the constitutional structure of the USSR. Already in 1921 Lenin had been disquieted by Stalin's and Ordzhonikidze's armed 'Sovietisation' of Georgia, hitherto an independent state under Menshevik jurisdiction. Lenin was dismayed at Stalin's heavy-handed approach to Georgian nationalist sensibilities. The affair worsened in the autumn of 1922 and even more serious disagreements emerged at that time when Stalin informed Lenin about his 'autonomisation' plan to incorporate the Ukrainian, Belorussian and Transcaucasian (Armenian, Azerbaijani and Georgian) Republics into the existing Russian Federation as 'autonomous' republics, but with little real independence and statutory powers. Stalin's ideas were more centralist than Lenin had envisaged and smacked of 'Great Russian chauvinism', one of Lenin's pet hates. His counter proposals, which served as the basis of the future federalised Union of Soviet Socialist Republics, were most ungraciously accepted by Stalin, who arrogantly accused Lenin of 'national liberalism'.[10]

The rift over the national question was just one component of Lenin's growing mistrust towards Stalin. Indeed, several historians, notably Moshe Lewin, have argued that Lenin was fighting a desperate last-ditch battle on many fronts to overcome Stalin's growing pernicious influence.[11] By late 1922 Lenin had become deeply anxious that personality and policy clashes could lead to a dangerous split in communist ranks. As part of his campaign to restore and consolidate unity, in December of that year a desperately ill Lenin dictated 'Letter to the Congress', a brief tract that became known as his 'Testament'. The 'Letter' contained *inter alia* short appraisals of six prominent figures, notably Trotsky and Stalin, who were described as 'the two outstanding leaders of the present C[entral] C[ommittee]', itself a remarkable judgement that belies Stalin's image as a 'grey blur'. Trotsky, though, 'has displayed an excessive self-assurance and shown excessive preoccupation with the purely administrative side of the work'. Lenin's assessment of Stalin has gone down in history as prophetic: 'Comrade Stalin, having become Secretary-General, has unlimited authority concentrated in his hands, and I am not sure whether he will always be capable of using that authority with sufficient caution.' Eleven days later, after Stalin had verbally abused Lenin's wife Nadezhda Krupskaia, who may have brought the coarse outburst to her husband's attention, Lenin added an angry postscript with far-reaching ramifications for the *Gensek*:

> Stalin is too rude and this defect, although quite tolerable in our midst and in dealings among us Communists, becomes intolerable in a Secretary-General. That is why I suggest that the comrades think about a way of removing Stalin from that post and appointing another man in his stead who....[is] more tolerant, more loyal, more polite and more considerate to the comrades, less capricious, etc.[12]

It is important to evaluate these passages carefully given the tremendous significance attached to them by later historians. Lenin did not categorically insist on Stalin's ouster; he made a suggestion. Neither did he intend that Stalin should be removed from his other positions in the party-state hierarchies, only the General Secretaryship.

Nevertheless, this was a searing condemnation and one that, in inauspicious circumstances, could have amounted to political death for Stalin. Furthermore, in March 1923 Lenin came close to breaking off all personal relations with Stalin, compelling him grudgingly to apologise for his behaviour. Most worryingly for Stalin, Lenin had left instructions that, following his demise, his 'Letter' should be read out to the next party congress, thereby effectively sealing Stalin's fate. In the event, party leaders, including Trotsky, decided that Lenin's words should only be made known to a select gathering of delegates to the Thirteenth Party Congress in April 1924, just three months after Lenin's decease. The General Secretary was essentially deemed indispensable, particularly as far as Zinoviev and Kamenev were concerned in their on-going bitter fight against Trotsky. Hence, Stalin survived. Indeed, he emerged in some ways even strengthened as his obsequious offers of resignation were turned down and an array of party dignitaries spoke in his defence.

If Stalin was to aspire to the supreme position, he had to build up a base of support among at least three constituencies: his co-leaders in the Politburo and Central Committee, influential provincial party secretaries and officials, and to a lesser extent rank-and-file party members. He did so better than any of his opponents. It is time to dispel the myth that Stalin was solely a master bureaucratic manipulator, a typical *apparatchik* beavering away in the background up to his neck in file cards and red tape. Stalin was doubtless a consummate 'machine politician', but he was far more than that. He expounded persuasive policies and held deep convictions on all the major, and many minor, domestic and foreign issues facing the Soviet Union.[13] What is more, he was able over time to project himself as an effective *leader* of that state, dutifully carrying out Lenin's behests while appearing to operate firmly within a collective framework. According to a prominent Russian scholar, 'Stalin was able to convince the party *apparat* that he alone personified the party's tradition of collective leadership contrary to the "old bosses" who thought only about personal revenge.'[14] Stalin's emphasis on 'organic' party unity as opposed to the inherently divisive actions of the various oppositions won him many adherents, while acting as a smokescreen for his own ambitions.[15]

Stalin's own account of the inner-party struggles alludes to aspects of this assessment. In private discussion with his closest colleagues on the occasion of the twentieth anniversary of the Bolshevik Revolution, the 'boss' implied

that he won because he was a 'man of the people'. He disingenuously
claimed that:

> his victory over the oppositions, and Trotsky in particular, had been
> improbable. He had been an 'unknown', 'lacking talent as a theoreti-
> cian'....a 'second-rater'....How had he defeated him?....Stalin attributed
> his victory to the mass of average Party members....who had supported
> him for his concrete achievements. Stalin likened them to officers, who
> had shown loyalty not to the Generals who have the best training, but to
> those who bring victory in battle.[16]

In addition, Stalin's analyses of the internal and external situation of the
country were generally convincing, though naturally not without flaws. His
work rate was prodigious, he appeared often as a studied 'centrist' trying to
steer the party clear of the extremism of his opponents and his policies
and theories, notably 'socialism in one country', attracted a relatively broad
audience, both inside and outside the party. As we saw in chapter one, he
consciously constructed an image of himself as a strong Russian 'proletarian'
leader capable of defending the integrity of the Soviet state, but who, as a
Georgian 'man of the borderlands', could appeal to the diverse ethnic minorities of the USSR. Trotsky's later acerbic observation that Stalin was 'the
outstanding mediocrity of our party' was in many ways wide of the mark.[17]
Stalin may not have been a first-rate theoretician, author or orator, but he
was an adroit political tactician with pragmatic ideas in his head. So much so
that by the mid-1920s 'the other Politburo members had come to rely on his
ability to analyze a situation and devise a course of action.'[18] He was also
without doubt a 'hard' Bolshevik quite capable of engaging in unprincipled
intrigue, muck-raking and back-stabbing. This was a formidable combination
for the tussles that lay ahead.

Stalin, Trotsky and the 'United Opposition'

This is not the place to rehearse in any detail the well-known events of the
vicious internecine power struggles of 1923–7.[19] A brief narrative will suffice.
In late 1923 with Lenin on his death-bed and the question of succession on
everyone's mind, Trotsky and his supporters launched a major attack on
the party majority led by Zinoviev, Kamenev and Stalin. These three battle-
hardened figures formed a loose triumvirate to counter the 'Bonapartist'
threat from Trotsky, who many in the party feared would use his position as

chief of the Red Army to instigate a *coup d'état*. It was a charge staunchly denied by the War Commissar. Trotsky's critique, first outlined in his *New Course* of December 1923, berated the ascendant party leadership for its undemocratic and bureaucratic practices, especially evident in Stalin's Secretariat, and for its economic mismanagement which had resulted in the so-called 'scissors crisis', a gross disequilibrium between industrial and agrarian prices leading to food shortages in the cities. Most damaging was Trotsky's assertion that the party was losing its revolutionary spirit and was becoming cut off from its mass base, its creativity stifled by the stranglehold of a 'conservative bureaucracy' solely interested in staying in power. To restore a healthy democratic essence to the party, it had to be regenerated by an influx of youth to counteract the ossification of the old guard. But these blistering forays, backed by several distinguished Bolsheviks, failed to garner mass support in the party either in 1923 or in subsequent years. Indeed, many historians have viewed Trotsky's defeat as effectively sealed by the winter of 1923–4. Why?

Firstly, the contradiction of Trotsky's position was palpable: he too had contributed in no small measure to the undermining of democratic practices and mentalities in the party during the Civil War, actions which he had seemingly conveniently forgotten. Secondly, it was common knowledge that he was a very late convert to Bolshevism and had opposed Lenin on more than one key issue both before and after the Revolution. Hence, his disagreements with the triumvirate could be convincingly construed as being fuelled more by hurt pride than objective realities and ultimately his policy preferences could be assailed as a 'Menshevik' deviation from Leninism. Thirdly, Trotsky's many opponents not unreasonably regarded his criticisms as exaggerated and his supposed solutions as vague. Fourthly, his recent work record was hardly exemplary, not exactly a ringing endorsement for a budding supreme leader.[20] Fifthly, in 1923–5 Trotsky was arguably fixated on his clash with Zinoviev and thus missed several opportunities to weaken Stalin's growing power, a tactical miscalculation of historic import. Finally, it is also possible that Trotsky's Jewish intellectual background worked against him, as undoubtedly did his notorious arrogance and aloofness which rankled his adversaries and predisposed him to seriously under-estimate all his rivals.

Above all, Trotsky and his supporters fell victim to the Leninist insistence on party unity and anti-factionalism. No matter how assiduously the Trotskyists refuted their 'factionalism' and professed their loyalty to Leninist principles, it was all too easy for Stalin and the party majority to accuse the Left Opposition of 'anti-party' activity for which they were then condemned and out-voted at congresses, conferences and Central Committee plena by delegates carefully selected and vetted by Stalin's Secretariat. Furthermore, at the apex of power Trotsky was faced not simply by the triumvirate, but by a veritable *semerka*, 'the seven', an informal grouping of Politburo members whose 'sole purpose was to conduct Politburo business without Trotsky's participation.' It was a body he had no idea existed until Zinoviev informed him in 1926.[21]

Trotsky's demise as a power contender came in stages. In January 1925 he was replaced as Commissar of Defence, his one and only power base, in October 1926 he was expelled from the Politburo and a year later was stripped of his membership in the Central Committee. At the Fifteenth Party Congress in December 1927 he was excluded from the party itself. Despatched into administrative internal exile in early 1928, his final humiliation came in January 1929 when the Stalinist dominated Politburo decided to send him into foreign exile, where he remained for the rest of his life. He ended his days in Mexico City in August 1940, brutally murdered with an ice pick delivered to the head by a Stalinist agent. Stalin had a long and unforgiving memory. Trotsky's fate demonstrates that crucial taboos were broken in the tense atmosphere of the mid-to-late 1920s. For the first time in the party's history members of the Opposition were overtly harassed, some even arrested, by the secret police. Moreover, as early as November 1927 Stalin had reportedly drawn an unprecedented parallel between dissidents and the USSR's foreign foes: 'persons propagating opposition views [should] be regarded as dangerous accomplices of the internal and external enemies of the Soviet Union and....[should] be sentenced as "spies" by administrative decree of the GPU [secret police].'[22] If authentic, Stalin's words provide a chilling foretaste of the accusations and practices commonly used in the years of the Great Terror, 1936–8.

The lengthy list of defeat after defeat for the Trotskyist Opposition, however, gives an unwarranted air of inevitability to the power struggles, as if Stalin's victory was somehow preordained. It is true that Trotsky's position was essentially weak, but his tentative alliance with Zinoviev from the spring of 1926, which resulted in the formation of the 'United Opposition', revitalised the Left and presented a real challenge to the emerging Stalin-Bukharin duumvirate. As early as July 1923 when ostensibly allied with Stalin in the triumvirate, Zinoviev had bitterly complained to Kamenev about the General Secretary's peremptory unilateral decision-making, his 'swinish tricks' and 'personal despotism', sourly concluding that 'in fact, there is no troika, but only Stalin's dictatorship.' Lenin had been 'a thousand times right' about Stalin.[23] The anti-Trotsky campaign would soon compel

Zinoviev to shelve these somewhat overstated criticisms, but Stalin was no doubt aware of his 'ally's' dismissive attitudes. Three years later he identified Zinoviev as a more serious rival than the marginalised Trotsky. In a letter dated 25 June 1926, Stalin declared that 'the Zinoviev group is now the most harmful' as it is 'arrogantly....preparing a schism.' As such, Zinoviev should be removed from the Politburo and the Comintern. In contrast, Trotsky was to be treated more indulgently on the calculation that he 'will once again become loyal'.[24] What Stalin outlined in his missive came to pass. By November 1926 Zinoviev had been expelled from the Politburo and relieved of his duties as chair of the Comintern.

Thereafter, the Trotskyist-Zinovievist critique of the domestic, foreign and Comintern policies of the party leadership was biting and potentially debilitating. The United Opposition's crusade against the Comintern's disastrous strategy in China in 1926–7 proved particularly embarrassing to Stalin and Bukharin, who had replaced Zinoviev as *de facto* head of the International. The decimation of the Chinese communists in April 1927 by Chiang Kai-shek's Guomindang nationalist forces was a devastating blow to the Comintern's 'united front' tactics, tactics which had been strongly endorsed by Stalin. Following the abject failure of the British General Strike in May 1926, the Chinese debacle confirmed for the United Opposition that the Stalinised Comintern was sacrificing world revolution on the altar of Russian national interests. For them, this was the logical consequence of Stalin's 'opportunistic' theory of 'socialism in one country', which I shall discuss in greater detail below. Just as worrying, perhaps, for Stalin were the indications he was receiving from ordinary Soviet citizens that popular support for the Opposition was relatively buoyant. In the autumn of 1926, for instance, many letters, though by no means all, addressed to Stalin expressed sympathy for Trotsky, one anonymous party member writing that 'the workers love Trotsky more than Stalin.'[25]

There was more than a grain of truth in the United Opposition's vocal barrage, but in the harsh realities of 1927, when revolution in the West appeared an ever more distant prospect, Trotsky and Zinoviev lay open to attacks of 'defeatism', 'splitting the party' and weakening the security of the USSR at a time of perceived imperialist threat. The famous 'War Scare' of that year, which elicited near panic in the party and Soviet society, may not have been totally engineered by the Stalinist leadership, but it certainly facilitated the backlash against the United Opposition. At the Central Committee plenum in October 1927, Trotsky and Zinoviev were even accused of the ultimate sin: 'carrying the factional struggle against the party and its unity to a degree bordering on the formation of a new anti-Leninist party in conjunction with bourgeois intellectuals.'[26] This intense pressure finally paid off. By the time the Fifteenth Party Congress convened in December, Zinoviev, Kamenev and one hundred and twenty of their supporters, faced with the threat of expulsion from their beloved Leninist party, renounced all further oppositional activity and unconditionally recanted. Trotsky and most of his adherents held firm. Nearly all were expelled from the Communist Party as 'factionalists' and 'Menshevik' tools of 'the bourgeois elements'.

Stalin, Bukharin and the 'Right Opposition'

By the end of 1927 the United Opposition lay in tatters, Trotsky was about to be banished into internal exile in the Kazakh capital Alma Ata and Zinoviev and Kamenev had ignominiously capitulated and would later be readmitted into party ranks. Soon many more former Oppositionists would lend their backing to Stalin's 'revolution from above' and rapid industrialisation. The Bukharin-Stalin duumvirate appeared rock solid, but this was to change dramatically and very rapidly. Within a few months profound differences began to surface between the 'Stalinists' and the Bukharinist 'Right Opposition', whose leaders included Rykov, Lenin's successor as head of the government, and Tomskii, boss of the Soviet trade unions. Domestic issues were at the fore, but Comintern strategies also bitterly divided the erstwhile friends and political partners. The outcome was that by late 1929 Stalin had emerged triumphant, nearly all 'right-wingers' having been removed from their positions of influence both at home and abroad.

The confrontation originated in the 'grain crisis' of winter 1927–8.[27] We shall discuss this crisis in more detail in the next chapter, but briefly Stalin and his allies maintained that the peasantry, the kulaks in particular, were consciously withholding produce from the market in an impudent attempt to force the authorities to raise grain procurement prices. As such, the kulaks were deemed to be holding the proletarian state to ransom. Stalin responded by implementing 'extraordinary measures' in the countryside. Essentially, this entailed a return to the forcible grain requisitioning of the Civil War years. Behind the scenes Bukharin and his allies in the Politburo insisted that the moderate NEP strategy should continue. Industrial and agrarian policies should be balanced and the peasantry should not be unduly antagonised. Hence, they baulked at the violence used in the villages and in the summer of 1928 Bukharin famously intimated to Kamenev that Stalin was 'a Genghis Khan....[whose] line is ruinous for the whole revolution....an unprincipled intriguer, who subordinates everything to the preservation of his own power.'[28] Stalin, the master of tactical in-fighting, bided his time, making the occasional concession to his opponents in an attempt to divide and rule. Most notably, he and his colleagues succeeded in manufacturing an 'anti-party', 'right-wing deviation' out of the new 'opposition'. As Tomskii ruefully remarked: 'They were gradually refashioning us by means of a special system, every day a little brushstroke – today a dab, tomorrow a dab. Aha....as a result of this clever bit of work they've turned us into "right-wingers".'[29] These machinations outraged the Bukharinists on the grounds that it was the *Stalinists*, not them, who were scrapping Lenin's NEP pursued by the party since 1921. They also demonstrate that control over language, terminology and labels played an important part in undermining the various 'oppositions'.

Stalin's position in any case was unassailable by 1928. He could count on the backing of five out of nine Politburo members (Molotov, Voroshilov, Kuibyshev, Rudzutak and the slightly wavering Kalinin), virtually all the 'candidate' members of that body, including Kaganovich, Kirov and Mikoian, and he held a commanding majority in the Central Committee. Like its Leftist predecessor, the 'Right Opposition' was thus conclusively out-numbered in the key party offices. What is more, Bukharin's will to resist was from the start open to doubt. At the beginning of June 1928, he had written revealingly to Stalin in connection with the forthcoming Comintern Sixth World Congress:

> Koba,....*I do not wish to and will not fight....give us a chance to hold the congress in peace; do not carry out any superfluous splits;....We'll end the congress....and I'll be prepared to go wherever you like, without any scuffles, without any noise and without any struggle.*[30]

In many respects Bukharin fulfilled his promises. Although he defended his corner in Politburo and Central Committee meetings, he and his associates did little to rally support inside the party and were duty bound not to seek succour outside the party. Bukharin had no real power base and was utterly convinced that an overt power struggle would have profoundly adverse effects both for the party and the country as a whole. In this regard, it is crucial to remember that the years 1927–9 were characterised by war scares and internal crises. It appeared to many Bolsheviks that the very existence of the Soviet state was in question. It is thus tempting to conclude that for the Bukharinists party unity and strength ultimately outweighed 'petty' factional considerations. Everything had to be done to ensure the USSR's survival in a dangerous world and unduly rocking the faltering Soviet ship was a step too far. Leninist iron discipline had to be upheld. These factors, rather than Bukharin's personal 'weakness' or 'intellectualism', seem to me to best explain Stalin's relatively straightforward triumph over the 'Right Opposition'.

For the Stalinists, the international communist movement could not be spared the assault on the Bukharinists. The fierce campaign against the 'right' in the Comintern thus complemented the attack on Bukharin in the Soviet party.[31] The differences between the antagonists centred on the definition and application of the highly controversial 'social fascist' theory adopted by the Comintern in the course of 1928–9. Already in 1927 Bukharin had detected the first signs of an end to 'capitalist stabilisation', an intensification of national and international conflict, the threat of war against the USSR and a consequent radicalisation among European workers. This marked the start of a new revolutionary 'Third Period' in Comintern history. Crucially, Bukharin linked these developments to the 'treacherous and malicious role of social democracy'.[32] The social democrats were turning into dangerous enemies of the communists for two reasons. Firstly, they were becoming the main social pillar of support for capitalism's 'rationalisation of production' and, secondly, the German Social Democratic Party (SPD) in particular was held in contempt for backing the 'imperialist' war plans of the 'anti-Soviet front'.

Up to early 1928, Stalin hove to the 'Bukharin' line in the Comintern, but during that year and especially in 1929 the Stalinists radicalised the concept of the degeneration of social democracy largely in order to defeat Bukharin and his supporters in the international communist movement. From Bukharin's original prognostication it was but a small step to deride the social democrats as 'social fascists', aiding and abetting the 'fascistisation' of the capitalist state, overtly repressing the 'revolutionary proletariat' and hence becoming, objectively, a more dangerous enemy than the real fascists. The influence of social democracy over the working class therefore had to be crushed if the overthrow of capitalism was to be achieved. The Comintern's 'ultra-leftist' tactics thus matched the 'class war' domestic policies unleashed by Stalin in 1928–9. Bukharin could not accept the Stalinists' crass identification of social democracy with fascism, but Stalin's radical stance gained the approval of many foreign communists, notably in the German party. And those who did not agree either resigned or were expelled without ceremony. Hence, Bukharin and his adherents were out-manoeuvred and out-voted at key Comintern meetings. Bukharin himself was finally excluded from its Executive Committee in July 1929. There followed a veritable purge of 'Bukharinists' in the Comintern apparatus and communist parties and in their stead were promoted solid 'Stalinist cadres'. The 'Stalinisation' process in the international communist movement was complete and from now on the Comintern was to be a more or less docile instrument of the Soviet state.

What was the result of Stalin's victory in the succession struggles? For a start, the scope for inner-party discussion and disagreement was severely curtailed. As Graeme Gill has argued 'from spring 1929, policy debate and argumentation were no longer conducted in an open, combative style.'[33] In many ways, the Stalinists had effectively declared an end to doctrinal and theoretical disputes: socialism was in the process of being constructed, it was a truly massive undertaking and therefore the party no longer required divisive ideological hair-splitting. In this atmosphere, diversity of opinion and freedom of expression were all but eliminated from the party lexicon. Action, not words, was now the order of the day. And any doubter or vacillator would be dealt with accordingly. As Bukharin, quoting Lenin, had warned at the Sixth Comintern Congress: 'if you are going to expel all the not very obedient but clever people, and retain only obedient fools, you will *most assuredly* ruin the Party'.[34] Even more portentous, Stalin was now free to initiate his intense industrialisation, collectivisation and 'dekulakisation' campaigns without any major opposition. The economy, social structure and ultimately the political system of the USSR were about to be transformed. 'Stalinism' was in the making.

Stalin, the Opposition and the New Economic Policy

It should be evident by now that Stalin's rise to supremacy was not only about personal power, manipulation and cunning chicanery. The inner-party dog-fights were at all times couched in ideological and policy-making garb. All aspirants to Lenin's mantle, including Stalin, had to elaborate positions on the 'big' questions of the day: NEP and the optimum road to socialism in the Soviet Union, the Bolshevik state's relationship with the working class and peasantry, the internal organisation of the party, and the fate of the revolution abroad. These were closely interlinked issues and the cause of bitter altercations among the protagonists. In the next two sections of this chapter I will examine the debates on the most contentious themes, the New Economic Policy and Stalin's theory of 'socialism in one country', before reaching an overall conclusion on the reasons for Stalin's triumph.

The fundamental question that exercised the Bolshevik elite in the early-to-mid 1920s was whether NEP was leading to the construction of socialism or to the restoration of capitalism. Introduced at the Tenth Party Congress in March 1921, Lenin's New Economic Policy was a radical attempt to forge social stability and encourage regeneration of the ravaged Soviet economy (large-scale industrial production in 1921 was a mere 21 per cent of the 1913 figure).[35] In his last writings the ailing Bolshevik leader advocated NEP as a viable long-term transition to socialism. However, in the party it was quite widely interpreted as a retreat from consecrated socialist principles, its market orientation seen as a deviation from the prime goal of 'building socialism'. For many Bolsheviks, and not just those on the 'left', NEP was an ideologically suspect innovation that represented a form of 'state capitalism', a notion even Lenin readily conceded. Hence, it would not be much of an exaggeration to claim that the party rather reluctantly accepted its provisions, an attitude which goes some way to explaining why its demise under Stalin in 1928–9 solicited relatively little opposition. The stipulations of NEP permitted the re-appearance of 'petit-bourgeois remnants': small-scale private entrepreneurs and traders in the urban areas (so-called Nepmen) and better-off peasants (*kulaks*) in the countryside based on a certain revival of the despised 'market'. There was scant central planning and unemployment grew in the course of the 1920s. The 'socialist' component of NEP was that the 'commanding heights' of the economy – heavy industry, wholesale trade, banking, foreign trade – remained nationalised and the peasantry had to fulfil state imposed quotas of grain and other procurements before they could sell any surpluses on the open market. As one expert has commented: 'NEP was a hybrid combination of petty capitalism and state regulation'.[36]

It seems that Stalin's initial response to NEP, unlike Trotsky's, was largely negative on the grounds that it signified a shift 'away from militant socialist revolution toward compromise with the class enemy', the peasant and the small-scale capitalist. Stalin, though, was wise enough to refrain from overt criticism of Lenin's departure from War Communism.[37] By the mid-1920s, in his public pronouncements at least, Stalin had altered his stance, giving the impression of being a committed, albeit ambivalent, exponent of NEP and he upheld this position until the crises of 1928–9. It is quite possible that privately he maintained a desire to make the 'great leap' to a fully socialist, rather than 'state capitalist', economy and his policies from 1928 onwards certainly attest to this attitude. But if so, he expended much energy and time in defending moderate economic polices against his Leftist detractors and it would appear safe to conclude that in the years 1924–7 Stalin's support of NEP was driven as much by conviction as by political and tactical expediency. Both the national and international conjunctures – that is, the need for social cohesion and economic consolidation at home and the 'relative capitalist stabilisation' and lack of revolutionary fervour abroad – provided the broader rationale for Stalin's equivocal adherence to NEP.

The basic point at issue between the Left Opposition and the 'party majority' was whether NEP could accumulate the necessary surpluses to fund the ultimate goal of the Bolsheviks: the industrialisation and modernisation of the USSR. Their disagreements have for this reason been dubbed the 'great industrialisation debate'.[38] On the one hand, the Left, spearheaded by the Old Bolshevik Evgenii Preobrazhenskii, argued strongly from 1924 onwards for a faster pace of industrialisation and more state planning to overcome the vagaries of the market. The resources for this huge task were to be gathered by what Preobrazhenskii called 'primitive socialist accumulation'. This meant that the peasantry should be subject to higher direct and indirect taxes and the terms of trade should be roundly in industry's favour. Essentially, it was a question of squeezing greater and greater quantities of cheap grain out of the peasantry, both to export and feed the hungry worker, while somehow ensuring social stability. Coercion of the peasant was specifically rejected. Recognising some of the contradictions in his own ideas, Preobrazhenskii reiterated the absolute necessity of revolution in the advanced West to alleviate the burdens of Russian modernisation. Trotsky and later Zinoviev defended Preobrazhenskii's theories, constantly warning of the 'kulak danger', the 'anti-worker' propensities of the party leadership and the gross inadequacies of its industrialisation programme, all of which, they asserted, threatened the degeneration of the party into a subordinate of the bourgeoisie. Their recommendations effectively signified the annulment of NEP, or at least Bukharin's and, to a lesser extent, Stalin's pro-peasant understanding of it.

By 1924–5 Bukharin had emerged as the principal adversary of the Left Opposition and the main advocate of a long-term moderate NEP strategy. Although all Bolsheviks could agree on the need for state planning, industrialisation and a 'modern' socialist economy, Bukharin insisted that Preobrazhenskii's 'primitive socialist accumulation' would seriously undermine the worker-peasant alliance that lay at the heart of NEP and ultimately risk the very existence of the Soviet state by fomenting peasant revolts. Rather than squeeze the more productive peasants, Bukharin sought to actively encourage the 'middle' and kulak elements, because it was precisely they who would provide the farm surpluses that would fund industrialisation. By definition, this would be a very gradual process, which Bukharin himself characterised as 'riding into socialism on a peasant nag'. Even more

controversially, in April 1925 he exhorted the peasantry to 'enrich your-
selves', a slogan that stuck in the throats of nearly all other Bolsheviks, Stalin
included, and one that he was soon forced to withdraw as ideologically
unsound. Nevertheless, it was Bukharin's conception of NEP and the road to
socialism that was ratified at key party congresses and conferences in the
mid-1920s, the opposition being incrementally debarred from representa-
tion and meaningful participation.

While upholding Bukharin's general line, Stalin tended to take a back
seat in the economic disputes with the Left Opposition, perhaps consciously
positioning himself as a unifying 'centrist'. He agreed that tax concessions to
the more prosperous peasants were advisable, but at the same time firmly
disassociated himself from Bukharin's more pro-peasant inclinations – 'the
slogan "get rich" is not our slogan' – and let it be known that the pace of
economic modernisation needed to be stepped up. It is tempting to conclude that for Stalin the issue of national security was more salient than the
subtleties of economic 'laws' and theories. Given the conditions of continuing 'capitalist encirclement' and the Bolsheviks' ideologically motivated
'siege mentality', the *tempo* of industrialisation became the burning question. When should the advance to socialist industry be resumed? How fast
should it proceed? These concerns were given renewed urgency at the time
of the 'war scare' in 1927. Above all, could full-scale socialism be built successfully in an isolated and embattled USSR? Or should world revolution
remain the cornerstone of Marxism-Leninism in the absence of which the
Soviet state was doomed to destruction? Thus, the whole imbroglio of
the international revolution and the Soviet Union's place within it came to
the fore by the mid-1920s. Stalin was to stamp his mark on these debates
with arguably his best known formulation – 'socialism in one country'.

Stalin and 'Socialism in One Country'

The General Secretary invoked his much-vaunted doctrine of 'socialism in
one country' for the first time in December 1924. It was a theory that was to
impact mightily on the internal policies, foreign diplomacy and Comintern
strategies of the Soviet Union, as well as become a major bone of contention
in the inner-party power struggles. Initially propounded rather tentatively,
Stalin seems to have drawn and expanded on Bukharin's earlier notion of
'growing into socialism'. In outlining his unorthodox theory, Stalin assiduously, albeit controversially, stressed its authentic Leninist credentials.
Lenin's 'law of the uneven, spasmodic, economic and political development

of the capitalist countries' signified that 'the victory of socialism in one country,....while capitalism remains in other countries,....is quite possible and probable'. However, Stalin could not allow himself to appear overly unorthodox and added: 'it goes without saying that for the *complete* victory of socialism, for a *complete* guarantee against the restoration of the old order, the united efforts of the proletarians of several countries are necessary.'[39] Stalin's emphasis was certainly innovative and potentially explosive. The construction of socialism in a single state – that is, in a 'backward' agrarian USSR – *was* possible without risking a peasant war, without succumbing to economic blockade and without the need for world, or at least European, revolution, hitherto for many Bolsheviks an axiomatic Leninist truism. Stalin's vague formulation of 'united efforts' scarcely recognised the necessity of revolution in other capitalist states. The only real threat to Soviet socialism, according to Stalin, was military intervention by the 'imperialist powers'.

The significance of this departure was not readily apparent, not even most likely to Stalin himself. No one at the time took much notice of the General Secretary's rare sally into the dizzy realms of theory and indeed Lenin's last writings did seem to suggest that an isolated socialist Russia based on peasant cooperatives was capable of maintaining an independent existence in a world of capitalist enemies. It is also the case that Stalin's main antagonists in the mid-1920s accepted parts of his analysis. Zinoviev, Kamenev and even Trotsky to a lesser extent admitted that Russia possessed sufficient resources to 'take socialist construction forward' and that the process of building socialism was ongoing in the Soviet Union. But the nascent 'United Opposition' ultimately rejected the notion that the *final* or complete victory of socialism was possible without successful revolutions abroad. For Trotsky, Stalin's autarchic idea of a single socialist economy isolated in an international capitalist market made a mockery of Marxist theory. Hence, the 'narrow national-mindedness' and 'national reformism' inherent in 'socialism in one country' appalled him, as did Stalin's and Bukharin's apparent downgrading of proletarian internationalism and the prospects of world revolution. These were articles of faith for Trotsky and Zinoviev on which the fate of Soviet Russia depended. As the latter put it in his much interrupted speech to the Fifteenth Party Conference in October 1926:

The final victory of socialism in one country is impossible. The theory of final victory in one country is wrong. *We are building and will build socialism in the USSR with the aid of the world proletariat.*...We will win final victory because revolution in other countries is inevitable.'[40]

By then such views found precious few adherents among his unsympa-
thetic listeners. Trotsky was even more categorical, asserting in 1929 that an
isolated proletarian state was doomed to collapse.[41]

Stalin's 'socialism in one country', it can be surmised, appealed to many
new raw party members, untutored, and not interested, in the finer nuances
of Marxist-Leninist philosophy. The 'Lenin Levy' of 1924–5 had resulted in
the mass enrolment of approximately 440,000 workers in the party. This may
or may not have been a conscious attempt by Stalin's Secretariat to flood
the party with 'loyal' proletarian members,[42] but what these recruits surely
understood was Stalin's emphasis on self-sufficiency, a scarcely veiled nod in
the direction of nationalist sentiment. In contrast to Trotsky's theory of 'permanent revolution', which he dusted off in the autumn of 1924 and which
appeared to presage only more upheaval and hardship for the long-suffering
Soviet people, Stalin's concept promised a distinct measure of stability and
'national' progress based on faith in the viability and potential strength of
the Soviet economy. This stance attracted the sub-elites and burgeoning bureaucrats, for whom 'Soviet patriotism sat easily with enjoyment of the fruits
of offices disbursed by the Secretariat.' In this way a 'Stalinist constituency'
was formed in the party, one which, as we have seen, grew with Stalin's 'left
turn' in 1928–9.[43] It is also likely, as two Russian scholars have recently
suggested, that Stalin's apparent 'refusal' to export revolution was 'a wise
decision, which found widespread support among the people', not just the
party faithful.[44]

What is more, Stalin's evaluation of the international conjuncture on
which 'socialism in one country' partly rested was persuasive. Elaborating
on his ideas in the course of 1925–7, Stalin reiterated the Leninist orthodoxy that world revolution was historically inevitable, but noted that the
revolutionary tide in Europe had temporarily ebbed, a realistic assessment
following the defeat of the 'German October' in 1923, setbacks in Bulgaria,
Poland and Estonia, and the failure of the British General Strike in May
1926. In Stalin's (and Bukharin's) estimation, these grave disappointments
for the Comintern were evidence of an insecure, but nevertheless palpable
'relative capitalist stabilisation'. Technological advances, rationalisation in
production, quantitative growth and the easing of international tensions in
the wake of the Dawes Plan and the 'Locarno spirit' meant that capitalism
had for the time being consolidated itself, delaying its inevitable demise. But
crucially for Stalin there were *two* stabilisations. In Soviet Russia, NEP had
facilitated the recovery of the economy and thus in his words a 'certain temporary equilibrium of forces' existed between the two competing systems, a
'period of "peaceful coexistence" between the Land of Soviets and the capi-

talist countries'.[45] What the USSR required now was a prolonged and tranquil period of socialist construction, free from the threat of 'imperialist intervention'. These prognostications must have appeared eminently reasonable and desirable to many Soviet and foreign communists, and together with Stalin's less savoury penchant for *otsechenie*, the 'chopping-off' of troublesome comrades, help us comprehend the multiple sources of his triumph both at home and in the Comintern.[46]

Why Stalin?

Why, then, did Stalin emerge victorious from the bruising battles of the 1920s? As with any complex historical process, we must eschew monocausal explanations and explore an intriguing combination of personal, organisational, socio-cultural and politico-ideological factors.[47] The 'heroic' interpretation of the rise of Stalin focuses on the personalities of the main actors. Stalin has consistently been portrayed as a stereotypical 'Asiatic': cunning, duplicitous, shameless and cruel, capable of carefully planning his road to supremacy. His overriding goal was dictatorial power and his various policy positions and 'theories' were merely smokescreens to mask the ultimate aim of smashing his rivals. Neither was he above stealing his opponents' programmes as in 1928–9 with the crash course of heavy industrialisation which the Trotskyists had been advocating for several years. The attributes of Stalin's leading antagonists have also been subject to much critical analysis.[48] Zinoviev is almost universally regarded as a self-important, even unpleasant, careerist with few political skills outside of his undoubted oratorical prowess. Kamenev appears generally as a second-string figure in the shadows of more illustrious colleagues, although recent work has challenged this overly negative assumption.[49] Views of Bukharin tend to be more positive. He was a respected theoretician and author with a genial personality for which he was well-liked in the party. In many ways he represented the 'human face' of Bolshevism. But his lack of guile meant that Bukharin, crucially, had little idea of political in-fighting and was inept at constructing the necessary organisational power base.[50] Trotsky, Stalin's most determined adversary, is depicted as suffering from acute personality defects and delusions of grandeur. Above all, he missed several opportunities to undermine Stalin's increasing authority, not least at the time of Lenin's 'Testament', and accepted the dangerous notion that 'the Party is always right'.[51] All without exception, including Lenin, are said to have grossly under-estimated the 'dull-witted' General Secretary until it was far

too late. The conclusion is clear: Stalin 'won' because he was the most de-
ceitful and ruthless and his rivals 'lost' because they were weak-willed and
easily misled and manipulated.

While personal characteristics, ambitions and failings obviously played a
sizeable role in Stalin's rise, it would be as well not to exaggerate their
significance, not least because the 'psycho-historical' approach tends to overestimate the extent any one individual can 'control' events and situations and
also because personalities are in part socially constructed and cannot be di-
vorced from surrounding 'reality'. The organisational and administrative
'reality' behind Stalin's triumph has already been examined in some detail in
the section 'Stalin as General Secretary' and needs no further commentary.
The more recent 'socio-cultural' interpretation does deserve serious attention. Associated with scholars such as Sheila Fitzpatrick and Moshe Lewin,
this view emphasises the 'formative experience' of the Civil War and its
legacy, the changing social and political composition of the Soviet working
class and the gradual bureaucratisation and ossification of the party-state
structures. As we have noted, the Civil War engendered a 'command-order'
mentality among the Bolsheviks and thrust the hard practical activists to the
forefront, displacing the more intellectually-minded strata. Stalin's *modus
operandi* tended to suit these newly promoted *praktiki*, who were used to carrying out orders unconditionally and to being obeyed in like manner by subordinates. What is more, it has been argued that in NEP Russia with the influx
of peasant migrants and *déclassé* elements into the factories the Soviet
working class became to a certain extent de-proletarianised and less politically conscious, thus forcing the party to substitute itself for the now barely
existent 'proletarian masses'. This in turn encouraged 'machine politics', undemocratic practices and bureaucratisation, culminating not in the 'dictatorship of the proletariat' but in the 'dictatorship of the leadership'. All these
developments facilitated and strengthened Stalin's grip on power. Indeed,
in Trotsky's estimation Stalin personified the counter-revolutionary ethos of
this emergent self-satisfied bureaucracy. He was the product of and therefore
needed by 'the tired radicals, by the bureaucrats, by the *nepmen*, the *kulaks*,
the upstarts, the sneaks, by all the worms that are crawling out of the
upturned soil of the manured revolution'.[52]

The politico-ideological interpretations of Stalin's rise examine the relationship between Leninism and Stalinism and place the power struggles
firmly in the acrimonious NEP debates over the optimum road to socialism.
It is commonly argued that Lenin's pre-revolutionary principle of 'democratic centralism', which effectively subordinated the party to the will of its leadership, his insistence on strict ideological purity and tendency to suppress

'heretics', his recourse to the Cheka and creation of the first labour camps, and his passionate belief in 'iron discipline' and centralisation, culminating in the infamous 'ban on factions' in March 1921 'furnished Stalin with powerful weapons in the succession struggle; disagreement became factionalism, factionalism became treason....One by one Trotsky, Zinoviev, Kamenev and Bukharin fell victim to the very political machine they helped to construct.'[53] In this view, Stalinism was the logical, even inevitable, outcome of Leninism. Although no one would deny the numerous lines of continuity between the Leninist and Stalinist phases of the revolution, such a teleological approach tends to under-estimate the scope for alternative routes of development and obscures the potential 'turning-points' in Soviet history. It also overlooks the important dissimilarities between the Leninist and Stalinist systems, not the least of which were the sheer scale of state terror under the latter, the targeting of loyal communists and the near total straitjacketing of freedom of expression and opinion within the party.

Finally, according to many scholars ideological considerations and stances contributed in no small measure to Stalin's ascendancy. In short, his 'centrist' position on NEP and the optimum road to socialism proved more operable, attractive and dynamic than either the 'Left's' anti-peasant industrialisation project, which threatened to engulf the USSR in deep social conflicts between town and countryside, or the 'Right's' pro-peasant 'socialism at a nag's pace', which risked a restoration of 'petit-bourgeois' capitalism. Stalin adapted to rapidly changing circumstances and was able to carry the majority of Bolsheviks with him. However, as Chris Ward has pointed out, this methodology 'cannot answer the question of intentionality – of whether or not Stalin manipulated ideological registers for other, hidden ends.' Perhaps, ultimately, Ward's overall verdict on Stalin's triumph is the most persuasive: revolution and civil war had given birth to a chaotic 'politics of permanent emergency' to which Stalin's administrative talents and authoritarian proclivities were eminently suited.

> Given Lenin's death (which threw the leadership into disarray), a modicum of popular support (evident amongst the metropolitan proletariat in 1928) and his mastery of the apparatus (staffed by the new cohort of sub-élites thrown up after 1917), circumstances ensured that inside the mutating body of the party-state [Stalin] would succeed and his rivals fail.[54]

How Stalin used this abundant power in a breakneck drive for 'modernity' is the theme of the next chapter.

Chapter 3: Moderniser

In 1928–9 Stalin and his leading colleagues launched a state-sponsored drive for 'modernity' of unprecedented violence, scope and pace. The overriding goal of this self-proclaimed 'revolution from above' was none other than to overcome Russia's perennial 'backwardness', to drag the USSR, kicking and screaming if necessary, into the twentieth century. All vestiges of the *ancien régime* were to be wiped out. This truly profound socio-economic and cultural transformation was designed to expand and modernise Soviet industry and agriculture at unheard-of tempos. An entire heavy industrial base was to be created almost from scratch and vast collective farms (*kolkhozy*) were to dominate the Soviet countryside. The USSR had to catch up and overtake the advanced capitalist states as rapidly as possible. This cataclysmic upheaval was aimed, above all, at ensuring the country's military security. And it all had to be done in a decade, not generations as in the 'bourgeois' west.

Just as importantly, Stalin's revolution *par excellence* had the professed goal of 'constructing socialism' in the USSR, thus fulfilling the historic mission of the Bolshevik Revolution. This socialist modernisation was to be rational, efficient and centrally coordinated via a series of Five-Year Plans. State planning, so it was believed, would overcome the anarchic booms and busts and social inequities of the capitalist market epitomised by the contemporaneous Great Depression. Private production, trade and distribution would be all but eradicated. 'Socialism' would bring about abundance and material well-being for every Soviet citizen. Socialised agriculture would be mechanised and productive, the new industrial enterprises would be supplied with the latest technologies and would pump out record quantities of iron, steel, machinery and eventually consumer goods. Cheap housing and free education and health care would be available for all. If everyone tightened their belts for a while, socialism would soon arrive. All that was needed was the requisite iron will, resolve and determination. Or in Stalin's words, 'there are no fortresses which Bolsheviks cannot capture'.[1]

That, at least, was the theory and the propaganda message. The reality was human suffering on a vast scale as the country was plunged into severe crisis in the years 1930–3. The prime victims, as ever, were the peasantry. Stripped of their land, they were herded, often at gunpoint, into collective farms where they toiled in conditions reminiscent of serfdom. Even worse, millions of them starved to death in the Great Famine of 1932–3 or were 'dekulakised' and shunted off into internal exile or the newly-created Gulag system of labour camps and colonies. The situation in the urban areas was better, but still the majority of industrial labourers lived and worked in dire poverty, hunger and shortage. By the mid-1930s the cultural and academic intelligentsia was harnessed to the goals of the state and creative and scholarly freedom was effectively annulled. The national minorities of the Soviet Union were subject to a gradual process of 'Russification' and aspects of the Tsarist past were evaluated more positively. The Communist Party itself became a near monolithic entity as independent or oppositional activity and ideas were suppressed. Stalin emerged as a dictator whose word was gospel.

These hectic life-shattering events force scholars to ponder some very difficult issues: why was full-scale collectivisation introduced in 1929–30 and with what consequences?; how did the peasantry respond to this unprecedented attack on their life-style?; was the Great Famine consciously engineered 'from above' to smash peasant and national resistance?; to what extent was the planned economy 'planned'?; how far did rapid industrialisation improve the lot of the Soviet population?; most relevantly for our purposes, what was Stalin's role in determining these momentous decisions?; conversely, how far did other actors, high and low, contribute to the 'Great Breakthrough'?; finally, what is specifically 'modern' about Stalinist socio-economic and cultural development in the period 1928–39 and can Stalin accurately be described as a 'moderniser'? These problems form the basis of this chapter, but I will also discuss two inter-related matters: Stalin's 'Cultural Revolution' and the subsequent 'Great Retreat', and the vexed 'national question'.

Stalin, Collectivisation and Famine

In the winter of 1927–8, the Soviet Union entered a grain crisis which threatened to leave the towns and Red Army hungry. Many Bolshevik leaders were convinced that the peasantry, especially the 'counter-revolutionary' kulaks,

..ately withholding produce from the state in the hope of extract-
..g higher prices. Stalin's temporary 'solution' to the agrarian crisis of NEP
in the early months of 1928 was to launch what became known as the 'Urals-
Siberian method' of grain extraction. These 'extraordinary measures', reminiscent of the requisitioning policies of War Communism during the Civil
War, turned out to be the first step in the state's violent assault on the multi-
million Soviet peasantry. The details of the Stalinists' tortuous path to collectivisation in 1928–9 do not concern us here. Suffice it to say that in
January 1928 Stalin made a crucial trip to the Siberian grain-growing areas
after which he seems to have decided definitively that coercion, forced collectivisation and dekulakisation were required to bring the peasantry once
and for all under party-state control. In addition, his experiences in Siberia
taught him that regional lower-level officialdom could not be fully trusted.
Indeed, he accused many bureaucrats of siding with the kulaks against the
party. At the same time, he discovered a measure of dynamic support 'from
below' among those local activists who embraced his advocacy of emergency
measures. Finally, the Siberian trip confirmed his deep suspicions of the
economic stranglehold of the kulaks, whom he regarded as a real threat to
the security of the state and to the party's monopoly of power.

Ominously, Stalin broadened these Siberian conclusions to encompass
the whole country. The only solution, he deduced, was a major purge of the
party (the Bukharinite 'right-wing') and a rapid advance to collectivisation.
In short, Stalin's sojourn in Siberia represented a significant radicalisation
of his anti-NEP inclinations, so much so that by early 1928 he had decided
that kulak power had to be smashed, that in the short term partial collectivisation was necessary and in the longer run total socialisation of agriculture
was imperative.[2] As the grain crisis continued, these views crystallised and by
the end of 1929 Stalin had convinced himself that the poor and 'middle'
peasants would join the new collectives voluntarily and the 'capitalist' kulaks
had to be 'eliminated as a class'.[3] Comprehensive (*sploshnaia*) collectivisation was now the order of the day.

Why was this momentous decision taken and more broadly why was
breakneck industrialisation unleashed? A complex combination of factors
accounts for Stalin's revolution. The historical context of Russian modernisation played a part, as did pressures 'from below', the international
climate and important socio-economic concerns. But in my estimation
politico-ideological determinants – the rapid advance to a 'socialist'
economy – informed the entire decision-making process. Ever since the
reign of Peter the Great, the state had been the prime sponsor of industrial
growth in Russia. In the 1890s, Sergei Witte, Tsar Nicholas II's Minister of

Finance, oversaw a period of rapid expansion which modernised production, increased output and created some of the largest factories in the world. Funding came mainly from grain exports, thus hitting the long-suffering peasants. However, despite the impressive growth Tsarist Russia remained relatively behind the developing economies of Western Europe, America and Japan. The point is that Stalin inherited a state-led model of modernisation bolstered by the collectivist 'statism' embedded in Leninism.

It is commonly assumed that Stalin was the decisive motor behind the 'revolution from above' and that all key decrees emanated from his office. There is much to recommend this interpretation, but it is not the full picture. Inputs and pressures 'from below', from local party activists and secretaries, 'radical' officials in economic agencies, militant young workers and Civil War veterans, appear to have influenced the leaders in Moscow. Anti-NEP sentiment was strong among many communists anxious to leap into 'socialism' as they understood it.[4] Also, the implementation of centrally prescribed orders, themselves often vague, was inordinately difficult to monitor in the chaotic days of early collectivisation. Stalin drove the campaign forward and initiated violent policies such as 'dekulakisation', but he acted on information derived from multiple sources and he could not control all local and regional responses. More than this, it has even been argued that some provincial officials opposed Stalin's agrarian plans and that his hold on power in 1928–9 was vulnerable.[5] Not all bureaucrats were as yet compliant 'yes-men'.

The international conjuncture is likewise vital for an understanding of the launching of the 'Great Breakthrough'. The 'War Scare' of 1927 may have been in part artificially created, but the reality of 'capitalist encirclement' was axiomatic for all Bolsheviks, especially Stalin. Armed conflict between 'imperialism' and 'socialism' was inevitable and it was *absolutely imperative* that the USSR be prepared sooner rather than later for this historic clash of civilisations. This was the 'state of siege' mentality that engendered the rapid pace of Stalinist modernisation. The foreign threat continued to inform Stalin's strategies even after the launching of forced collectivisation. What most alarmed the political and military elites in late 1929 and early 1930 was the possibility of an external attack on the USSR at a time of virtual civil war in the Soviet countryside. Intense peasant resistance combined with foreign pressures appear to have fostered a 'perception of vulnerability' among fearful party leaders, a perception which partially accounts for the temporary suspension of the collectivisation campaign in March 1930.[6]

Economically, the Stalinists were correct to link agricultural advancement, industrial progress and military security. The central idea was that

massively enhanced grain collections, combined with improved mechanisa-
tion and production on the *kolkhozy*, would permit increased exports on the
world market, which in turn would mean that desperately needed finances
could be ploughed into industrialisation. Economic historians have never
agreed on the practicality and effectiveness of this strategy and whether resources and investment moved from the village to the town or vice versa.
Some insist that a continued balanced NEP-style policy would have resulted
in solid industrial growth rates into the 1930s without the need for the horrendous violence and excess deaths of Stalinism. This is an attractive proposition which may well hold water, but it is one which attenuates the role of
Bolshevik ideology, an ideology that was intent on radically transforming
the world. Collectivisation and planned state-led rapid industrialisation
quite simply signified 'socialism', the overcoming of capitalist and 'petit-
bourgeois remnants' in town and country, the fulfilment, no less, of the
Revolution. For Stalin and many Bolsheviks, the peasants, notably the
kulaks, were holding the Soviet state and workers to ransom by withholding
grain from the urban areas.[7] They must be taught a lesson they would not
forget in a hurry. In this sense, 'dekulakisation' and collectivisation were
two sides of the same coin. What is more, collectivisation extended party-
state control to the huge hinterlands of the USSR, a political aim of
immense significance for the Stalinists since under NEP the peasantry and
much of the countryside enjoyed a fair measure of autonomy. From now on
the state could directly appropriate grain from the collectivised peasantry
without the circumventions and negotiations of NEP.

Collectivisation, begun in earnest in December 1929, meant that land,
equipment, tools and livestock were to be pooled into collective farms often
encompassing entire villages. This revolutionary drive to 'modernity' was
implemented by squads of party activists, secret police detachments and
approximately 25,000 worker volunteers, who scoured the countryside persuading, cajoling and if necessary coercing peasants into the collectives. The
whole process was so disruptive, improvised and threatening to the socio-
economic order that Stalin called a halt in March 1930 in his famous article
'Dizzy with Success' in which he hypocritically stated that 'collective farms
cannot be set up by force' and characteristically shifted the blame to 'over
zealous' and 'blockhead' local comrades.[8] The immediate result was that
hundreds of thousands of peasants quit the collectives ensuring the sowing
and harvesting of grain. Once the harvest was gathered in the autumn of
1930, collectivisation was reintroduced with a vengeance and by the end of
the decade over 90 per cent of households were enrolled in some 250,000
kolkhozy. If forced collectivisation was not bad enough, it was accompanied

by a violent programme of social surgery, 'dekulakisation', which aimed to rid mainstream society of what the Stalinists regarded as 'counter-revolutionary' and 'anti-socialist elements'.[9] It has been calculated that in the years 1930–1 about 1.8 million peasants (not all of them 'kulaks') were deported in cattle trucks to inhospitable areas of the USSR, many of them perishing in their new 'homes'. A further 400,000 households were uprooted but remained in their own districts. As many as 390,000 people were arrested, most sent to labour camps, and approximately 21,000 were shot.[10]

The peasantry responded to the terrible hardships of forcible collectivisation with widespread resistance, sometimes armed and often led by women. All sub-strata of the peasantry participated in the mass disturbances (*massovye vystupleniia*), many of which assumed threatening dimensions, especially in the first half of 1930. In that year alone there were reported 13,754 outbreaks of mass unrest compared to 709 in 1928 and 1,307 in 1929. These demonstrations, riots and even full-scale uprisings involved over 2.5 million peasants. In addition, there were 13,794 'acts of kulak terrorism' claiming 3,155 victims among Bolshevik activists and Soviet officials.[11] This was an unequal state-society conflict, bordering on civil war in some regions. It is little wonder that Stalin later intimated to Churchill that collectivisation in some ways represented a greater challenge to the Soviet regime than the Second World War. Peasants not only bitterly resented the imposition of collective farms, but more generally saw the onslaught as an attack on their traditional ways of life and culture. The abolition in 1930 of the village commune, the *mir*, the closing of thousands of churches, the melting down of church bells and the persecution of local priests elicited an angry response, and fears that the all-pervasive state would take over ownership of livestock signalled an orgy of slaughter and consumption of cattle, sheep and pigs. Soviet livestock figures did not fully recover from the mass killings until the 1950s and passive peasant resistance and foot-dragging remained more or less constant throughout the 1930s and beyond. Arguably, the principal peasant reaction was to escape the hated collectives by migrating to the burgeoning towns and industrial areas. Approximately 19 million did so between 1926 and 1939, a demographic shift of unprecedented scope that altered the face of the Soviet Union and placed immense strains on over-stretched municipal authorities.

How successful was collective farming? Although *kolkhoz* production figures fluctuated in the 1930s partly dependent on climatic conditions, collectivised agriculture continued to be the Achilles heel of the Soviet economy right through to the Gorbachev era. Average agricultural production in the years 1937–9 exceeded the 1928 level by at most 9.5 per cent and was actually lower per head of population. Even more striking, it has been calculated that in 1940 total personal consumption of Soviet citizens was approximately seven per cent lower than in 1928.[12] In the shorter term, however, the chaos of collectivisation and the Politburo's insistence on maintaining high levels of grain exports resulted in a catastrophe of Biblical proportions – the famine of 1932–3.

Stalin's precise role in the Great Famine is a matter of conjecture among historians. Robert Conquest, acclaimed author of the classic *The Harvest of Sorrow*, is scathing on the General Secretary. Reminding his readers that 'the Soviet collectivisation terror took more lives than were lost by all countries, on all fronts, in the First World War', Conquest emphasises Stalin's 'criminal responsibility….[his] special brand of hypocrisy [and] deception', nowhere more manifest than in his crass denial that the famine existed. Stalin and his associates knew that their decrees would result in famine, they knew in 1932–3 that mass starvation stalked the Ukraine, Kazakhstan and other areas of the USSR and yet still issued orders 'to ensure that the famine was not alleviated, and to confine it to certain areas.' More controversially, Conquest insists that the famine was engineered by the Stalinists as part of a deliberate programme to smash nationalism once and for all particularly among the Ukrainian peasantry and intelligentsia. As for the number of victims, Conquest calculates that about 14.5 million peasants perished as a consequence of dekulakisation and the famine, approximately seven million from starvation. What is more, 'these are conservative figures.'[13]

Conquest wrote his book before the Soviet archival gold-rush. It is certainly the case that official documents and statistics from party-state archives need to be handled very carefully, but they do suggest a slightly more complex picture. The recognised authorities on the Great Famine, Robert Davies and Stephen Wheatcroft, concur that the new archival records 'do not change it [Conquest's interpretation] fundamentally', although they do find it 'one-sided'. Stalin was indeed well aware of the effects of his 'ruthless and brutal' policies in the countryside and on one occasion he even used the word 'famine' to refer to them.[14] However, Davies and Wheatcroft reject the notion that the Stalinist leadership consciously sought to induce famine as a means of crushing Ukrainian nationalism. The crisis 'was unexpected and undesirable.' In addition, they point out that in the summer of 1932 Stalin proposed lowering the grain collection plans in the Ukraine and in nearly all other regions by a total of three million tons (approximately 14%), but it was far too little, too late. Generally, Stalin was scornful of regional officials who requested even higher reductions. Finally, Davies and Wheatcroft estimate that 5.7 million people died of hunger in the years 1930–3, implicitly arguing that Conquest's totals are implausibly high. Whether we accept higher or lower variants, 'this is an enormous figure' only exceeded in the twentieth century by the famine in China after 1958.[15] The bottom line is that collections and exports of grain were maintained at high levels despite the compelling evidence of starvation. Stalin's responsibility for this murderous policy is undeniable.

Collectivisation of Soviet agriculture represented 'revolution on a massive scale: social, political, cultural and economic'.[16] It was carried out as a veritable military operation on the home front in an atmosphere of war scares and internal breakdown. It is hardly surprising that the soldier's tunic, boots and breeches became *de rigueur* for all leading Stalinists at this time. When assessing Stalin's input, it is difficult to avoid the conclusion that the whole process of intense social upheaval accompanied by large-scale coercion against perceived 'enemies' closely suited and reflected the General Secretary's 'class war' mentality and his revolutionary Bolshevik commitments. Stalin's 'revolution from above' resulted in a truly fundamental transformation of Soviet life far outstripping the changes ushered in by Lenin's October Revolution. Stalin could now portray himself in his burgeoning cult as the 'builder of socialism', the standard bearer of Marxism-Leninism, the anointed 'Great Leader' bent on fulfilling the historic goals of 1917.

Stalin and Rapid Industrialisation

The main economic rationale of collectivisation was to raise funds and investment for the increasingly rapid tempos of industrial development demanded by the Stalinist leadership from 1928 onwards. If Stalin ever lived up to his adopted name it was in the period of the First Five-Year Plan (1928–32) when the production of steel, steel and more steel seemed to take possession of him and his coterie. Light industry and consumer goods production were not to be forgotten, but the Stalinists were obsessed with iron, steel and machine-building. The 1930s was a decade when entire cities and heavy industrial sites, such as Magnitogorsk in the Urals, were forged from scratch, when millions of peasants turned themselves painfully into urbanised labourers, when living standards reached rock bottom and when the state was forced to devise and re-devise mass mobilisation strategies in order to keep workers' shoulders to the wheel. For the Stalinists, the pressure of time was paramount. The USSR was surrounded by predatory enemies, war was imminent and the socialist bastion could only defend itself with a modern heavy manufacturing base and an up-to-date military. This was no time to ask questions, to doubt the party's 'general line'. Any vacillator was objectively aiding the capitalist and imperialist foe. Hence, the ever-increasing rates of projected industrial growth (what some observers have termed Stalin's 'gigantomania') and the ratcheting up of inner-party discipline, rigidity and repression. Stalin's path to dictatorship was thus inextricably linked to the imperatives of industrialisation and collectivisation.

There was no historical precedent for Stalin's modernisation, because his was to be a *socialist* modernisation. Socialism, as understood by many thousands of budding Stalinists, was conceived as an end to the private ownership of the means of production, distribution and trade, the virtual eradication of market forces and the rational use of advanced technologies, many initially at least imported from the West. Above all, socialism equalled the introduction of a planned economy elaborated by 'experts' in government agencies and ministries, but one that was unremittingly overseen by Stalin and his top associates. For the 'boss', this state-run and state-owned economy represented socialism, the logical embodiment of Marxism-Leninism and the crushing of 'capitalist elements' in the Soviet Union. In 1928–9 it certainly signified the curtailment of the NEP mixed economy, although this was not officially recognised at the time. Indeed, paradoxically, the individual sector in small-scale industry and in private household plots and collective farm markets precariously survived the ravages of Stalinist statism. Other integral components of this 'socialist industrialisation' were a war against so-called 'bourgeois specialists' and the education and promotion of a new cohort of Stalinist cadres drawn largely from younger working-class and peasant strata. Upward social mobility was to be an important hallmark of Stalin's revolution, but it was more than matched by horrendous downward mobility as the use of forced labour in the Gulag system of camps and colonies played a significant, albeit costly, role in economic expansion.

How far was the Stalinist economy 'planned'? Planning was considered a key distinguishing feature of socialism, but theory bore little relation to reality, especially during the First Five-Year Plan. According to Soviet economists in the State Planning Committee (Gosplan), socialist planning meant that materials, investment and capital equipment would be rationally and centrally allocated to the various branches of the economy; within the longer-term Five-Year Plan, detailed quarterly and annual production targets would be laid down for all industrial enterprises and for the economy as a whole; wages and prices of goods would be decided centrally, not by the despised 'capitalist market'; distribution and trade would be brought under state control out of the hands of rapacious 'Nepmen' and other 'petit-bourgeois elements'; and virtually everyone would be employed by the state. This highly bureaucratised and centralised system survived basically intact until the 1980s, but already in Stalin's day the weaknesses were glaringly apparent. Imbalances, bottlenecks, pilfering of state property, gross supply shortages, an inherent attention to quantity rather than quality, massive labour turnover and waste of human and material resources, strict wage egalitarianism and a consequent lack of incentive among workers, the creation of 'black' markets and other illegal means of procurement of scarce goods and equipment (even train robberies!), the falsification of output figures by enterprise managers, unseemly scraps between entire industrial regions to get their hands on state investment, local self-protection cliques and evasion strategies, all this and more epitomised and undermined the supposedly 'planned' nature of the chaotic First Five-Year Plan. Greater stability, efficiency and productivity prevailed during the Second Five-Year Plan, but the system remained in many ways dysfunctional.

Stalin's involvement in this crash industrialisation programme was constant. Although he often delegated responsibility to close associates such as Molotov, Kaganovich and Ordzhonikidze, only he could change the course of the campaign. Even minor details of trade deals and negotiations rarely escaped him.[17] He was desperate during the First Five-Year Plan not to squander hard-earned finances on trivialities; for instance, in April 1930 the Politburo on his insistence refused to send a Russian football team to England on the grounds that it was 'a waste of money'.[18] At the same time, he could take arbitrary and expensive decisions if political considerations demanded them. In November 1931 he ordered the purchase of 50,000 essentially superfluous barrels of British herrings because 'well known political circles in England' had requested it.[19] Above all, Stalin pressed for the introduction of modern technology in order to catch up with and surpass the advanced capitalist countries. He reiterated again and again the urgency of the task ahead, exhorting the need for more effort and sacrifice. As he famously asserted to a gathering of industrial managers in early February 1931:

One feature of the history of old Russia was the continual beatings she suffered because of her backwardness. She was beaten by the Mongol khans. She was beaten by the Turkish beys. She was beaten by the Swedish feudal lords. She was beaten by the Polish and Lithuanian gentry. She was beaten by the British and French capitalists. She was

beaten by the Japanese barons. All beat her – because of her backwardness, military backwardness, cultural backwardness, political backwardness, industrial backwardness, agricultural backwardness....We are fifty
or a hundred years behind the advanced countries. We must make good
this distance in ten years. Either we do it, or we shall be crushed.[20]

The rhetoric was inspiring and left no room for doubt or doubters.
Neither was it coincidental that Stalin listed first 'military backwardness'.
The very survival of the Soviet state was at stake. In the event, the 'capitalists'
did indeed give Russia ten years to industrialise, not that Stalin knew this in
1931.

It is notoriously difficult to measure the growth of the Soviet economy in
the period 1928–41, and hence evaluate Stalinist industrialisation, not least
because of the falsification of official Soviet statistics. In the maze of competing figures and theories, I have relied on the work of R. W. Davies, the
leading economic historian of the USSR.[21] There can be no doubt that major
advances were made in the course of the first three Five-Year Plans
(1928–41). Overall, it is likely that industrial output trebled between 1928
and 1940, an annual growth rate of almost ten per cent. The total number of
industrial enterprises rose from 9,000 in 1929 to 64,000 in 1938. In particular, there was a vast expansion of capital goods and machine-building industries: an impressive iron and steel sector was developed in the Ukraine and
the Urals, the show-case being the huge plants at Magnitogorsk, the socialist
'model city'[22]; massive tractor factories were established in Stalingrad,
Kharkov and Rostov; and there was a huge expansion of the Donbass coal industry, of the oil fields in Baku and Grozny, and of electric and hydro-electric
power stations, notably the Dnieper dam complex. It was decided for security
reasons to relocate and develop a sizable part of Soviet industry in the east,
in the Urals, Siberia and Central Asia, thereby making the country less
vulnerable in the event of attack in the west. Crucially, armaments and
defence sector production, particularly aircraft and tanks, grew twenty-eight
fold between 1930 and 1940. The darkening international climate in both
Europe and Asia massively spurred armaments production and it is no exaggeration to say that the perceived threat of war underlay the forced pace of
Stalinist modernisation.

Other positive phenomena can be gleaned from the whirlwind of change.
Unemployment became a thing of the past by the end of 1930 and women
entered the workforce in huge numbers, notably during the Second Five-
Year Plan. By January 1935, almost eight million women were employed in
the main branches of the national economy compared to 3.3 million in

1929.[23] We need to be very careful when assessing this development. Women were often compelled to take up employment by the miserable wages of their menfolk, were regularly subject to harassment and abuse by their male colleagues and endured a debilitating 'dual burden' – industrial labour plus the bulk of domestic drudgery. Nevertheless, many welcomed the opportunity to participate in public life and a few even made it to positions of responsibility in the party-state hierarchies. It should also be noted that many workers, men and women, and even large numbers of foreign engineers escaping the traumas of the Great Depression, enthusiastically responded to the rallying call of the party and genuinely believed that they were 'building socialism'. Some, such as the norm-breaking Stakhanovites not to mention the embryonic 'red bourgeoisie' of the *nomenklatura*, enjoyed the privileges of better salaries, housing and consumer goods, and were thus despised by their poorer comrades in the factories and mines.

In general, the undoubted achievements of Stalinist industrialisation were gained at the cost of intense human suffering. Living and working conditions in the new urban areas were primitive, labourers toiling long hours and regularly sleeping in over-crowded barracks, on the shop-floor or in earthen huts. Real wages declined markedly in the 1930s as inflation took hold, trade unions were emasculated and brought under strict state control, draconian labour legislation was enacted to regiment the workforce and limit job mobility and the social infrastructure in the nascent cities was minimal. Above all, there were gross shortages and people went hungry, especially in the first half of the decade. Rationing was introduced in 1929 and not ended until January 1935. It is true that Stalinist leaders occasionally made concessions, such as the 'neo-NEP' of 1932 and the extension of the private agricultural plot in 1935, that laws were often undermined and not easily enforceable, that Soviet citizens were ingenious in finding ways round the crass deficiencies, trying as best they could to negotiate the heavy demands of the Soviet state, and that Stalin himself was at times keen to make consumer, even luxury, goods more readily available – an unusual insight into Stalin's methods of rule epitomised by his 1935 declaration: 'Life has improved, comrades. Life has become more joyous.'[24] Regardless of these ambiguous developments, the everyday existence of the vast majority of the Soviet people remained extraordinarily hard throughout the 1930s.

For Stalin, evidently, the price was worth paying. By 1941 he had the basis of a modern industrialised economy and an efficient well-equipped army. The inevitable social and political backlash – and there was much discontent in the early 1930s ranging from anti-Stalinist platforms in the party to workers' strikes and mass peasant resistance – could be neutralised by a judicious mixture of the 'carrot and stick', generally the latter. At the Seventeenth Party Congress in January 1934 Stalin trumpeted 'the final victory....of the socialist system of economy' and the elimination of 'capitalist elements', and in 1936 with the adoption of the 'Stalin Constitution' it could be proudly declared that the USSR was now a fully-fledged socialist state on the road to communism.[25] This was a militarised *étatist* 'barracks socialism' that bore few similarities to the more libertarian and egalitarian tenets of Marx, even Lenin. But for millions of Soviet citizens it was *socialism*; for the younger generation it was all they knew and many internalised it. Many others adapted it, circumvented it, even subverted it. All did their best to survive the turmoil that was Stalinism.[26]

Stalin, Cultural Revolution and the 'Great Retreat'

Stalin's policies from 1928 did not only aim for a vast economic transformation of the USSR. Together with forced collectivisation and rapid industrialisation went a 'cultural revolution' of far-reaching proportions. In the years 1928–31, this cultural revolution was part and parcel of a broader 'class war' against 'bourgeois enemies' of socialism. In the opinion of many historians, the campaign was initiated by Stalin in order to unleash militant 'leftist' forces against his arch opponents of the day, the Bukharinite 'rightists'. In this interpretation, the cultural revolution was but one component of a general shift to the 'ultra-left' (including economic, foreign and Comintern policies) more or less cynically manipulated by Stalin as a means of besmirching and defeating his political rivals in his quest for total power. Once this had been achieved, a process often referred to as the 'Great Retreat' witnessed the introduction of more traditional socio-cultural policies and values, a process damningly termed by the exiled Trotsky 'the Revolution betrayed'.[27] How to explain these vicissitudes and Stalin's role in them? To what extent did the 'Great Retreat' actually signify a turn away from 'modernity' and the revolutionary goals of 1917?

According to the renowned authority Sheila Fitzpatrick, 'the purpose of Cultural Revolution was to establish Communist and proletarian "hegemony", which in practical terms meant both asserting party control over cultural life and opening up the administrative and professional elite to a new cohort of young Communists and workers.'[28] The starting point was the Shakhty Trial of 'bourgeois specialists' and engineers in May 1928. The trial, carefully orchestrated by Stalin, was designed to show that the non-communist technical elite could not be trusted, was essentially anti-regime and lacked the requisite revolutionary enthusiasm to fulfil the huge economic and industrial tasks that lay ahead. Emboldened by the leadership's anti-intelligentsia and anti-expert rhetoric, militant 'proletarian' activists in the party's youth section, the Komsomol, and in the arts, sciences and academia launched fierce attacks on 'bourgeois' specialists, artists and professors. Radical and highly contested theories similar to those of War Communism during the Civil War became fashionable in many fields, epitomised by ideas such as the 'withering away' of the law, money and the school and the creation of a strictly 'proletarian' culture. Stalin's attitude to these utopian schemes was equivocal. He was prepared to give them some space as long as the party required the intemperate radicalism, dynamism and revolutionary will typical of the First Five-Year Plan, but in high culture, for instance, he rejected a purely 'proletarian' art (whatever that was in practice) which he believed would be too exclusive, sectarian and divisive. He and his colleagues were not, however, always able to control the excesses of the young cultural revolutionaries, whose internecine wrangles and in-fighting produced mayhem in cultural and academic bodies throughout the country, severely straining the Stalinist bosses' patience.

Only after 1931–2 was the party leadership capable of establishing a measure of order in the arts with the creation of institutions like the Union of Soviet Writers. Thereafter a new cultural orthodoxy emerged known as 'socialist realism'. Stalin himself fully participated in the elaboration of the new theory together with the illustrious author Maxim Gorky and other cultural and political luminaries. Writers, Stalin famously claimed in October 1932, were 'engineers of human souls' whose job was 'to show our life truthfully, on its way to socialism'.[29] That is, Soviet art and culture should be realistic, accessible to ordinary people and shorn of western 'formalism', abstraction and the *avant-garde* experimentations of the 1920s, but should also carry a definite political and mobilising message – the party guiding the masses along the road to socialism. This was in essence a propagandistic conception of art, typified by depictions of happy collective farm workers celebrating over tables laden with meat, fruit, vegetables and other consumables. But it was a project shared by many, if not all, in the cultural elite who genuinely believed that literature, painting, poetry, film and music could perform crucial ideological and social goals while remaining 'true to art'. Though much modified, Stalinist theories and practices of 'socialist realism' survived as core principles of Soviet culture until Gorbachev's reforms of the late 1980s.

It might well be argued that Stalin's 'cultural revolution' was not primarily concerned with culture *per se*. Just as vital from the leaders' point of view was the rapid creation of a new 'proletarian' elite capable of administering the gargantuan bureaucracies, enterprises and institutes that were mush-rooming everywhere under the First Five-Year Plan. The aim was to break the state's reliance on 'bourgeois' experts by advancing a solid cohort of lower-class 'Stalinist cadres'. Hence, the acquisition of educational and tech-nical skills assumed crucial significance in these years. State-sponsored mass literacy campaigns meant that by 1939 the bulk of Soviet citizens could read and write. Hundreds of thousands of workers and peasants, not all of them communists, were plucked from the shop-floor and village, rushed through two-years' basic training in a polytechnic and churned out the other end as engineers, technicians, middle-level officials, teachers and a host of other professions. It was the era of the *vydvizhentsy*, the upwardly mobile promo-tees who composed the new 'worker-peasant intelligentsia'. Future Soviet dignitaries such as Khrushchev, Leonid Brezhnev and Aleksei Kosygin were among the beneficiaries of these policies (and in more macabre fashion of the Great Purges). Many others like them formed a social base of support for the regime and for Stalin personally, the very existence of which belies the commonly held 'totalitarian' thesis.[30] The forging of a new 'proletarian' elite was seized on by Stalinist propagandists as yet more evidence of the fulfilment of original Leninist goals. Had not a fundamental task of the October Revolution been to create a 'workers' state', run by and for the workers?

Just as the breakneck economic policies of 1928–31 had resulted in wide-spread chaos, disorganisation and gross imbalances and had to be combated by the more temperate strategies and production targets of the years 1932–7, so the upheavals associated with the 'cultural revolution' forced the Stalinist Politburo to rethink its priorities. In sum, the process known as the 'Great Retreat' was set in train. The 'Great Retreat' is a powerful, but debat-able, notion first coined by the anti-communist émigré scholar Nicholas Timasheff in 1946.[31] Timasheff's main thesis was that from 1934 the con-spicuous failure of Stalin's radical economic, social and cultural policies to gain popular support, combined with the looming threat from Japan and Nazi Germany, compelled the Soviet leaders to seek more traditional pre-revolutionary methods of achieving economic efficiency, popular legitimacy and social cohesion. The starting point for this reversal, according to recent research, was Stalin's 'Six Conditions' speech of June 1931 in which he de-nounced *inter alia* wage equalisation, 'expert-baiting' and 'bad organisation of labour', all of which were impeding 'the modern requirements of production'.[32] Thereafter, in all fields of endeavour the radical Marxist 'cultural revolutionaries' were repressed, their 'utopian' schemes vilified and, in Timasheff's opinion, the 'Communist Experiment' was tacitly abandoned in favour of conservative policies such as strengthening the family, outlawing abortion, reintroducing conventional teaching methods and harsher norms of discipline in schools, reclaiming aspects of the hitherto excoriated Tsarist past and appealing to Russian nationalist sentiment. In the arts, as we have seen, 'modernist' forms were rejected and a return to classical realist nineteenth century styles was imposed. The assault on religion was toned down. In the economy, following Stalin's speech, wage egalitarianism was eschewed and pay differentials revalidated, one-man management was reintroduced and the relative status of 'bourgeois specialists' was renewed.

There is much to recommend Timasheff's path-breaking analysis. On the surface, it does indeed appear that the unprincipled Stalinist leaders reverted to pragmatic, anti-revolutionary and anti-modernist strategies, reneging on the promises and theses of Marxism-Leninism. The reactionary attitudes towards women and the family seemingly encapsulate this negation and it is tempting to see Stalin's reported male chauvinism behind the conservative legislation of the mid-1930s. However, interpreted in a different way the picture becomes more complicated and a hybrid compound emerges. As Erik van Ree has noted on the Stalinist attitude to the 'woman question':

> As in the old days, motherhood was restored as woman's honourable mission, culminating in a veritable cult with medals and other decorations. Freedom of abortion and easy divorce were among the casualties of the new policy. At the same time, there was no restoration of the man as the head of the family. The Stalinists rejected male leadership as an obscurantist principle. Nor was the woman pushed back out of the workplace into the house. In contrast to the old days, women were in the ideal case expected to be both productive workers and mothers.[33]

In similar vein, David Hoffmann has convincingly argued that the idea of a 'Great Retreat' from socialism towards pre-revolutionary ways is problematic given 'the Stalinist leadership's continuing commitment to social transformation and the creation of a New Soviet Person'. This attempt to instil socialist values 'contrasts sharply with the social conservatism of tsarism'. What is more, although 'Stalinist propaganda relied on some traditional institutions and appeals....it did so for distinctly modern mobilisational purposes'; that is, to rally society behind the goals of the socialist state.

Indeed, in Hoffmann's view it was the purported attainment of socialism in the mid-1930s that allowed the Stalinist elite to use traditional values and culture to support and further the new order. Hence, 'the family, previously suspected of perpetuating bourgeois beliefs, could now be trusted to promote socialism among children [and] ....patriotic appeals, elsewhere used to foment bourgeois nationalism, in the Soviet Union inspired defense of the socialist motherland.' All these examples of 'social interventionism and mass politics' were integral components of what Hoffmann defines as generic 'modernity'.[34]

The overall mission of the Bolshevik Revolution, its very essence one might say, was none other than to create the 'new Soviet person', an ideal citizen raised and educated under socialism, 'modern', 'clean-living' and 'cultured' in outlook, rational in deed, untainted by 'bourgeois' egotistical motivations or religious sentiments and, above all, collectivist in spirit and dedicated to state goals. If we believe van Ree and Hoffmann among others, Stalin's commitment to the forging of this 'new Soviet person' and to social-ism in general (at least his version of it) remained constant. The outcomes were often highly ambivalent – gender equality, for example, was never achieved either in the Soviet home or workplace. But the 'modernist' thrust of his socio-cultural policies can be identified in the quest to mobilise, 'civilise' and unite a diverse population for the overriding tasks of economic development and military preparedness.

Stalin and the National Question

Stalin retained a lifelong interest in the 'national question' ranging from his influential pre-revolutionary writings, some of which were discussed in chapter one, to *Marxism and the Problems of Linguistics* published in 1950. His background as a 'man of the borderlands' and member of an oppressed national minority no doubt partly explains this commitment. But just as relevant is the fact that the Soviet Union was a multi-ethnic, multi-cultural entity and therefore the Bolshevik rulers, if they were to survive and 'build socialism', had to devise strategies to win over the diverse peoples of the 'empire'. In order to attract the non-Russian minorities Lenin even sanc-tioned national self-determination up to and including the constitutional right of secession for member republics of the USSR, an extremely radical measure which few Bolsheviks, Stalin among them, took seriously (although Poland and Finland did become independent in 1918). What was the essence of Stalin's beliefs on the crucial national issue? In public at least, he never forswore the classical Marxist canon that nations and nationalism, products primarily of the capitalist economic base but also of deep-seated cultural phenomena, were ultimately doomed to extinction with the inevitable rise of socialist internationalism and global revolution. However, more than most Bolsheviks he realised that this was a long-term, even distant, prospect and that distinct national identities would continue to exist under socialism. He encapsulated this idea in a speech in May 1925 in which he asserted that 'the universal human culture towards which socialism is marching' is 'proletarian in content and national in form'.[35]

In practice, what this meant was that Stalin envisaged a strong centralised socialist state with strictly limited political and economic powers for the constituent republics and regions of the USSR, but, importantly, a state which granted relatively broad autonomy to ethnic minorities in matters of language, culture, education, and, above all, the elevation of 'national' indigenous cadres and intelligentsias to positions of power in their own localities. Thus Stalin, before the mid-1930s at least, categorically rejected the assimilation of the non-Russian peoples into the dominant Russian culture. These concessions, worked out largely in concert with Lenin, became collectively known as *korenizatsiia* ('indigenisation'), a strategy that lay at the heart of Soviet nationality policy from 1923 to the early 1930s and in some respects even beyond. They created what one expert has termed the 'Affirmative Action Empire', the ultimate aim being to disarm 'bourgeois' supra-class nationalism by permitting expression of national cultures and languages in national territorial units, although not separate from Russian culture and within an overall proletarian socialist framework. In this way, 'socialist nations' would emerge supportive of the Soviet state and its Marxist-Leninist ideology and these entities would eventually fuse into one nation with one language.

'Indigenisation' was in its day an innovative and bold attempt to partially decolonise and de-Russianise the lands of the former Tsarist Empire by merging nationalist demands for cultural autonomy with socialist demands for a politically unitary state. However, from the mid-1930s these moderate progressive policies fell victim to Stalin's growing sense of 'capitalist encirclement'. In an atmosphere of war scares and heightened international tensions, several Soviet ethnic diasporas were perceived, and fearsomely repressed, as 'enemy peoples' and selected aspects of the Tsarist past and Russian nationalism were reincorporated to bolster social unity. For many scholars, this 'Russification' campaign, part of the general 'Great Retreat' outlined above, proves that Stalin was at core a traditional Russian nationalist, an interpretation which I think is debatable.

In the 1920s, the *korenizatsiia* policy enjoyed a fair degree of success despite opposition from Communist Party activists and rank-and-file members. It facilitated the creation of national intelligentsias and political elites, upheld the maximum development of national literatures and languages, some of which had to be codified from scratch, promoted the construction of national museums, operas, academies of science and film studios, supported the flourishing of non-Russian folklore and mass media, and encouraged nationals to join their republican Communist Parties and participate in republic, regional and municipal administration. As a result, and surprising as it may seem, Russian officials were often replaced by national cadres, notably in Georgia and Armenia,[36] and oppressive 'Great Russian chauvinism', as Lenin had insisted, was generally deemed the main danger, not local nationalisms. But *korenizatsiia* was deeply contradictory. On the one hand, it was designed to overcome 'bourgeois'-inspired aspirations of national separatism and bring about the 'merger of nations', but on the other it overtly fostered the blossoming of national cultures and indirectly stimulated the growth of national consciousness and 'nation-making' among millions of non-Russian citizens, a potential political threat to the territorial integrity of the Soviet state which the Stalinist Politburo could ill afford to ignore.

Indeed, by the early 1930s the negative effects of the 'indigenisation' policies became worrying to the central leadership in Moscow. Stalin was particularly anxious about the cultivation of what he derogatively called 'national communism', a disease which, in his mind, afflicted his homeland, Georgia, and the Ukraine above all. Already in 1923 he had accused Ukrainian communists of striving for a loose 'confederation' with wide powers for the constituent republics *vis-à-vis* the central government. Less than a decade later, such 'Ukrainisation' seemed to be seriously undermining the principle of strict political and economic centralisation in the USSR. Some Ukrainian leaders, according to Stalin, were becoming more 'national' than 'communist', prioritising local needs and interests over those of the Soviet state. Many would pay with their heads during the Great Terror. What is more, mass resistance to collectivisation had been worst in the Ukraine and had not been adequately countered by the republican authorities. These manifestations of 'national separatism' and political weakness were totally unacceptable, especially during the famine crisis of 1932–3 when many Ukrainian officials criticised Moscow's grain procurement plans. As the 'boss' made abundantly clear in a letter to Kaganovich in August 1932:

> Things in the Ukraine have hit rock bottom. Things are bad with regard to the [Ukrainian] *party*....This is not a party but a parliament, a caricature of

a parliament....Unless we begin to straighten out the situation in the Ukraine, we may lose the Ukraine....rotten elements [in the Ukrainian CP]....will waste no time opening a front inside (and outside) the party, *against* the party. The worst aspect is that the Ukraine leadership does *not* see these dangers.[37]

Largely as a consequence of these profound apprehensions, linked as they were to external threats (in this case Marshal Pilsudski's authoritarian government in Poland), Stalin launched a vicious attack on so-called 'national communists', notably the Ukrainian 'Old Bolshevik' Mykola Skrypnik, who under intense pressure committed suicide in July 1933. Later Stalin would inaugurate campaigns to promote 'Soviet patriotism' and the primacy of the Russian language and culture, campaigns which had adverse effects on all nationalities of the USSR. These tendencies were combined with an ongoing process of increased centralisation and a concomitant decrease in the autonomy of the Union republics.

What did this 'Russification' drive from 1934–5 entail? Firstly, it should be noted that not all rudiments of *korenizatsiia* were jettisoned. Indeed, according to Terry Martin, three of its main provisions – the training and promotion of indigenous cadres, the strengthening of national territories and the fostering of distinct national identities – survived slightly modified throughout the 1930s, amounting to what he calls a 'silent *korenizatsiia*'. But in other important aspects Stalin's policies represented a major reversal. Russian, for instance, became the dominant language in government, the party and higher education in nearly all areas of the USSR and by 1938 it was the sole language in the Red Army.[38] Most significant was the recrudescence of traditional Russian culture and nationality, epitomised by the partial rehabilitation of Peter the Great, Ivan the Terrible and other Tsarist dignitaries hitherto vilified by the Bolsheviks, the Pushkin Centenary celebrations in 1937, and the raising of the Russians officially to the rank of 'first among equals' in the Soviet family of nations. Stalin evidently believed that the restored centrality of the Russian people, its history and culture would function as a cement to bind the multi-ethnic Soviet Union together at a time of imminent war. It was a strategy that would serve him well in the 'Great Patriotic War' and was to become even more pronounced after 1945 in an era of Cold War tensions.

It cannot be denied that from the mid-1930s Stalin elevated the Russians over other Soviet peoples; he may well have regarded himself as a latter-day Peter the Great industrialising and modernising Mother Russia and as a born-again Ivan the Terrible sweeping the country clean of 'enemies', but the USSR – 'his' creation – was not a state dominated by the gentry, Orthodox priests, Tsarist bureaucrats and other privileged, largely Russian, elites. It was a modern, technologically and socially developing socialist state and economy that had educated, trained and promoted a new leading cohort from a working class and peasantry that had previously been exploited and humiliated. Stalin was not defending age-old oppressive 'backward' Russia – that 'prison house of nations' – but a dynamic modern entity that was rushing pell-mell towards fully-fledged socialism. That was the message of Stalinist propaganda, and it seems to have struck a chord with many, though by no means all, Soviet citizens.[39] If the heroes, symbols and myths of the Tsarist past could be selectively adopted to strengthen the USSR in dangerous uncharted waters, and if the historic 'greatness' of the Russians could be used to bind the diverse Soviet peoples together, then so be it. But it seems to me that Stalin was not a Russian nationalist in the sense that he consistently and materially privileged the Russians over all others or sought to assimilate the indigenous populations into Russian culture. Russians suffered as much as most other ethnic groups during the Great Terror; they were certainly not spared his wrath. More positively, his long-standing advocacy of *korenizatsiia*, his attempt to modernise, socially and economically, the under-developed non-Russian regions of the USSR and his concern to integrate them into the 'Soviet family of nations' demonstrate more than a lukewarm commitment to raise the prestige and status of the ethnic minorities.

In conclusion, on the question of Stalin's ideological predispositions I agree with Arfon Rees, who has argued convincingly that:

> Stalin's Russian nationalist pronouncements appear to be more than simply manipulative devices, but it would be a mistake to see them as symptomatic of an alternative ideology which displaced Marxism-Leninism as the guiding principle behind the regime....the significant aspect of Stalinist ideology was not the extent to which it adjusted to a nationalist perspective....but the extent to which....a Marxist-Leninist perspective, modified over time, remained the dominant ideology.[40]

Stalin was a Marxist who, unusually, understood the appeals of nationalism and the resilience of national identities. Hence, his nationality policies, ever adapting to changing circumstances, were a complex compound, typified by the seemingly incongruous slogan 'socialist motherland'. His overriding aim was to devise practical strategies for the unity and defence of this Soviet 'socialist motherland'.

Stalin as Moderniser?

The nature of Stalin's 'modernity' is a difficult conceptual issue which I have partially addressed above in the section on the 'Great Retreat'. It begs many questions: how should 'modernity' be defined?; what is the meaning of a 'modern' state and society?; does 'modernity' merely imply economic, industrial and technological progress?; or should it include political, social and cultural change?; does it not also include the inculcation of 'modern' notions such as science, rationality, efficiency, hygiene and 'cultured living'? Most problematically, how to assess Stalin's understanding of, and commitment to, 'modernity'?

As far as economics are concerned, it has been cogently argued that the collapse of the USSR and Marxism-Leninism in the 1980s and early 1990s demonstrated the fundamental failure of the Stalinist planned economy to tackle the changing technological demands of 'modernity'. 'Modern' economies, by definition, are capitalist and market-driven, based on private ownership, free trade, consumer demand, entrepreneurial dynamism and scientific creativity, the very opposite of the hyper-centralised, inflexible and wasteful 'command economy'. This conclusion may or may not be accurate, but it is certainly teleological. Stalin's insistence in the 1930s on the rapid expansion of heavy industry, machine-building and indeed on state intervention in the economy was the epitome of 'modernisation', as then understood. How could a 'modern' state be overwhelmingly agrarian? How could a 'modern' economy be left totally to the vagaries of the market without state regulation? The Stalinists were not alone in their emphasis on the state; even progressive Conservatives in Britain in the 1930s and beyond accepted the positive role the state could play in the economy, health care, education, housing and many other areas. The crucial difference was that Stalin's rampant 'statism' knew no bounds and he used it to create an authoritarian monster that politically was in many ways more akin to a pre-modern personalised autocracy than a modern constitutional polity.

Recently historians have addressed these issues through an examination of Stalinism's relative 'modernisation' or 'neo-traditionalism'. Those scholars, such as David Hoffmann and Yanni Kotsonis who depict the essential modernity of Stalinism, or more exactly of Soviet socialism, defend their thesis by emphasising the universal trends common to modern European systems that were replicated in the Soviet experience: 'the spread of bureaucracy and state control, efforts to manage and mobilize the population, scientism and attempts to rationalize and categorize society, and the rise of mass politics.' Many of these innovations were closely linked to the need to gain knowledge of, and mobilise, the population's military capacity in an era of 'total war'. While recognising the unique features of Stalinism, particularly its militant anti-capitalism and its use of class-based mass terror, and accepting the periodic recourse to 'neo-traditional' practices, Hoffmann insists on placing Soviet socialism, even in its Stalinist guise, firmly in the 'modernist' camp.[41]

These views are challenged by the 'neo-traditionalists', chief among them Terry Martin, who maintains that the Soviet 'neo-traditional society' produced 'a variety of practices that bear a striking resemblance to characteristic features of traditional pre-modern societies.' These included the continued existence of an estate-based rather than a class-based society, the importance of informal, paternalistic and personal relationships between rulers and ruled, the reliance on ranks, titles, uniforms, honours and other status symbols and a hierarchical distribution of privileges and information according to political status. Above all, Martin argues that Stalinist nationality policies in the 1930s turned national identity into an ascribed 'primordial and essential attribute, not simply a historical and contingent one'; that is, national identity came to be regarded as innate and immemorial as opposed to being a by-product of modern capitalism. Martin concludes suggestively: 'Modernisation is the theory of Soviet intentions; neo-traditionalism, the theory of their unintended consequences.'[42] Robert Service in his recent biography of the 'boss' has written more straightforwardly and categorically that 'Stalin, far from being the clean-limbed titan of modernity, was a village sorcerer who held his subjects in his dark thrall.'[43]

Obviously, the debates are not as simple as I have intimated, and both sides recognise contradictory currents and trends and the coexistence of both modern and traditional elements. Indeed, Hoffmann has suggested that the two concepts are not mutually exclusive.[44] It would be foolhardy, then, to squeeze Stalin and all his competing policies and ambivalent attitudes into the 'modernity' box. His personal tastes in art, music and literature were basically classical and he rarely enthused about contemporary Soviet cultural productions (Mikhail Bulgakov's play *The Days of the Turbins* was the main exception). The vicious headline in *Pravda* in January 1936 attacking Shostakovich's opera *Lady Macbeth of Mtsensk* as 'Cacophony, not Music' was almost certainly inspired by Stalin's aversion to 'modernist' atonal music.[45] His repressive and occasionally obscurantist policies in academia and the natural sciences often badly retarded development – his support for the renegade and charlatan geneticist Trofim Lysenko, who espoused a totally erroneous theory of heredity, springs to mind here.

However, it seems to me that we can isolate important modernist propensities in Stalin and Stalinism. Above all, his commitment to advanced industrial technology and production, his strategies for mass mobilisation, mass education, 'mass culture', even mass participation (albeit not in our understanding of democratic mass politics) and his ideologically-driven conviction that the state should be the prime agent of the modernisation process. All are quintessentially 'modern' phenomena that distinguish twentieth-century regimes from earlier state and societal formations. Even Stalinist policies that have often been attacked as conservative and reactionary can be interpreted as attributes of a 'modern' state. Hence, it might be argued that the selective rehabilitation of the Tsarist past and the appeals to Russian nationalism, discussed above, represented a specific Soviet version of what Eric Hobsbawm and Terence Ranger have famously termed the 'invention of tradition', the search for a usable past that many European states undertook from the late nineteenth century as a means of creating social cohesion and papering over the class divisions and conflicts that threatened the established order.[46] This was a 'modern' strategy previously unappreciated by political elites. Even Stalin's dictatorial power was dependent on modern means of communication and organisation. It is to this theme – Stalin as dictator – that we now turn.

Chapter 4: Dictator

On 7 November 1937 at a private banquet marking the twentieth anniversary of the Bolshevik Revolution, Stalin uttered the remarkable words:

> Anyone who attempts to destroy the unity of the socialist state....is a sworn enemy of the state and of the peoples of the USSR. And we shall destroy any such enemy, even if he is an old Bolshevik; we shall destroy his entire kith and kin. Anyone who threatens the unity of the socialist state, either in deed or in thought – yes, even in thought – will be mercilessly destroyed.

Stalin concluded with the chilling toast: 'To the final destruction of all enemies...!'[1] This quotation, together with many other pieces of evidence gleaned from the former Soviet archives, shows conclusively the transformation of Stalin's power from that of leading oligarch to personal dictator and the decisive role of terror in that shift. He could now decide the ultimate fate of many thousands of people, including his closest colleagues and relatives. By mid-1937 mass repression had become a central plank in Stalin's form of governance and personalised power. How to account for this momentous development? Was it simply a product of Stalin's deranged megalomania and psychopathic personality? Or were there broader 'objective' socio-economic and political factors at work? How and why did Stalin's power change over time, from, say, 1928 to 1938? Did Stalin continue to seek a measure of collegiality? How did the functions of the Politburo evolve? How were decisions actually taken? Were there still limitations to Stalin's authority? How important was Stalin's 'cult of personality' in securing his power and legitimacy? These are among the key issues to be addressed in this chapter, with particular emphasis on the role of terror as a prime method of Stalinist political and social control.

From Chief Oligarch to Dictator

We have already seen in chapter two that in the 1920s Stalin was able to concentrate enormous power in his hands by a variety of means, fair and foul. But at the time of the 'second revolution' he was not yet a dictator, if by this is meant a ruler who can impose his own decisions, disregard alternative elite opinion and whose power is not constrained by formal laws or informal bargaining. This momentous transition occurred gradually in the course of the 1930s and came to fruition during the years of the Great Terror, 1937–8. In explaining this process, a few words on human agency are required. Stalin's road to dictatorship was not simply a product of his conscious will, a result of a deliberate plan of action to curb the authority of his colleagues and eliminate all rivals and potential sources of opposition. There can be little doubt that Stalin was driven by an insatiable power lust and his personal motives should in no way be under-estimated. However, systemic factors played a vital role too. Much recent research has emphasised the close inter-linkages between the crises of the 'revolution from above' 1929–33 and the path to terror and Stalin's dictatorship.

The picture painted is one of a Stalin obsessed with creating a unitary modernised homogeneous communist utopia, but increasingly frustrated by division, social flux, insubordination, diversity and clandestine opposition in the party, state and society, all compounded by a darkening international climate. In these circumstances, Stalinist leaders found it difficult to tame the autonomous urges and self-protection networks of party-state officials, professional organisations and citizens alike. The outcome was an incremental radicalisation of methods of political and social control culminating in the Great Terror. Mass repression and the elimination of 'enemies' were thus to an extent systemically generated, products of the inevitable crises of stage-managing an inordinately rapid modernisation of Soviet state and society.[2] In brief, the historical context should never be forgotten when assessing Stalin's rise to dictatorship. However, two highly relevant caveats are necessary to complicate this picture. Firstly, the immense strains of the 'revolution from above' were not 'objective' criteria independent of human action, but were in the main self-imposed by an impatient Stalinist hierarchy that was intent on fundamentally uprooting Soviet life by 'constructing socialism' in as short a time as possible. Secondly, by 1936–7 Stalin was directing state coercion towards perceived recalcitrant strata in his own party and entourage in a largely successful attempt to achieve personalised power. This was a truly radical Stalinist innovation. To be sure, Lenin had sanctioned state-sponsored coercion, but never violence against members and leaders of the Communist Party.

An examination of the changing nature of Stalin's mode of governance and of the role of the Politburo, the supreme decision-making body in the Soviet party-state system, will elucidate the transformation in Stalin's power from chief oligarch to dictator, although, as we will see, there is nuanced disagreement among scholars on the scale and methods of Stalin's dominance. The stereotypical image of Stalin as an isolated omnipotent 'oriental' despot imposing his will unilaterally on colleagues, the party and society needs to be qualified, but it palpably bears much resemblance to reality. For a start, he was effectively free of many of the political, constitutional and social checks and balances that limit the prerogatives of the executive in liberal systems (the Soviet 'parliament' was not democratically elected on a multi-party basis and was basically a rubber-stamping institution; the judiciary and courts were not independent of the political leadership and the concept of the rule of law had shaky foundations in Bolshevik theory; the pervasive secret security forces, which by the mid-1930s were becoming a 'state within a state', were ultimately accountable only to Stalin; the press and other means of mass communication were strictly censored and alternative sources of information were formally banned; there were no autonomous legalised non-party 'pressure groups' in Soviet society that could seek to influence government policy; in short, there was no clearly defined pluralistic 'civil society' in the USSR, whereby power is negotiated between a legitimised central authority and a consenting social polity and in which civil liberties are guaranteed in practice, not just in theory. Moreover, the Communist Party itself was far from a 'normal' political organisation in that its officials managed state, regional and municipal affairs from the power centres in Moscow, Leningrad and Kiev to the outlying hinterlands of Siberia and Central Asia. The party was highly secretive, disciplined and hierarchical. The Leninist canon of 'democratic centralism', fiercely applied under Stalin, was designed to ensure that no 'factions' could appear in the party to contest the policies and decrees of the leadership. Bolshevik political culture was, then, in many ways authoritarian and anti-democratic. In such a body, the power of the *vozhd'* was bound to be immense, the rights of his underlings severely restricted.

However inauspicious these political mentalities and constitutional provisions may have been, they did not signify the inevitable emergence of an omnipotent single dictator. Indeed, in the late 1920s and into the 1930s Stalin's closest associates, while certainly recognising him as *primus inter pares*, were not yet totally dependent on him and considered themselves to be weighty actors in their own right with powerful offices to defend. Molotov, as head of government, and particularly Ordzhonikidze, as

Commissar of Heavy Industry, are known to have cross swords with the 'boss' on several occasions and the latter, who had known Stalin since the Koba days in Georgia, tended to regard him as an authoritative 'older brother' with whom he could wrangle. As late as 1936–7, Ordzhonikidze had serious altercations with Stalin about the extent of repression in government offices and it is highly probable that he committed suicide in February 1937 after one such verbal clash. It is true that some in Stalin's entourage were more vassal-like in their attitude – Kaganovich ('a 200 per cent Stalinist', according to Molotov), Voroshilov and Aleksandr Poskrebyshev, Stalin's long-time personal secretary – would come into this category, but they were the exception before the mid-to-late 1930s.[3] In his personal communications prior to this period, Stalin was capable of persuasion and compromise, even a measure of friendly self-deprecation. In September 1931 he reciprocated Ordzhonikidze's sense of familiarity: 'Don't reprimand me for being rude and, perhaps, too direct. Still, you can reprimand me as much as you want.'[4] With one or two colleagues he would very occasionally use jocular nicknames – 'Molotovich', 'Molotshtein' – and address them with the informal 'ty' form ('thou'), but even these signs of affability were dispensed with by the mid-1930s.

At an institutional level, Politburo meetings were regularly convened, almost one per week on average in the years 1928–32.[5] The same went for the Secretariat and Orgburo. There are few extant minutes of Politburo sessions, but there is plenty of evidence of internal disagreement and open discussion, especially on issues concerning the allocation of scarce resources and investment. Stalin acted as the supreme arbiter in these interdepartmental conflicts, some of which were deep-seated and personalised. When deemed necessary the decision-making elite was broadened to include selected experts and specialists. Central Committee plena were not yet well rehearsed set pieces and debate could be quite lively. Furthermore, Stalin willy-nilly had to delegate much responsibility and his input in specific policies and campaigns varied. It is remarkable to learn that Stalin and the Politburo 'were quite unable to control many major agricultural processes', that Stalin had relatively little influence on certain crucial initiatives, such as the Stakhanovite movement, and that 'whole spheres of economic activity – for example, heavy industry – were in practice largely delegated to Stalin's colleagues', in this case Ordzhonikidze. Although 'his authority in economic matters grew with the increase in his personal power', Stalin had to select carefully the areas to be directly involved in. Grain requisitioning was a constant preoccupation, as were security, capital investment issues and, contrary to received wisdom, foreign policy.[6] He also chaired the Politburo sub-commission on culture and the arts, revealing a serious interest in ideology and the power of words. Consequently, he had his fingers in most pies, but not all. These institutional arrangements and division of labour in the Stalinist hierarchy have led some scholars to the guarded conclusion that before 1932, and to a limited extent even after, 'a residual tradition of "collective leadership" remained in the party'.[7]

This semi-collegial atmosphere gradually dissipated after the intense crises of 1932–3. The experience of virtual civil war with the peasantry during forced collectivisation, the resultant Great Famine, the suicide of his second wife, the revelation of inner-party discontent and opposition, and the worsening international situation in both Europe and Asia, all these traumatic events hardened Stalin's mental landscape, altered his relations with top associates and deepened his suspiciousness and vindictiveness. This process, uneven and at times contradictory, was undoubtedly also driven by Stalin's conscious resolve to relieve himself of the constraints mentioned above. Whatever the case, after 1932 he rarely, if ever, permitted open dissent. Indeed, according to three leading experts 'no case has so far been found of even one of his decisions being challenged by another Politburo member after August 1932.'[8] His manner with colleagues became far more brusque and self-assertive. If in 1931 Stalin had been prepared to banter with Ordzhonikidze, by July 1933 he was labelling him 'a rotten conservative, who supports the worst traditions of the Right deviationists.'[9] Stalin also became adept at issuing unilateral decrees in the name of the Central Committee or other leading bodies. For example, the notorious repressive law against theft of socialist property in August 1932, which elicited tentative opposition among one or two Politburo colleagues, was penned personally by Stalin and the decision to abolish bread rationing in October 1934 was taken unilaterally by the 'boss', albeit on information supplied by various government agencies.

Formal Politburo sessions declined from 43 in 1932 to a mere four in 1938 and voting was increasingly done 'by poll' (*oprosom*) of members on the telephone or in writing. Already by the early 1930s, it appears the Politburo had ceased operating as the prime site of drafting resolutions, its role being largely to ratify and record previously approved memoranda. As for meetings of the Secretariat and Orgburo, they too became far less frequent with Stalin scarcely bothering to attend after 1928. Leninist party regulations were flouted with only three party congresses being held in the 1930s (1930, 1934 and 1939). These gatherings tended to be a rubber-stamping exercise with precious little real debate. Likewise, Central Committee plena, though still regularly convening, became ritualised affairs concerned more with the humiliation of oppositionists and less with open discussion of substantive issues.[10] From the mid-1930s policy tended to be thrashed out in small subcommissions, often summoned to Stalin's Kremlin office, or, especially in the post-war period, in informal late night soirees at his *dacha* in the outskirts of Moscow. Normal 'constitutional' channels of decision-making were, thus, largely circumvented. This permitted Stalin to set agendas, hand pick his accomplices and hence more easily divide and rule. An inner core of leaders emerged, composed in the early-to-mid 1930s of the ever-present Molotov, Kaganovich, Mikoian, Voroshilov and Ordzhonikidze, later supplemented by Zhdanov, Malenkov, Beria and Khrushchev. Other Politburo members, such as Andreev, Kalinin, Rudzutak and Kosior, were in effect sidelined. Although many of these trends had their origins in the 1920s and there is no strict dividing line in 1932, there is undoubtedly a gradual personalisation of power in Stalin's hands from the early 1930s onwards. It is also clearly the case that Stalin, unlike Hitler, was very much a 'hands-on' leader embroiled in daily decision-making even on what appear relatively trivial matters.

Stalin's power did not only derive from his ability to control the decision-making procedures and emasculate his co-decision makers, but also from his position at the pinnacle of a vast secret communication and intelligence gathering network. There has been much speculation that during the 1920s and early 1930s Stalin's personal secretariat and the Central Committee's Secret Department became fused, a process regarded by some historians as pivotal in his acquisition and maintenance of power. Stalin's personal assistants, such as Ivan Tovstukha, Lev Mekhlis and Poskrebyshev, held leading posts in the secret apparatus continuously from 1922 to just before Stalin's death. Precisely because the party's secret sectors and departments played a crucial role in the communication and security system, the placement of 'his' men permitted Stalin to raid the party archives for 'dirt' on his rivals, to gain access to top secret information on a whole array of party and state issues, to have this material analysed and synthesised by a dedicated 'think-tank', to influence personnel management and control, and to check up on decision implementation, a key aim for Stalin. Apparently, he even had tapped the telephones of loyal courtiers like Molotov. The Danish expert on this theme, Niels Erik Rosenfeldt, has concluded cautiously that the secret apparatus was not full-proof, but 'in the struggle for power and communication control it certainly gave [Stalin] an initial advantage over any possible political rival'.[11]

Some scholars, however, have complicated this picture of an increasingly dictatorial and personalised political system under Stalin. Stephen Wheatcroft has suggested that a 'Team-Stalin' operated more or less collegially until the late post-war period of 'High Stalinism' when there was a marked shift towards a 'degenerate tyranny'. Stalin, far from jealously reserving all decision-making functions for himself, sought considerable group participation, both inside and outside the Politburo. Wheatcroft proposes that:

> in the 1930s and early 1940s, Stalin had a very broad circle of acquaintances, and he spent a considerable time meeting and working with others....Stalin was for most of his active political life a party animal. He appears to have thrived on social interaction. His working style was as part of a working collective or editorial team, rather than as a 'loner'.[12]

The anchor of this relatively wide Stalinist decision-making system, at least until the early 1950s, was the relationship between Stalin and Molotov. More than any other individual, Molotov was Stalin's right-hand man and the main 'survivor'. In addition, Wheatcroft agrees with T. H. Rigby's polemical argument that Stalin, rather than being intent on totally destroying his elite comrades, was with notable exceptions a 'loyal patron'.[13] Aside from Molotov, many other top associates survived Stalin's unpredictable wrath: Kaganovich, Mikoian, Voroshilov, Kalinin of the 'Old Guard' and Beria, Malenkov, Khrushchev, Zhdanov and Bulganin of the 'new' elite. The image that emerges from Wheatcroft's analysis is that Stalin was head of a stable 'consultative bureaucratic oligarchy' which lasted almost until his death in March 1953.[14]

While this 'Team-Stalin' interpretation serves as a useful corrective to the crass 'one-man tyrant syndrome' resonant in the popular mind, it is misleading, in my estimation, to imply that at the heart of the Stalinist power structure there existed a distinct and meaningful interaction among more or less equals. Wheatcroft accepts that the system was dominated by Stalin and if so it must be asked how was this hegemony manifest? Judging from the recently published correspondence between Stalin and his top aides, the former's word was gospel in the inner elite on any issue. Even when on his extended summer working vacations in the south, his written comments and decisions were often incorporated verbatim into Politburo decrees.[15] And what is meant exactly by 'consultation'? Surely there could be no dialogue worth the name if Stalin's interlocutors were fearful of openly expressing their own opinions, if they moulded their ideas and advice to suit what they thought the 'boss' wanted, and if the threat of demotion, arrest and, after 1936–7, death hung over them? And this was no idle threat. According to the testimony of one eyewitness, sometime in the spring of 1941 Pavel Rychagov, a high-ranking Red Air Force commander, attended a meeting chaired by Stalin to discuss the poor performance of Soviet aircraft. When asked by Stalin to explain the recent spate of plane crashes, Rychagov snapped: 'The accident rate will get even worse because you force us to fly in coffins.' The room, apparently, went deathly silent as Stalin padded around puffing his pipe. 'You shouldn't have said that!', he eventually muttered twice in hushed tones.[16] Rychagov was arrested a few days later and shot in October 1941. In this atmosphere of repression and scapegoating, it can only be concluded that Stalin's 'colleagues' must have become basically docile executors of his will. In many ways, then, Stalin's authority rested on the threat, and reality, of terror.

Stalin's 'Class War' Mentality

Before discussing the Great Terror of 1936–8, it should be emphasised that repressive policies had defined Stalinist rule from at least the late 1920s. A major explanation for this is Stalin's 'class war' mentality, a mindset that accentuated the ever-present spectre of the 'enemy from within', be it an expropriated kulak, an anti-social 'hooligan', a disgruntled priest, a former White Guardist, or even a disloyal party-state functionary. One of Stalin's most infamous theoretical principles was that of the 'ever-sharpening class struggle'. The argument, carefully rehearsed on many occasions from 1928 onwards both publicly and in private, was that as socialism approached in an era of capitalist encirclement so the resistance of the 'dying exploiting classes' would inevitably increase, thus demanding greater state coercion and vigilance. By 1937 this idea, which one suspects made eminent sense to many battle-hardened Bolsheviks, had become an immutable law of Stalinist politics forming the ideological underpinnings and starting point of the Great Terror.[17]

Stalin's propensity for strong-arm tactics was well-known in party circles. As we have seen, during the Civil War he had ordered the execution of many 'class enemies' and 'counter-revolutionaries', although he was hardly alone here. On occasions in the 1920s Stalin had displayed a worrying penchant for *otsechenie*, the 'chopping off' of troublesome communists. In a speech to a Comintern gathering in 1926, he talked of the need 'to take the surgical knife in hand to cut off certain comrades', and while he recognised that these 'methods of vivisection' were applicable 'only in extreme cases', his use of such terminology cannot be coincidental.[18] Indeed, many foreign communists were expelled from their parties in the mid-to-late 1920s for

Trotskyite, Zinovievite or Bukharinite tendencies. In 1928, Stalin had overseen the trial of fifty three 'bourgeois specialists' and engineers accused of
sabotage in the Shakhty area of southern Russia. Five were executed.

Ample archival evidence from the early 1930s testifies to Stalin's increasingly
morbid, suspicious and vengeful mental landscape. A few examples will suffice.
In August 1930 he demanded in a letter to Molotov that the leading economists Nikolai Kondratiev and Vladimir Groman together with 'a whole group
of wreckers in the meat industry must definitely be shot' as anti-Soviet activists.
Stalin's inhumanity and utter contempt for ordinary citizens are clearly shown
in his insistence that 'several dozen common cashiers' should be included in
the list of executed.[19] Later, in July 1932, Stalin informed Kaganovich and
Molotov that the recent wave of 'plundering' and other economic crimes was
organised 'in the main by *kulaks* (dekulakised) and other *anti-social* elements,
who are striving *to shatter our new order*'. They should be sentenced 'at a
minimum to ten years imprisonment, and as a rule to the *death* penalty.' Stalin's
violent response reveals the ease with which he relied on the organs of state
security to '*eliminate* and send to *concentration camp* (individually)' the
'wretches' who preached flight from the collective farms. Likewise, 'hooligans'
disrupting rail transport should be 'shot on the spot' by armed detachments of
the OGPU (secret police), who up till then had been '*sleeping* (fact!).'[20]

In particular, the sources establish beyond doubt the General Secretary's
constant search for vigilance against 'slothful smug' bureaucrats in the party-
state apparatuses. For instance, at the Central Committee Plenum of April
1928 Stalin warned of the dangers of the party resting on its laurels, of
wanting 'to sleep a little' after the defeat of the Trotskyist-Zinovievist United
Opposition at the Fifteenth Party Congress.[21] This notion of 'sleeping' on
the job became a constant refrain over the next few years. In a note to
Kaganovich in mid-August 1934 Stalin berated the People's Commissariat of
Foreign Affairs (NKID) for its conciliatory attitude to Japanese anti-Soviet accusations: 'We need to flog the NKID for its somnolence, blindness and
myopia. But instead we lag behind the yawners from the NKID....You can't
yawn and sleep when you're in power!'[22] Stalin's repeated recourse to the
'yawning and sleeping' metaphor conceals a more sinister aim – the constant
verification and periodical purging of insubordinate or inefficient officials.
Already in September 1930 in a missive to Molotov he had coined a barely
translatable phrase which typified his methods of personnel management:
'inspecting and checking up by punching people in the face' (*proverochno-
mordoboinaia rabota*).[23]

What emerges very clearly from the documents is Stalin's tireless quest,
never fully realised, for total control over the *nomenklatura* and party-state

organs. His correspondence with Kaganovich in the early-to-mid 1930s abounds with negative assessments of the Soviet bureaucracy, above all those ministries concerned with the economy. In time, those guilty of defending departmental (*vedomstvennye*) interests took on for Stalin the connotations of a political opposition, encroaching on his personal power. There is hardly a single letter to Kaganovich in which Stalin does not rebuke his Politburo colleagues for 'yawning', 'dropping off', or 'yielding' to the attacks of the bureaucracy. A common refrain is: 'Don't ask about my health. If you wish me good health, then maintain maximum vigilance and don't allow yourself to be led by the nose by those departmental heroes'.[24] Whenever difficulties arose in any branch of the national economy, Stalin's invariable response was to curse the complacency and even sabotage of leading bureaucrats. A fine example concerns the People's Commissar of Communications, M. L. Rukhimovich. Writing to Kaganovich on 19 September 1931, the General Secretary launches into the hapless minister and his supporters:

> The resolutions of the CC [Central Committee] *will be shelved* as long as there sits in Transport a gang of self-admiring and self-satisfied bureaucrats of the Rukhimovich type, scoffing like Mensheviks at the decrees of the CC and spreading demoralising scepticism. This gang must be smashed in order to save railway transport. Let me know if you need my help in this affair. If you can manage without my help, break this gang before it's too late. If you search hard enough you can always find in our party new people, believers in our cause, who can successfully replace the bureaucrats.[25]

Stalin's ominous reference to 'Menshevik' attitudes demonstrates how readily he compared organisational incompetence with disloyalty to the party leadership, which in turn bordered on political opposition and class betrayal. Anyone stamped with this epithet was sooner or later to pay the price, either in terms of demotion, expulsion or later arrest and execution.[26] His broader aim was to intimidate other functionaries by severely punishing Rukhimovich: 'Then everyone will realise that the CC is not joking and talking rot about the general line. They will realise and tighten up [*podtianutsia*]'.[27] It is well established that scapegoating was a prominent feature of Stalin's tactics, both to deflect popular frustration from himself and the regime and to set precedents to deter any future 'doubter'. The archival sources certainly attest to this aspect of Stalinism. What is more, Stalin on several occasions announced his distaste for bureaucratic 'families', 'clans' and 'feudal lords' who paid lip service to the party line but in practice hindered its development by gaining 'a certain independence from the CC.'[28] Stalin evidently saw in this embedded patron-client system a threat to his personal power and insisted that these self-protecting 'families' had to be broken up and replaced by fresh young talent.

Stalin seems, however, to have crossed a significant threshold sometime after the assassination of the Leningrad party boss, Sergei Kirov, on 1 December 1934. Up to then the purges of communists, both Soviet and foreign, had remained administrative, not physical. The Stalinist state had restricted the ultimate penalty to overt 'counter-revolutionaries' and 'wreck-ers', composed largely of 'kulaks', 'bourgeois specialists' and former Mensheviks. But in the course of 1935–6 Stalin must have convinced himself that an array of Old Bolshevik oppositionists, most notably Zinoviev and Kamenev who were accused of involvement in Kirov's murder and were linked to the arch-demon Trotsky, posed a serious threat to his rule and hence had to be eliminated. By late 1936 and early 1937, these 'enemies' had been extended to include 'disloyal' party and state officials and from August 1937 mass repression of 'socially harmful elements' and suspect ethnic minorities became the norm. Stalin's role in the Great Terror of 1937–8 is the theme of the next section.

Terror: The Primacy of Stalin

Scarcely any historian today would doubt that the Georgian dictator must bear prime responsibility for the mass arrests and executions that were un-leashed on Soviet state and society in 1937–8 and would broadly agree with Robert Tucker's assessment that he was the Terror's 'director general'.[29] But Stalin's role in the carnage is only one question that has divided experts. For many decades scholars have been preoccupied with the origins, processes and outcomes of the Terror. Not surprisingly, there is no consensus. There is disagreement on Stalin's motivations, aims and plans, the influence of other key actors and institutions, the intended targets of state violence, the number of victims, the input 'from below' of local officials and the popula-tion as a whole, and the short- and longer-term impact of mass repression on Soviet society. In the 1980s and into the 1990s adherents of the rival 'totali-tarian' and 'revisionist' schools slugged their way through a cantankerous and ultimately sterile debate, the former stressing the terroristic essence of the Stalinist state and Stalin's controlling hand, and the latter concentrating on 'centre-periphery' tensions, the chaotic and dysfunctional elements of the Stalinist system and its manifold interactions with Soviet society.[30]

Neither of these two paradigms was 'right' or 'wrong': both elucidated fundamental truths about Stalinism. The totalitarians correctly identified the monist urge of the Bolsheviks to gain mastery over social processes and human destinies. The revisionists accurately concluded that intention 'from above' was often foiled by unforeseen reaction 'from below', which in turn demanded ever more draconian 'solutions' from the leadership.[31] I cannot hope to address, let alone answer, all these imponderables and controversies. Instead, I focus on Stalin's input in the purges and discuss the most recent interpretations of the Terror, which demonstrate that rather than being a unitary phenomenon possessing a single overriding aim, it was a multi-faceted process composed of separate but related political, social and 'national' dimensions, the origins and goals of which were differentiated, but which coalesced in the horrific wave of arrests and executions of 1937–8.

It has been recognised for many years that Stalin's personal role in the Terror was profound. He signed hundreds of 'death warrants' containing thousands of names; in September 1936 he appointed Nikolai Ezhov, a known hard-line adversary of 'anti-party elements', as head of the NKVD; he initiated and carefully orchestrated the three Moscow Show Trials of August 1936, January 1937 and March 1938 as a result of which his old Bolshevik rivals Zinoviev, Kamenev and Bukharin *inter alia* were shot in secret police cellars[32]; he participated in some of the interrogation sessions of leading prisoners; he even had arrested several members of his own extended family and close relatives of his colleagues, presumably in an attempt to test the loyalty of his subordinates; and, together with his propagandists, he set the overall tone and atmosphere of the Terror: the xenophobic suspicion of foreign 'spies' and 'agents', the all-pervasive fear of 'wreckers', 'saboteurs', and 'double-dealers', and the endless exhortations to uphold 'Bolshevik vigilance' in the face of 'enemies of the people'. Stalin pulled no triggers, but metaphorically there are oceans of blood on his hands.

Recently declassified documents from hitherto inaccessible Soviet archives have extended our knowledge of Stalin's nefarious activities. He despatched telegrams to local authorities demanding that 'enemies' should be peremptorily shot; he oversaw the secret trial of Marshal Tukhachevskii and the decimation of the Red Army command in May–June 1937; he confirmed the composition of the *troiki* (three-man sentencing bodies); he sanctioned the routine use of 'physical methods' (torture) to extract confessions; he ordered the organisation of show trials in each republic and region; he regularly adhered to local requests to extend the quotas of victims; and he ratified the dismissal and arrest of numerous central and regional party officials.[33] These actions were often agreed by the 'quintet' of leaders, Stalin, Molotov, Ezhov (later Beria), Kaganovich and Voroshilov, who managed repression strategy in 1937–8. In this way, Stalin incriminated top colleagues in his murderous policies. Their occasional scrawled comments on surviving manuscripts do not make for edifying reading:

> A pack of lies! Shoot him!   Stalin.
> Agreed.   Molotov.
> Agreed.   Blackguard! A dog's death to a dog.   Beriya.
> Maniac.   Voroshilov.
> Swine!   Kaganovich.[34]

Stalin's overall responsibility for the terror is now a non-issue for historians. As the former 'revisionist' and world-renowned expert, J. Arch Getty, has written: 'he played the leading role....his name is all over the horrible documents authorizing the terror.' But for Getty 'that role remains problematic and hard to specify.' Distancing himself from those scholars who perceive Stalin as adroitly planning the entire purge process, Getty maintains that the archival record shows 'too many twists and turns, too many false starts and subsequent embarrassing backtrackings to support the idea that the terror was the culmination of a well-prepared and long-standing master design....[Stalin] seems not to have decided on a wholesale massacre until early in 1937.'[35] In this scenario, Stalin responds *ad hoc* to events as much as he initiates them. He is a relatively weak, sometimes panicky, leader fearful of domestic and foreign encirclement, who blindly lashes out in 1937–8 against an ill-defined array of 'enemies'.

It is true that Stalin's actions were subject to change and vacillation, and certainly he and other elite communists were apprehensive about the hostile environment. It is also the case that no evidence has been unearthed that definitively proves the existence of a long-term Stalinist plan to remove physically all opponents. Getty is probably right here. But there is conclusive evidence, discussed in the next section, that in 1937 Stalin and his top political and secret police aides issued orders to target and round up specific strata of the population. This seems to contradict the picture of Stalin blindly lashing out against ill-defined enemies and suggests more than a degree of premeditation. What is more, Stalin had proven himself a committed exponent of state violence since at least the late 1920s. As we have seen, he had demanded death penalties for 'bourgeois wreckers' at the Shakhty Trial of May 1928. He had called for the 'elimination of the kulaks as a class', had supported harsh measures against a series of party 'oppositionists' in the early 1930s (Syrtsov and Lominadze, the Riutin Platform, and Smirnov,

Tolmachev and Eismont), and had personally imposed the strictest legal sanctions after Kirov's assassination in December 1934. This demonstrates that the logic and technologies of terror were in place well before 1937 and that Stalin's instinct, regardless of the occasional 'liberal' interlude in the mid-1930s, was for repression rather than concession.

The 'boss', though no doubt influenced by hawks like Ezhov, was the real power broker, the master manipulator of situations, individuals and institutions. Only he could start the mass arrests and executions; only he could rein them in, as he did in November 1938.[36] Indicative of this position is the hard-hitting conclusion of a recent archival based article by Michael Ellman on rural repression: 'The *raion* [district] show trials which took place in September–December 1937 were initiated by Stalin personally and the (chief) sentences were decided by Stalin personally.'[37] David J. Nordlander argues along the same lines, referring to 'Stalin's crucial agency....[and] authoritarian impact' on the destruction of the Bolshevik party.[38] We do not need to view Stalin as some kind of omnipotent and omniscient tyrant to appreciate his signal input in the whole terror process.

Terror: Social and 'National' Dimensions

Little was known about the social aspects of the terror until relatively recently. The studies of historians such as Paul Hagenloh and David Shearer have documented the inter-relationship between, on the one hand, social disorder and evolving NKVD strategies to contain it in the early-to-mid 1930s, and, on the other, the onset of mass arrests in the summer of 1937. Hagenloh perceives the Great Terror as 'the culmination of a decade-long radicalization of policing practice against "recidivist" criminals, social marginals, and all manner of lower-class individuals who did not or could not fit into the emerging Stalinist system.'[39] Shearer maintains that the threat of social instability posed by criminals, hooligans, other 'socially harmful elements', and even armed bandit gangs, was taken extremely seriously by secret police chiefs. By 1937 the lethal triumvirate of social disorder, political opposition and national contamination had raised fears among the increasingly xenophobic party and police elites of a broadly based anti-Soviet 'fifth column', linked to foreign agents and spies. In response, Stalinist leaders launched the massive purge of Soviet society in 1937–8 in order to destroy what appeared to them to be the social base for armed overthrow of the Soviet government. Shearer concludes that mass repression under Stalin was not solely a means of combating the state's enemies; it became a

'constitutive part of Soviet state policy.'[40] Another American historian of
the younger generation, Amir Weiner, has detected the prevalence of
'biological-hygienic' terminology – 'vermin', 'pollution', 'filth' – in Stalinist
discourse of the 1930s and 1940s in its emphasis on purifying Soviet society
by removing 'unfit human weeds.'[41]

The now infamous NKVD Order No. 00447, ratified by the Politburo in
late July 1937, launched the mass operations against 'former kulaks, criminals, and other anti-Soviet elements'.[42] It has been calculated that under the
terms of this order, which remained in force until November 1938, between
767,000 and 800,000 people were convicted.[43] The order cold-bloodedly
and precisely listed by region of the USSR the number of executions (category no. 1 – 75,950) and eight to ten year sentences in the Gulag (category
no. 2 – 193,000) which were to be carried out.[44] In reality, these figures were
over-fulfilled, the Politburo regularly acceding to the requests of local NKVD
leaders to extend the quotas of mass arrests. Thus, one of the most interesting conclusions of the new research is that, contrary to received wisdom
about the elite nature of the victims of the Great Terror, in strictly numeri-
cal terms the bulk of those repressed were 'ordinary' non-communist
citizens, 'kulaks', workers, and various 'social marginals': recidivist criminals,
the homeless, the unemployed, all those who deviated from the social norms
of the emerging Stalinist 'utopia'. To this extent, the Terror must be seen,
in part, as an exercise in social cleansing undertaken on a truly massive
scale.

Another characteristic of Stalinist terror which has only recently been explored in any detail is the 'national', or ethnic, component.[45] It is now
known that beginning in the summer of 1937 the NKVD launched 'national
sweeps' of specific categories of foreigners and Soviet citizens of foreign
extraction. Central and East Europeans were particularly badly hit, but so
were Koreans, Chinese, Afghans and many other minorities. The 'Polish
Operation', based on NKVD Order No. 00485 ratified by the Politburo on
7 August 1937, resulted in the arrest of around 140,000 people, a staggering
111,000 (approximately 80 per cent) of whom were shot.[46] Similar campaigns were directed against Germans, Finns, Balts and many others who
were perceived to be real or potential 'spies' of hostile states and agents of
foreign anti-Soviet intelligence services, although the percentages of those
shot were generally lower than in the Polish case. Jews formed a relatively
high proportion of those repressed, but this may or may not have reflected a
conscious anti-semitism. They were well represented at the top levels of
various organisations and therefore may have been disproportionately targeted. A substantial number of victims were members of foreign communist

parties affiliated to the Comintern in Moscow. This body was decimated by the purges, as a new documentary collection shows all too persuasively and depressingly.[47] Such was the scale of the 'national operations' that from about February 1938 they became the prime function of NKVD activity, more pervasive than the campaigns associated with Order 00447.

These examples of Soviet 'ethnic cleansing' have led some scholars to compare Stalinist and Nazi exterminatory policies. The terminology of 'Stalinist genocide' employed by one or two specialists suggests a close relationship and moral equivalence between Nazi and Soviet terror. If we view the latter in the 'intentional' v. 'functional' framework, it appears that both elements of motivation were applicable: the 'intended' victims were the 'traditional suspects' (peasants, political opponents, and supporters of the Tsarist regime) and the 'functional' ones were invented in the specific context of developments in late 1936 and 1937, consisting of replaceable elite cadres and alien nationals. War or its expected imminence, therefore, radicalised repressive policy in both dictatorships.[48] However, while recognising the enormity of Stalinist repression, I tend to agree with those historians who emphasise the uniqueness of the Holocaust – 'the only example which history offers to date of a deliberate policy aimed at the total physical destruction of every member of an ethnic group. There was no equivalent of this under Stalinism.'[49]

Finally in this section, it is necessary to discuss another recent, and in many ways controversial, approach to the Terror. This is one associated with the broader 'cultural turn' in Stalinist studies, which consciously shifts the focus away from 'high politics' and the party-state elites to the diverse means by which individual Soviet citizens internalised, rationalised and negotiated the values, mentalities and goals of the dominant Stalinist ideology. Scholars such as Oleg Kharkhordin, Jochen Hellbeck and particularly Igal Halfin have argued that the sources of the Terror should be located as much in the psyche of ordinary people as in the conscious aims of the Stalinist hierarchies. Halfin has proposed that, by identifying with the official party discourse, many individuals 'engaged in Communist "self-fashioning", thus turning the messianic aspirations of the state into their own intimate affair.' The idea that Soviet society was largely conformist, practising 'self-inspection', 'self-policing', virtual 'self-purging', is deeply challenging as it subverts the totalitarian commonplace that the omnipotent communist state confronted the atomised 'liberal' citizen in an unequal and stark battle. Standing much existing historiography on its head, Halfin boldly claims that the Great Purge of communists had unintended consequences and did not represent an 'unprecedented breakdown of all moral behavior', but rather 'rested on an ethical system' in which 'grand-scale violence could make moral sense' as a quest 'to bring human-ity to moral perfection.' The disturbing conclusion is that 'less a state policy than a state of mind....Party terror was the result of a never-ending interro-gation of the self.'[50]

This view goes a long way in exonerating Stalin and his henchmen for the homicide of 1937–8 by suggesting that all communists, from the highest to the lowest, participated in and, to varying degrees, supported the violent purging of their own ranks. They were complicit by internalising the all-pervasive party discourse and moral logic on the existence of ubiquitous 'enemies of the people'. In J. Arch Getty's terms, this represented the 'self-destruction of the Bolsheviks'. This unsettling notion helps us comprehend the mindset of millions of communists and is a salient reminder that the Terror had multiple causes, affected individuals in different ways, was per-petuated by various means and hence cannot be reduced to the evil machina-tions of one man alone. However, it seems overdrawn in its emphasis on the almost lemming-like nature of party members, willingly consenting to and colluding in their own demise. What is more, this interpretation offers no explanation for the fate of the hundreds of thousands of *non*-communists caught up in the meat-grinder of Stalinist repression.

Terror: Motivations and Outcomes

The key question of motive remains. Why did Stalin launch the mass arrests of loyal party-state bureaucrats after the notorious February–March 1937 Central Committee Plenum?; why the extension of the Terror in the summer of that year to include 'socially harmful elements'?; why the vicious assault on ethnic minorities that escalated in late 1937 and continued well into 1938? Traditional explanations for the strictly political aspects of the Terror em-phasise Stalin's power lust, his determination to liquidate all real and per-ceived rivals in a paranoiac drive for autocratic rule. Large numbers of 'Old Bolsheviks', former oppositionists and a host of unreliable elements – 'wreck-ers', 'saboteurs', 'spies' – were targeted in what became a frenzy of blood-letting. By eliminating these undesirables and replacing them with totally devoted 'yes-men', Stalin's power base would be mightily strengthened. This argument is not without validity. At the Eighteenth Party Congress in March 1939, Stalin reported that over 500,000 young recruits had taken up leading posts in party and state offices,[51] the vast majority, presumably, owing alle-giance to the General Secretary. Furthermore, as Graeme Gill has pointed out, the new Central Committee elected at the congress marked the rise to dominance of the post-revolutionary generation and was a 'striking illustration of the way in which the political power of the Old Bolsheviks had been destroyed.'[52] As noted above, beginning in the 1980s this Stalin-oriented approach was challenged by the 'revisionists', who saw a certain systemic rationale behind the seemingly irrational waves of repression.

Stalin's motives remain, and will continue to remain, obscure. What is more, he did not, nor could he, decide everything. Indeed, a convincing consensus is emerging which stresses the multiplicity of factors, both internal and external, and the inter-relatedness of the Stalinist 'revolution from above' of the early 1930s and the Great Terror of 1937–8. The latter was inextricably linked to the massive industrialisation campaigns and the forced collectivisation of Soviet agriculture from 1928–9 onwards. The intense social flux and dislocation, the rising crime levels, the peasant resistance to collectivisation, the urban tensions attendant on breakneck industrialisation, the limited success of the initiatives on the 'nationality question', and the contradictory pressures on the bureaucracies and other elites, which engendered insubordination, deceit and local and regional self-defence cliques and networks, all these 'outcomes' of the Stalinist 'revolution from above' created conditions that were propitious for the hunt for 'enemies'. Add in Stalin's not inconsiderable personal power goals and paranoia and the in-built need for scapegoats to 'explain' the dire state of Soviet material consumption, and the origins of large scale repression become more explicable.

The launching of the mass operations in the summer of 1937 appears to be directly related to reverses in the European and Asian arenas, demonstrating the inextricable ties between domestic and foreign events. In particular, the lessons of the Spanish Civil War induced an atmosphere of panic in the Kremlin and incited the Stalinists to seek 'enemies' at home and abroad.[53] The Soviet leadership's fears of a 'fifth column' among party, state and military elites, who in the event of war could count on broadly based support among 'socially harmful elements' and 'hostile' national minorities in the USSR, seems to explain the dramatic extension of mass arrests and executions. In his later years Molotov, admittedly not the most objective and disinterested of commentators, insisted that it was this threat of a 'fifth column' which caused, and in his opinion justified, the purges.[54] More persuasive is Stalin's interjection in Ezhov's speech to the Central Committee plenum in February–March 1937. Ezhov was discussing the dangers of the 'wrecker' when Stalin piped up: 'And he will save up his strength *until the moment of war, when he will really do us a lot of harm.*'[55] In his own address to the plenum, Stalin revealed his deep distrust of foreigners and 'spy mania':

> Is it not clear that as long as capitalist encirclement exists there will continue to exist among us wreckers, spies, saboteurs and murderers, sent into our hinterland by the agents of foreign states?[56]

The logic of Stalin's words is that in a highly tense international climate epitomised by ever-present war scares these 'spies' would enlist the support of ethnic diasporas in the USSR – Poles, Germans, Balts, Finns, Koreans – who were suspect because of their presumed common ethnic ties to hostile states and populations. Indeed, in April 1938 the authoritative French-language weekly *Journal de Moscou* encapsulated the prevailing xenophobia: 'it would be no exaggeration to say that every Japanese living abroad is a spy....and every German citizen....is a Gestapo agent.'[57] It would appear, then, that the fear of a 'fifth column' is the crucial link between the three dimensions of the Great Terror: political, social and 'national'. It is in the context of the looming war threat and the Stalinists' grave concerns for the security of the Soviet state that the mass repressions of 1937–8 can be best understood.

Although the most recent writings reaffirm to varying degrees the 'primacy of Stalin' in the launching of the mass repressions of the late 1930s, this conclusion does not imply that 'centre-periphery' tensions, regional inputs and variations, and other broader factors should be overlooked. Clearly, even as 'omnipotent' a dictator as Stalin could not inspire or control everything that occurred in his vast domain, if by the word 'control' is meant his ability 'to create a rational and well-functioning political-economic system and to ensure that every citizen displayed the desired pattern of behaviour.'[58] It has been argued that an important determinant of the mass arrests was the anxiety among local and regional leaders that Soviet power was under threat from the millions of ex-kulaks, White Guardists and other multifarious 'anti-Soviet elements', now enfranchised by the Stalin Constitution, whose votes in the proposed secret-ballot Supreme Soviet elections of December 1937 might destabilise the regime.[59] Linked to this approach is the marked tendency to shift attention from the decision-making processes in Moscow to the implementation of those decisions in the provinces, often demonstrating unintentional, and sometimes contradictory, outcomes.[60] The same appears to be true of the repression in cultural organisations, an emerging theme among researchers.[61] It also seems appropriate to take ideological concerns more seriously than hitherto. Mass purging was motivated not only by Stalin's

desire to strengthen his power base, but also by a perceived need to 'revolutionise' and transform Soviet society by crushing once and for all counter-
revolutionary 'socially harmful elements' and 'class enemies'. Likewise, the
attack on the sprawling bureaucracies can be construed as an attempt to
smash the 'bourgeois' and 'Menshevik' lethargy of party-state functionaries.

Another interesting issue is how the Terror was received by different sections of Soviet society. Many 'ordinary' citizens, it seems, perceived the repression of communists as an essentially positive phenomenon: the despised
'them' devouring each other.[62] Moreover, the language and images of
'enemies', 'wreckers' and 'spies' reflected a society, still largely rural, in
which traditional notions of evil spirits and nefarious demons were deep-
rooted and in which social and ethnic antagonisms were ubiquitous.[63] From
a longer-term perspective, it might be asked what was the psychological and
demographic impact of mass repression on Soviet wartime performance and
popular attitudes. One prominent 'revisionist' has asserted that the morale
of the Red Army, and of the Soviet people in general, during the Great
Patriotic War was not unduly undermined by the Terror of the late thirties,
though this hypothesis requires closer inspection.[64] Finally, much more
clarity is needed on the winding down of the purges after November 1938.
Why did Stalin and Molotov decide to rein in Ezhov and the NKVD and limit
mass arrests? Recent evidence suggests that by the autumn of 1938 the
Stalinist leaders had become aware of the dysfunctional aspects of repression and sought to restore a modicum of 'normality' to party, state and
economic life.[65]

The outcomes of the Terror were manifold. The sheer numbers involved
are awe-inspiring. Of the 1,996 delegates to the Seventeenth Party Congress
in 1934, no fewer than 1,108 were arrested of whom 848 were executed. Out
of the 139 Central Committee members elected at that congress, 98 were
eventually destroyed. As for regional party secretaries, 319 out of 385 were
repressed. The Ukraine was particularly badly hit. Of the 200 Central
Committee members of the local party, a mere three survived. Archival
figures published in Gorbachev's era of *glasnost'* (openness) indicate that
786,098 people were shot in the USSR between 1930 and 1953, of whom
681,692 were executed during the Great Terror of 1937–8.[66] In addition to
these deaths, very large numbers perished in the Gulag system of labour
camps.[67] Official statistics suggest that around 3.5 to 4 million people were
detained in labour camps, 'special settlements' and internal exile in the
years of the Terror, the number rising to five million in the early 1950s.
Many scholars have speculated that the real totals were substantially higher.
In the absence of definitive data, however, it seems prudent to acknowledge

the archival figures as basically accurate. But whether we accept the high or low figures, Stalinist terror represented an unprecedented assault on a state and society in peace time. What is more, horrendous as they are, these bald statistics obscure the unimaginable depths of human misery, the families ripped apart, the innumerable orphaned children, the mental and physical torture of prisoners, the uprooting of entire peoples from their homelands, the trampling on human integrity and dignity. These were the ruinous consequences of Stalin's terror.

They were not, however, the only consequences. In socio-economic terms, industrial relations and discipline in the factories and enterprises were severely disrupted as workers were encouraged to denounce their managers and foremen as 'wreckers', 'double dealers' and 'saboteurs'. This contributed in no small way to a marked decline in production in many branches of the economy. Most importantly, the assault on the Red Army officer corps massively weakened Soviet military capacities (or at least this was the general perception in Europe at the time) at an absolutely crucial juncture and may well have cemented Hitler's resolve to launch an early invasion of the USSR. Hence, at precisely the time Stalin was preparing for war he was decisively undermining Soviet defensive capabilities. What appears to us to be the total irrationality of the Terror hides, paradoxically, several highly rational purposes for the 'boss'. Above all, he used state coercion at different levels to create and maintain his personal dictatorship: to remove physically all real and putative opponents and potential rivals (Old Bolsheviks, military elites and party oppositionists); to scapegoat state and party bureaucrats for the failings of the economy and material consumption and thus divert discontent from himself and the leadership; to eliminate whole layers of perceived insubordinate and inefficient cliquish officials who could hinder his drive for autocratic power and to replace them with a younger more malleable 'Stalinist' cohort; and to bind his colleagues even closer to him through collective guilt and test their loyalty by the selective persecution of relatives and loved ones.

But for Stalin terror also had far broader applications, becoming the dominant mode of governance: to spread fear among the general population in an attempt to ensure conformity and mass mobilisation; to promote solid 'proletarian elements', untarnished by bourgeois education and ethics, into positions of authority; to activate the 'masses' through means of 'anti-bureaucratic', pseudo-populist campaigns of denunciation; and to cleanse the country of social misfits, malcontents and malefactors, who, so it was believed, posed a challenge to the communist utopia by their very existence. In my estimation, however, the primary purpose of the Terror was to bolster state security at a time of impending threats to Soviet national integrity by targeting suspect political, social and ethnic groups. Compulsion, repression and ultimately mass terror were certainly not the sole methods adopted by Stalin to subjugate the party and country at large, but I would argue that they remained his core governing principle from the late 1920s through to his death in 1953.

Limits of Tyranny

Stalin's murderous assault on targeted strata of Soviet party, state and society during the Great Terror stands as irrefutable testimony to his burgeoning tyranny. But this does not mean that constraints and limitations on his power were totally eliminated. By focusing on these parameters, my intention is not to turn Stalin's authority on its head and over-emphasise his weakness and fear of enemies and rivals, but rather to challenge popular stereotypes of the omnipotent despot. As indicated above, his powers were vast and he took a daily interest in a broad array of state policy, particularly issues of internal security, personnel management and defence. He was a prodigious worker, unlike the 'lazy dictator' image of Hitler. That said, several instances of power limitation can be identified. First, at a very basic level, are what can be called 'common sense' notions. There were only twenty four hours even in Stalin's day and he was a fallible single human being, not the God projected by the cult. He had to deal with a relatively rudimentary state of communications (for example, before 1935 there was no high-frequency telephone link between Moscow and his holiday location in the south[68]) in a country that covered a sixth of the globe. Stalin was also faced with the 'normal' dilemma of all politicians: how to respond to unforeseen events and unintended outcomes, both at home and abroad. In short, it is self-evident that, hard as he may try, he was unable to control fully the manifold political, social, economic and cultural processes at play in Soviet state and society.

Secondly, there was a dire lack of competent human raw material. The vast bureaucracies of the USSR were often staffed with ill-educated, poorly trained and potentially insubordinate provincial 'cliques', which the Moscow bosses, much to their irritation, found difficult to command in any sustained fashion. This is summed up in Stalin's grumble of June 1937: 'It's thought that the centre must know and see everything. No, the centre doesn't see everything; it's not like that at all. The centre sees only a part and the rest is seen in the localities. It sends people, but doesn't know these people 100%

and you must check up on them.'[69] Even if we agree that Stalin was being somewhat disingenuous here, he was still alluding to a real dilemma, which Moshe Lewin has aptly encapsulated: 'Despotism depends on, but cannot trust, the bureaucracy'. The mass purge of communist officialdom at all levels of the central and regional administrations could not completely free Stalin from these in-built constraints. Stalin 'the capricious supercentralizer was giving away power by default; each "little Stalin" could be destroyed but was immediately replaced.' Furthermore, in Lewin's estimation, Stalin's despotism, based on arbitrary methods, emergency powers and *ad hoc* agencies, clashed fundamentally with the routine and predictable modes of operation favoured by the vast bureaucracies. The result was a bloated largely inefficient party-state apparatus, which in turn demanded more centralisation and arbitrary intervention, which in turn meant greater inefficiency – a veritable Catch-22 syndrome.[70] A clear distinction should be drawn, then, between a hyper-centralised form of decision-*making*, in which the 'boss' became increasingly dominant, and a multi-layered process of decision-*implementation*, according to which Stalin could not be sure his policies were being enforced.

Stalin's vengeance was thus exacerbated by the disturbing awareness that he was dependent on the bureaucrats to implement state policy and to provide him with accurate information on a whole array of issues. Here was a dictator whose authority had grown inordinately, but one who was still reliant on potentially idle, recalcitrant and cliquish strata of functionaries, whose inclination was to dissimulate, dissemble and feet-drag. Stalin must have regarded this dependency as an insufferable curb on his personal power. If so, his decimation of the party-state organs and managerial elites has its origins not so much in psychological phenomena – relevant though these certainly are – but in the ineluctable dilemmas of twentieth-century dictators whose grandiose plans for state-building are modified and impeded by a cowed, but resilient and self-protecting bureaucracy.

Thirdly, it is possible to identify various forms of resistance, non-compliance and dissent towards Stalin's rule. The limited popular appeal of Marxism-Leninism, the ambivalent reception of the 'Stalin cult', and the existence of alternative non-conformist views among fairly wide strata of the Soviet population[71] suggest a complex differentiated relationship between the leadership and society and the relative inability of the regime to mould citizens into 'new Soviet persons'. It seems that resistance, broadly defined and not always passive, was a permanent fixture on the Soviet scene, even in Stalin's heyday. From workers' strikes[72] and bandit gangs[73] to gender dissent[74] and the black market,[75] Soviet citizens refused to comply fully with, and sought to mediate, the rules of the game as best they could.[76]

Finally, it could be speculated that Stalin too was a kind of victim of the system he had created. Khrushchev reportedly overheard the 'boss' mutter in 1951: 'I'm finished....I trust no one, not even myself.'[77] Had the Soviet leader gained a disturbing realisation of his own impotency? Or should we dismiss this statement as the musings of a deranged old man? It would appear that towards the end, and probably well before, Stalin could trust neither his closest colleagues, nor the party, nor, at the most fundamental level, the Soviet people. As Lewin has argued, 'Stalin's morbid and pervasive suspiciousness toward his entourage was a permanent condition.' His power position was therefore 'not just a conquest but also a trap into which he had allowed himself to fall.'[78] Do we have here, then, a dictator who was so consumed by Byzantine court intrigues and conspiracies, so ensnared by the web of secrecy, lies and deception that he felt powerless to enforce his will, or even totally unable to discern the causes of regime malfunctions? By seeing 'enemies' everywhere and by personalising defects in the system, he was incapable of determining the real causes of crises in the economy and elsewhere, thus effectively preventing solutions to these crises. Indeed, he could not delve too deeply into the 'objective' reasons for the problems, as this would inevitably undermine the system and the very policies with which he himself was so closely identified.

By considering the limits and parameters of Stalin's power, I do not want to give the impression that he was an 'ordinary' political leader, that he was helpless to cut the ties that bound him and that he was a prisoner of impersonal 'objective' circumstances. Surely, Stalin's dictatorship offers as clear-cut a historical example as possible of an individual who was able to concentrate immense power in his own hands, to use, and massively abuse, that power for his own purposes, to ride rough-shod over the views and interests of an entire society, and to impose on that society his own ideological preferences. My point, rather, is that power is never total, is often contradictory, and that at times Stalin may even have experienced a degree of powerlessness in the face of intractable forces. In this sense, the traditional 'totalitarian' perspective of the 'all-powerful' ruler is overly simplistic, uni-dimensional and unnecessarily restrictive.

The Stalin Cult

The emphasis in this chapter so far has been on state coercion and terror as a means of securing Stalin's hegemonic position. However, another pivotal factor must be brought into the equation: what Khrushchev would later call the 'cult of personality'. Stalin's cult, assiduously disseminated by a state propaganda system of mythical proportions, rose in parallel to his personal dictatorship, but when discussing it in relation to Stalin's emergence as un-rivalled *vozhd'*, a perennial conceptual problem is that of conscious human agency. How aware was Stalin of the ability of the cult to mould the hearts and minds of Soviet citizens? How far did he deliberately manipulate and manufacture his own image and identity for political purposes? What were his attitudes to the cult and what, in his opinion, were its functions? Notions of carefully planned conspiracies may seem to be stretching a point. Indeed, if we follow Vadim Volkov's approach to the regime's cam-paigns for 'civilised living' (*kul'turnost'*) from the mid-1930s, it appears these practices and policies 'did not derive from any unified explicitly for-mulated political project. Their unity can better be seen with reference to their social and individual effects, their long-term consequences, rather than from the point of view of intentional projects of political authorities.'[79] The cult, it appears, is an altogether different proposition. There is plenty of evidence to show that Stalin was fully cognisant of its mobilising powers and legitimising properties and that he actively intervened in its invention and consolidation. He was by far not the only player in this process, but in Arfon Rees' opinion 'the strategy of creating a leader cult was deliberate and calculated.'[80]

It is widely assumed that the Stalin cult originated in December 1929 on the occasion of the General Secretary's fiftieth birthday celebrations. Closely based on the Lenin cult of the 1920s, it had manifold functions: to underpin Stalin's image as the 'Lenin of today', to bind the party and people to the new beneficent Leader and by extension to the state, to identify the achievements of the regime with himself, and to project a father-like persona, ever-caring for his 'children', the Soviet people. As 'Leader, Teacher, Friend' and 'Father of the Peoples', Stalin's paternalist image personified the supposed harmonious relations among the diverse ethnic groups of the Soviet 'family'. The cult thus sought to provide a symbolic source of security and stability at a time of profound and rapid socio-economic change. By the mid-to-late 1930s it also had the important goal of inculcating 'Soviet patriotism' and a willingness to defend the 'so-cialist motherland' in the war that everyone knew was coming.[81] The cult fluctuated in the course of the 1930s, being less pronounced in the early part of the decade, but by the time of the Terror and beyond Stalin was accorded an almost God-like status, culminating in the grotesque pane-gyrics of the late 1930s and the post-war years. Epithets such as 'Sun-Man' and 'Creator' abounded. All forms of media were used to promote the cult: cinema, photography, posters, oil painting, sculpture, songs, poetry, prose, folklore, drama and crafts and it was not uncommon for Stalin himself to regulate the artistic production of his image. Totalitarian theorists of the Cold War period equated Stalin with the other 'charismatic' twentieth-century dictators, Hitler and Mussolini, and argued that his mythic cult, combined with ubiquitous Marxist-Leninist propaganda, served to indoctrinate Soviet society and prevent the articulation of alternative ideologies.[82]

While eschewing Cold War rhetoric, Robert Tucker, a leading expert on the cult, has reasserted its centrality not only for the Stalinist system as a whole, but for Stalin personally. Tucker has claimed that Stalin not only used the cult as a vital political support, but he was psychologically dependent on it: 'Stalin needed a cult as a prop for his psyche as well as for his power. He craved the hero worship that Lenin found repugnant.'[83] It is true that in the course of the 1930s Stalin oversaw and sanctioned a massive expansion of personal adulation which, presumably, he could have curtailed by lifting the telephone. But ultimately Tucker's psychological interpretation is unprovable. No doubt Stalin's studiously professed modesty was largely disingenuous and was itself a component of the cult, linked as it was to Lenin's legendary diffidence. But it does appear that Stalin held ambivalent attitudes to his burgeoning cult status. On several occasions he discarded its more extreme manifestations and complained that it nourished feelings of servility and grovelling in the people. He adamantly refused the suggestion that Moscow be renamed 'Stalinodar', recommended that a hagiographic account of his childhood be burned, dropped his name from formulations such as 'the party and teachings of Lenin and Stalin', rejected the idea of holding a Stalin art exhibition and struck out sycophantic passages from speeches, official reports and cultural productions. One example of the latter is Stalin's missive dated 27 January 1937 to Boris Shumiatskii, the head of the Soviet film industry, in which he insists that all 'references to Stalin must be eliminated' from the script of the film *Velikii grazhdanin* ('The Great Citizen') and replaced with the words 'the CC of the party.'[84] He was particularly concerned not to permit details of his private life to be divulged in the media.

The latest research on this phenomenon suggests that the 'boss' adopted an orthodox Marxist approach to the idea of cults. They were acceptable as long as they promoted the leader as representative of the historical 'cause', of the party or wider social forces. Stalin's encouragement of the Lenin cult should be seen in these terms. While recognising the cult's political and ideological benefits, he was also aware of its latent incongruity with mainstream Marxist thought. Hence, he regarded the emphasis on the individual *per se* as an 'unbolshevik aberration which was open to abuse by opportunists and potentially detrimental to the education of the new intelligentsia. It continued to exist primarily because of its appeal to the culturally backward masses.'[85] Stalin reportedly stated in 1935 that ordinary people needed a tsar to worship[86] and thus he looked on the cult as a mobilising and legitimising force for a poorly educated population, its quasi-religious overtones reflecting widespread traditional practices and beliefs. It was correspondingly less effective, so he intimated, among trained party cadres and the new elites.

The cult also had an important function in strengthening Stalin's position among his top colleagues and in consolidating the collective identity of the 'Stalin clan'. Indeed, it appears that Kaganovich and Voroshilov among others played a key role in initiating the cult in the late 1920s and many Politburo members and regional secretaries enjoyed their own mini-cults. In this sense, the personality cults were mutually reinforcing and, initially at least, gave coherence and cohesion to a leading Stalinist cohort that rarely felt immune from political opposition and civil unrest.[87] Voroshilov's fawning attitude to the 'boss' is graphically illustrated in a letter he sent to another Stalinist luminary, Enukidze, in June 1933:

> A remarkable man, our Koba. It is simply incomprehensible how he can combine the great mind of the proletarian strategist, the will of a statesman and revolutionary activist, and the soul of a completely ordinary kind comrade, who bears in mind every detail and cares for everything that concerns the people he knows, loves and values. It is good that we have Koba.[88]

Even if we allow that Voroshilov may have been subconsciously writing for a wider audience, this obsequious out-pouring is symptomatic of the power of the cult to influence even elite figures in the Stalinist hierarchy.

Popular attitudes to the cult, on the other hand, are notoriously difficult to evaluate and no doubt ranged from genuine belief to wilful indifference to semi-overt ridicule and mockery. Sarah Davies best sums up the reception of the cult:

> People selected certain aspects of it, and rejected or ignored others; they appropriated those aspects of it which served their own purposes; they familiarised it so that it harmonised with their own preconceptions; they distorted its messages, criticised it directly, and subverted it in a more indirect manner.[89]

It would seem logical to conclude that the cult's main base of support came from party activists and the younger upwardly mobile social strata, the officials, managers, engineers and middle-level technocrats. These ex-workers and peasants were the prime beneficiaries of the Stalinist 'revolution from above' and had the most to gain by internalising, willingly or otherwise, the slogans and discourses of the cult. Nevertheless, certain intellectuals, educated workers and even some party members were critical of the cult's more absurd elements and in this sense it could have counter-productive consequences. Among the bulk of the peasantry, since forced collectivisation Stalin's image was overwhelmingly negative and there is little reason to assume the cult seriously altered this perception. In general, however, by profoundly personalising the Soviet political order and effectively emasculating the party as the fount of ideological orthodoxy, by using the omnipresent image of Stalin to embody and glorify the state, by providing a direct populist link between the Leader and the masses, by portraying Stalin as the benevolent purveyor of 'gifts' to the Soviet people, and by regulating the interpersonal dynamics among his 'inner circle', the cult massively strengthened Stalin's power position and helped to secure the legitimation of his system of rule. The cult also afforded a basic rationalisation for the Terror in that it so closely aligned Stalin with the regime and with communism, the very goal of the Bolshevik Revolution, that any opposition to him was tantamount to treason.[90] And what does any state do with traitors?

With the cult at its most intense in the late 1930s and early 1940s, Stalin and the entire Soviet polity were about to be plunged into their most severe test: the Second World War, or as it is still called in Russia today, the 'Great Patriotic War'. Stalin as 'Warlord' is the theme of the next chapter.

Chapter 5: Warlord

A week after the momentous and unexpected Nazi invasion of the USSR on 22 June 1941, Stalin reportedly blurted out to his shocked colleagues: 'Lenin left us a great inheritance and we, his heirs, have fucked it all up!'[1] Regardless of the expletive, this statement reveals Stalin's despair at the calamity that had befallen his creation. The 'infallible' Leader had inexplicably failed to foresee or adequately prepare for Operation Barbarossa. He had obstinately refused to accept the veracity of his own military intelligence that accurately dated the German attack. He had declined to mobilise the Soviet armed forces on the western fronts. He bizarrely held to the idea that the attack when it finally came was a 'provocation' against Hitler's wishes. Even as he uttered the words above, he was overseeing a disaster of immense proportions as the *Wehrmacht* tore through the Soviet countryside, capturing and killing up to 5.9 million Red Army troops in the first six months of the fighting and eliminating an estimated ninety per cent of the Soviet tank strength.[2] In addition, the *Luftwaffe* virtually destroyed the Red air force on the ground. Hitler's betrayal of the Nazi-Soviet Pact was taken as a personal humiliation by Stalin, who had deluded himself to the last minute that the *Führer* would not voluntarily create a second front and would not launch his legions before 1942.

And yet the debilitated 'boss' rapidly regained his composure, supervised a truly massive reorganisation of the Soviet economy and society onto a war footing, turned himself into a more than competent military Supreme Commander and after the colossal Battle of Stalingrad culminating in early 1943 led his people and armies to a historic victory in the 'total war of the century'. How did he achieve this? What concrete policies did he adopt? What was his involvement in, an understanding of, military strategy? How did his relations with the top Red Army officer corps change over time? How best to interpret the many historical controversies aroused by Stalin's actions (and inactions) in the vital months of August 1939 and May to July 1941? Ultimately, did the USSR emerge triumphant because, or despite, of 'Uncle Joe'? These are among the main issues to be discussed in this chapter, but I will begin with an evaluation of Stalin's pre-war international diplomacy, concentrating on the key period 1933–41. .

Stalin's Foreign Policy and the Road to War

In contrast to the view that posits a stark dichotomy in Soviet foreign policy under Stalin – either a fundamental commitment to *realpolitik* and conventional 'balance of power' diplomacy or an ideologically-driven quest to expand the boundaries of communism – I would argue that both *realpolitik* and ideology were ever-present in a shifting and delicate symbiosis, albeit one which is extremely difficult to delineate and disentangle. In this I wholeheartedly agree with the Italian expert, Silvio Pons, whose extensive research on Stalin's international policy has revealed that:

> There is growing evidence of an interaction between doctrine and geopolitical thinking, and these are not necessarily incompatible. Stalin's unprincipled pragmatism was not detached from his ideological vision, as it was rooted in strategic thinking originating in the Bolshevik doctrine about the inevitability of war.[3]

Stalin's foreign policy in the 1930s was based on three underlying premises. Firstly, all capitalist states were potential or real enemies of the Soviet Union; secondly, the requirement to preserve the national security of the Soviet state in both Europe and Asia by a policy of dividing the 'great powers' was paramount; and, thirdly, the 'inevitable war' had to be avoided as long as possible in order to modernise the Soviet armed forces. More assertively, Stalin was also interested in recovering the 'lost lands' on the western peripheries of the USSR (the Baltic republics, Bessarabia, even areas of Finland) and was not averse to opportunistic machinations to achieve his ends. The central dilemma was: how best to realise these, in part, contradictory and conflictual aims in the rapidly changing and dangerous international climate of the 1930s and early 1940s?

Ever since the October Revolution, foreign relations had presented a major headache for Bolshevik leaders.[4] There was an inherent dualism in their strategies. Should a traditional *modus operandi* be sought with the capitalist powers, whose economic and trading potential was much needed by the struggling Soviet Union, or should national security be based on fomenting world revolution by means of the Comintern and its affiliated communist parties? In the 1920s, both strategies were pursued simultaneously in an unprecedented, but ultimately ineffectual, attempt to combine *realpolitik* and Marxist ideology. The overriding priority established by Lenin was to use skilful diplomacy to prevent the formation of an anti-Soviet western coalition and this was partly achieved by wooing Weimar Germany, the other main international pariah. Up to 1920 at least, Lenin was also convinced that revolution in Europe and in the colonies was on the immediate agenda. As we have seen in previous chapters, Stalin had rarely placed much faith in the revolutionary élan of the western proletariat, but even the chief advocate of 'socialism in one country' never totally refuted the Leninist goal of world communism. He remained sensitive to prospects of revolutionary change (the British General Strike and the Chinese Revolution) and certainly harboured a deep class-based mistrust and anathema of capitalist states and their 'imperialist' representatives. Two somewhat coarse letters to Molotov exemplify this attitude. In the first, dated 9 September 1929, Stalin reflects on recent negotiations with the British Labour Government: 'Remember we are waging a struggle (negotiation with enemies is also struggle), not with England alone, but with the whole capitalist world....We really would be worthless if we couldn't manage to reply to these arrogant bastards briefly and to the point: *'You won't get a friggin' thing from us.'* In the second missive from January 1933 Stalin congratulated his friend's speech on foreign relations, saying: 'The confident, contemptuous tone with respect to the "great" powers, the belief in our own strength, the delicate but plain spitting in the pot of the swaggering "great powers" – very good. Let them eat it.'[5]

All Soviet leaders, particularly Stalin, were haunted by what Pons has called 'the inevitable war'. The foreign interventions during the Civil War had left an indelible 'siege mentality' among the Bolsheviks. It was axiomatic that the USSR's many enemies were merely biding their time until the next concerted attempt to overthrow Soviet power. This underlying fear of a western-led coalition intent on waging war on the Soviet Union was undoubtedly exaggerated and often stoked for political purposes, notably in the 'War Scare' of 1927, but was a genuine perception of a Marxist-Leninist truism: no capitalist state could rest easy until the 'land of socialism' had been crushed. Palpable threats began to emerge in the 1930s. In the Far East, Japan's invasion of Manchuria in 1931 raised the alarm bells in the Kremlin and the Nazis' rise to power did nothing to alleviate the Stalinists' sense of isolation and vulnerability. After 1933, Stalin's two main foreign policy options were either to seek a continued *rapprochement* with Germany on the basis of their mutual hostility to the Versailles settlement and bourgeois 'old Europe' or work for 'collective security' with the democratic western countries against the German threat bolstered by a broad cross-class 'Popular Front' combining communists, social democrats, radicals and other anti-fascist forces. By late 1933 and more systematically in 1934–5, Stalin and the Politburo decided to pursue the 'collective security' line personified by the Soviet Foreign Minister Maksim Litvinov, an Anglophile diplomat, but not a member of Stalin's 'inner circle'. Typically, however, Stalin did not wish to burn his bridges. Never one to close off alternatives, Stalin, supported by influential close colleagues such as Molotov, maintained a surreptitious interest in upholding sound relations with Germany.[6] Indeed, some historians have averred that a Nazi-Soviet alliance was the long-term, but unstated, goal of Stalin's diplomacy in the 1930s, the ultimate aim being to encourage a war between the Nazis and the western democracies from which the USSR would emerge the real power broker in continental Europe with substantial territorial aggrandisement.[7]

This argument is cogent, but problematic. Too much time and energy were invested in the 'collective security' policy for it to be considered little more than a ruse. In 1935 the USSR signed important mutual assistance treaties with Czechoslovakia and France, the Soviet Union was the only major power to send military aid to the anti-fascist Republicans in the Spanish Civil War, and it entered into security negotiations with a lukewarm Britain and France as late as the summer of 1939. This does not mean that Stalin was unambiguously committed to a 'collective security' line that precluded amicable relations with Nazi Germany, nor that he was a principled adversary of all forms of fascism, Soviet cordiality with Mussolini's Italy being a fine example.[8] He was primarily concerned to devise a strategy (or strategies) that could best defend the existence of the USSR. As he said at the Seventeenth Party Congress in January 1934:

We never had any orientation towards Germany, nor have we any orientation towards Poland and France. Our orientation in the past and our orientation at the present time is towards the U.S.S.R., and towards the U.S.S.R. alone....And if the interests of the U.S.S.R. demand rapprochement with one country or another which is not interested in disturbing peace, we take this step without hesitation.[9]

Stalin was intimating *inter alia* that a future Russo-German reconciliation could not be ruled out if it served the security requirements of the Soviet state. This was precisely the situation by August 1939.

The Molotov-Ribbentrop Pact is one of the most infamous and contentious diplomatic dealings in modern history: why did Stalin 'sup with the devil'? There are no easy answers and historians are sharply divided in their interpretations,[10] but recent Russian archival evidence suggests that it was Hitler who in May 1939 took the initiative in improving political relations between the two countries and that Stalin unequivocally accepted Berlin's overtures only in mid-August 1939 after convincing himself that the protracted trilateral negotiations with Britain and France, under way in Moscow, were going nowhere. From the Soviet perspective, with 'collective security' now definitively in tatters, the only realistic option was a deal with Nazi Germany that would guarantee, at least temporarily, Soviet territorial integrity and divert the *Führer's* attention West. In this understanding of events, Stalin's German policy appears more *ad hoc* than planned, more reactive than active. Inherent in his thinking was the orthodox Leninist premise that the USSR should not become embroiled in a 'capitalist' war, which Stalin believed would be prolonged and would hence exhaust his enemies. This can be inferred from his comments delivered at a Kremlin gathering on 7 September 1939. Basing his ideas on the 'Marxist dialectic', Stalin noted:

> We see nothing wrong in their [capitalist states] having a good hard fight and weakening each other. It would be fine if at the hands of Germany the position of the richest capitalist countries (especially England) were shaken. Hitler, without understanding it or desiring it, is shaking and undermining the capitalist system.[11]

More fundamental in Stalin's calculations was his recognition that the Red Army, despite the massive remilitarisation programmes of the 1930s, was in no position to combat the *Wehrmacht*. For Stalin, time was of the essence. By coming to an agreement with Hitler, vital months, perhaps years, would be gained to re-equip the Soviet armed forces for the Nazi invasion that he knew was in the offing. Such were the perceived benefits of, and rationale for, Stalin's tortuous diplomatic manoeuvrings in these critical days.

The Nazi-Soviet Pact signed in Moscow on the night of 23 August 1939 comprised two sections, one public and the other known as the 'Secret Protocols'. The former stipulated that relations between the two countries were to be based on non-aggression, neutrality and mutual consultation, effectively leaving Hitler free to attack Poland which he did on 1 September precipitating war with Britain and France. The secret agreements, the existence of which was officially denied by the Soviet Union until the Gorbachev era, established separate 'spheres of influence' in Poland and the Baltic republics. On 17 September, the Red Army occupied the eastern half of Poland, including large areas of Western Ukraine and Western Belorussia, and in August 1940 all three Baltic states, Estonia, Latvia and Lithuania, were 'voluntarily' incorporated into the USSR after Red Army and NKVD incursions and various strong-arm ultimatums. Stalin's policies in these lands have been described as a 'revolution from abroad', implying again a mixture of conventional *realpolitik* and ideological and political transformation.[12] As he cynically observed to Georgi Dimitrov, the head of the Comintern, at the above-mentioned meeting on 7 September 1939: 'what would be the harm if as a result of the rout of Poland we were to extend the socialist system onto new territories and populations?'[13] Stalin, by means of armed territorial aggrandisement and ruthless repression in the annexed regions, had seized the opportunity to extend the borders of Soviet-style socialism, the overarching aim being to secure the USSR's western boundaries. He was banking on a 'war of attrition' in the West, but with the totally unexpected rapid fall of France and several other European states in the spring and early summer of 1940, he was forced to turn to appeasement of Hitler in order to stave off a Nazi invasion. Stalin's controversial role in the immediate events leading up to the war in the East will be discussed below.

As Teddy Uldricks, a leading American expert, has wisely cautioned: 'the Kremlin pursued a diplomatic course that was neither morally nor ideologically consistent. Moscow's policy, like that of the democracies, was neither pure and noble nor diabolically cunning.'[14] Stalin, who was the final architect of Soviet foreign policy, had to devise an international strategy in highly complex, fluid and dangerous circumstances. He could trust none of his protagonists, all of whom Bolshevik orthodoxy told him were real or potential enemies. Thus, with the western democracies effectively rejecting an anti-German alliance with the USSR, what is universally regarded as an unconscionable, unprincipled and sordid deal between two despots was probably the only way out for a Stalin desperate to defend the Soviet state. That said, viewed in a broader historical framework, Stalin's turn to Nazi Germany in August 1939 undoubtedly helped open the way to World War II and the Soviet dictator must take his full share of the responsibility for this calamitous denouement.

Stalin and Operation Barbarossa

There are several persistent myths about Stalin's actions, motivations and intentions in the immediate pre- and post-invasion period that recent archival discoveries have elucidated, if not always totally debunked. The first of these concerns the so-called 'Icebreaker' controversy and relates to Stalin's military and geopolitical strategies in the weeks before the Nazi assault. In 1988 Viktor Suvorov, the pseudonym of Vladimir Rezun, a former Soviet intelligence officer who defected to the West in 1978, published a book entitled *Icebreaker: Who Started the Second World War?* It was a tract that was to cause something of an international sensation. In it Suvorov argued that the Soviet leader was planning to launch an attack on Germany in early July 1941 with the aim of completing Lenin's original goal of European-wide communist revolution. In this sense, Stalin is construed as the revolutionary aggressor and Hitler the unlikely victim. Indeed, Suvorov's claim merely re-iterated the *Führer's* justification for Operation Barbarossa as a pre-emptive strike against a belligerent USSR. The ramifications of Suvorov's thesis are truly profound, suggesting that the Nazis were fighting a preventative war and defending European civilisation from the barbaric Asiatic hordes. In re-sponse, scholars in Russia, Germany, America, Britain, Israel and elsewhere rushed to take sides in the bitter disputes that inevitably followed. Most, but by no means all, refuted Suvorov's largely unsubstantiated theories.[15]

Is there any solid evidence for this assertion of a planned Soviet offensive against Germany in the summer of 1941? In a recent meticulously re-searched article, Evan Mawdsley has shown firstly that ever since the Civil War Red Army military strategy had involved an 'offensive mode of action', had denigrated defensive operations on Soviet soil and had envisaged that any invader would be rebuffed at the borders and any fighting would be done on enemy territory. It was an overall doctrine that Stalin strongly en-dorsed, so much so that in the late 1930s he failed to maintain the reloca-tion of Soviet industry to the east, a decision that was to prove most costly. Secondly, on 5 May 1941 the 'boss' delivered a toast to new military gradu-ates in the Kremlin in which he urged the need 'to go from defence to offense....The Red Army is a modern army, and a modern army is an offen-sive army.' Finally, in light of these authoritative comments, on 15 May 1941 the Commissar of Defence, Semen Timoshenko, and the Chief of the General Staff, Georgii Zhukov, drew up a top secret draft memorandum which was almost certainly brought to Stalin's attention and which proposed 'a sudden blow against the enemy, both from the air and on land'. These are pieces of evidence avidly seized on by the 'Suvorovites'.

However, as Mawdsley convincingly demonstrates they are ultimately in-
conclusive and by no means support the idea of an imminent Soviet 'offensive war'. For a start, the 15 May document was unsigned and remained in
draft form. Furthermore, by all accounts Stalin adamantly rejected
Timoshenko's and Zhukov's plans. According to Zhukov reminiscing years
later, Stalin 'immediately exploded when he heard about the pre-emptive
blow....against the German forces. "Have you gone mad?"....he barked out
irritably.' Timoshenko's rendition has Stalin ranting at a stunned Zhukov
accusing him of being a warmonger and promising the Red Army leaders
that 'if you provoke the Germans on the border, if you move forces without
our permission, then bear in mind that heads will roll.' These words may be
apocryphal, but there is little doubt that Stalin was not enamoured of his generals' optimistic scenario. More relevant is the fact that 'military measures
that would have been essential for the lead-up to a "sudden blow" were not
carried out. Above all, there was no full-scale hidden mobilization'.[16] And
even if there had been a serious concentration of forces, transport, fuel and
other logistics, would the Red Army have been fully prepared for a strike in
early July, a mere seven weeks after the May plan? The answer can only be
'no'. It seems to me that Suvorov's notions should be laid to rest.[17]

If Stalin was not concocting a military offensive in the summer of 1941,
then what *was* his strategy towards Germany? It was a mixture of diplomatic appeasement and resistance with prime emphasis on the former.
A word of caution is in order here: we cannot crawl into Stalin's head and
be totally sure of his intentions. As Molotov later intimated, '"Stalin believed, Stalin thought...." As if anyone knew exactly what Stalin thought of
the war!'[18] His policies were shifting, having to adapt to rapidly changing,
often inauspicious, circumstances. That said, it can be postulated with
some surety that his overarching goal remained constant: to postpone the
inevitable war as long as possible to give the USSR time to re-equip and
modernise its armed forces and prepare the Soviet population. But how to
achieve this vital delay? Stalin was not a duped and naive believer in
Hitler's goodwill and neither was he under any illusions about the threat
posed by Germany. But he was convinced, apparently, that with Hitler
bogged down in a 'war of attrition' with Britain he could by clever diplomatic manoeuvrings appease the *Führer* and hence put off the Nazi attack
that he knew was coming. Stalin simply couldn't conceive that Hitler
would open a second front in the East without having first defeated
Britain in the West. He remained inveterately suspicious of the British,
who, he believed, were bent on embroiling Russia in a conflict with
Germany to ease their plight or, even worse, were capable of signing a

separate Anglo-German peace accord that would permit one or both
parties to turn their attentions east. Stalin's misguided attempt to chart
these treacherous seas and contain the Nazi threat took the form of
fulfilling his economic and trade obligations to Germany and, above all,
not provoking the *Führer* by front-line military mobilisations which in
May–June 1941 could only be interpreted as incendiary. Given the relative
unpreparedness of the Red Army, it was in some ways a rational policy
and Stalin's options, as in August 1939, were severely limited. But he obstinately clung to his appeasement policy to the bitter end, wilfully ignor-
ing reliable intelligence, both domestic and foreign, that the Germans
were mobilising for war.[19] Stalin had disastrously misunderstood Hitler's
utter conviction to launch an early 'war of annihilation' in the East,
a truly historic miscalculation which almost cost the Soviet people their
independent state and national existence.[20]

Stalin's actions, or more accurately inaction, after 22 June 1941 have also
been the subject of much speculation, confusion and myth.[21] For many years
it was widely held that for the first ten days of the Nazi attack Stalin, having
cut himself off from his colleagues in his *dacha* in a state of near breakdown,
abrogated all leadership responsibilities and issued no directives until early
July, thus leaving the USSR effectively rudderless in its moment of direst
need. What is more, it has been asserted that the members of the Politburo
even considered arresting Stalin at this time, a drastic step for which there is
no concrete evidence aside from Mikoian's impressionistic memoirs.[22] Reality
is far more complex. While certainly tired, demoralised and bewildered by
the increasingly grim and chaotic news from the fronts, Stalin, initially
demanding that the Red Army should carry the fight into enemy territory,
remained firmly in charge and active, at least until 29 June. It has been conclusively established from the list of Stalin's Kremlin visitors that he did not
become a paralysed recluse after 22 June 1941. On the contrary, at 5.45am
that day he received in his office Molotov, Beria, Zhukov and Timoshenko
among others. At 7.00am Dimitrov was summoned to the Kremlin and later
penned these remarks in his diary: 'Striking calmness, resoluteness,
confidence of Stalin and all the others.'[23] The meetings went on for eleven
hours and more than twenty orders and decrees were issued, including
Molotov's radio address to the Soviet people announcing the start of the war.
A string of top level political and military dignitaries continued to come and
go throughout the next few days, Stalin working more or less round the
clock. Also contrary to received wisdom, Stalin's image continued to be prop-
agated in the Soviet press in the early days of the war. Neither the 'real' Stalin
nor the cultic version went into hiding in this dark period.

The visitors' books indicate no meetings on 29 and 30 June, the two days when, in the opinion of most scholars, a depressed and fearful Stalin fled Moscow for his *dacha* only to be persuaded by his timorous colleagues to accept Beria's plan to set up an emergency war cabinet, the State Defence Committee (GKO), with Stalin at its head to direct the entire Soviet military effort. Roy and Zhores Medvedev, two leading Russian historians, refute this line of reasoning arguing that, according to Zhukov's memoirs, an infuriated Stalin twice attended gatherings at the Commissariat of Defence on 29 June. They also insist that the GKO was created at *Stalin's* initiative at an impromptu Politburo session convened by him at his *dacha* on 30 June, but they offer no evidence for this assertion. The whole episode is mysterious and Stalin never later referred to it. It seems likely that by absenting himself in these crucial days he was yet again testing the loyalty of his subordinates and showing them his indispensability. It is also possible, however, that he experienced more than a measure of self-doubt, guilt and dejection, expecting to be blamed for the calamities his policies had brought about. As Molotov recalled, 'He was a human being, after all.'[24]

Whatever the case, Stalin returned to a rumour-ridden and panicky Moscow on 1 July with renewed energy and optimism.[25] The leadership crisis was over and on 3 July he finally addressed the Soviet people for the first time since the Nazi invasion. His message, delivered in a rather halting tone, was nonetheless inspiring. Hailing the people uncharacteristically as 'Comrades! Citizens! Brothers and sisters!....my friends!', Stalin stressed that the German armies were not invincible, that a scorched-earth policy must be implemented to make conditions 'unbearable for the enemy', that the Soviet masses 'will rise up in their millions' supported by 'loyal allies' in Europe and America, and that ultimate victory in 'our patriotic war of liberation' was assured. He also warned ominously that all 'disorganisers of the rear', 'cowards', 'panic-mongers' and 'deserters' would be immediately hauled before 'the military tribunal' and that 'spies' and 'diversionists' must be exterminated.[26] It was a foretaste of the drastic repressive methods that would be used throughout the conflict to ensure total unity behind the government. In the weeks after this speech Stalin concentrated enormous power in his hands. In addition to his posts as party General Secretary, Chairman of the Council of Ministers and head of the GKO, on 10 July he was appointed Supreme Commander of the Soviet armed forces, on 19 July he took over as Commissar of Defence, and on 8 August he became chief of the Supreme High Command (Stavka). He was apparently loath to take on so many titles, presumably wishing to avoid blame for any future military disasters. Indeed, he would regularly seek to divert criticism by scapegoating and repressing his military subordinates. But he had to demonstrate his commitment to saving the country and from now on he was overlord of the Soviet 'total war' effort.

Stalin as Warlord

Stalin's involvement in martial affairs dated from the Civil War. As discussed in chapter one, his was a rather undistinguished and controversial record, but unlike many Bolshevik leaders he did have some first-hand experience of military action and tactics. In the 1920s Stalin, as one of the leaders of the Soviet state, necessarily had to keep abreast of military thinking and particularly defence production and budgets, but his role in policy-making was limited. This situation began to change with the 'war scares' of the mid-to-late 1920s and the continuing tense international situation in both Europe and Asia into the early 1930s. Specifically, Stalin's victory over the moderate 'Rightists' in the party and the launching of the First Five-Year Plan meant that 'by the end of 1930, the Stalinization of Soviet defense policy making would be complete, and Stalin's personal domination of defense matters cemented in place.'[27] This dominance was institutionalised with the creation of a new Defence Commission composed exclusively of loyal Stalinists, including the 'boss' himself. Stalin now had effective control over all the most important decisions on national security. Crucially, throughout the 1930s this signified a steady rise in Soviet military production and a modernisation of the entire military machine with rapid growth from 1938 onwards. This gradual 'militarisation' of the Soviet economy reflected the Stalinists' priority on defence in an atmosphere of looming war threats.

The perennial 'big question' that has exercised scholars for decades is: could the Soviet Union have defeated Nazi Germany in 1941–5 without Stalin's 'revolution from above' and its millions of victims? Could the necessary military-industrial base have been laid by more balanced economic policies without the horrors of collectivisation and the massive sacrifices of the Five-Year Plans? Unsurprisingly, economic and military historians are still unable to come to a consensus on this counterfactual argument. Morally, there can be no justification for Stalin's murderous 'class war' policies, the mass purges and the untold misery and suffering inflicted on the Soviet people. In many ways, this is the bottom line. That said, there were certainly no easy answers to the fundamental dilemma facing Bolshevik leaders after 1917: how to industrialise an overwhelmingly poor rural country, surrounded by hostile powers, and with underdeveloped cultural and educational levels? Where to get the resources in the absence of foreign loans? Stalin had a 'solution' to this conundrum, albeit an utterly draconian one. Furthermore, although several western experts have projected a 'Bukharinite' solution to the crisis, it will never be known for sure if more moderate economic strategies than Stalin's could have achieved the same or better growth rates in the 1930s and early 1940s. In strictly utilitarian terms, we can say that Stalin's violent crash industrialisation and 'militarisation' programmes may not have been as spectacularly successful as some suggest, but it is clear that significant progress had been made compared to the mid-1920s. For instance, it appears that on the eve of war Soviet tank, aircraft and artillery stock and the USSR's general defence-industrial capacity were superior than many, including Hitler, realised.[28] In the words of one leading authority, 'the Soviet ability to deny victory to Germany in 1941 was rooted in pre-war preparations', notably high military spending.[29] It might also be claimed that Stalinist insistence on a planned and highly centralised 'command economy' was a prerequisite for the Soviet war effort. The experiences of the 1930s laid the foundations of efficient and disciplined economic management in the 1940s.

Another key aspect in any estimation of 'Stalin as warlord' is his uneasy relations with the Soviet military elite. As an avid student of ancient and modern history, Stalin's readings would have told him that political leaders, especially aspiring dictators, need to be wary of their generals. In the power struggles of the 1920s, Trotsky was perceived as a potential 'Napoleon Bonaparte' whose control over the Red Army posed a threat to all other Bolshevik leaders. In the 1930s, Stalin became morbidly suspicious of his senior military commanders, persuading himself that many were 'Trotskyites', 'spies' and 'foreign agents' plotting to overthrow him and the regime. The fabricated 'Tukhachevskii trial' of May–June 1937 and the subsequent purges of the armed forces were the outcome.[30] At a leadership level, the Red Army was decimated with three out of five marshals executed and 720 out of the 837 army and navy commanders appointed in 1935 shot or sacked and replaced by inexperienced ill-educated cadres.[31] The scale of the mass arrests of lower-ranking officers may not have been as catastrophic as conventionally believed,[32] but it is difficult to overestimate the deleterious impact of the purges on the Red Army as an effective professional fighting force. Moreover, as Richard Overy has concluded 'the crisis was used to restore political dominance over [the] Soviet armed forces'[33] and can only have had a crippling effect on the relationship between Stalin and his top officer corps. From now on, any sign of independence or non-conformity on the part of the latter could be construed as traitorous with fatal consequences. These attitudes seem to have persisted well into the 'Great Patriotic War', stifling initiative and creativity.

Stalin determined military strategy in the war years just as he determined political and diplomatic policies. Historians, while inevitably divided in their interpretations of Stalin's military acumen, tend to agree on the broad periodisation of the war. There is near consensus that the second half of 1942 marked a crucial turning-point. Stalin is almost universally assailed for the gross failures and calamities of the early stages of the war, for the encirclement of Leningrad and near capture of Moscow, and for the disastrous counter-offensive of early summer 1942. But after the Battle of Stalingrad he is accredited with learning from his mistakes, transforming himself into a competent and adroit military leader capable of collaborating with his generals, while adopting more moderate domestic policies to mobilise mass support for the war effort. Beyond this, however, scholars differ in their emphases, sometimes quite starkly.

A selection of quotations will clearly indicate these marked divergences of opinion on Stalin's wartime role and conduct. Dmitrii Volkogonov, a Soviet era military specialist who after 1991 became a kind of court historian under Boris Yeltsin, wrote much on Stalin's activities during the war. His assessments are blunt and, having had access to top secret archival documents, seemingly authoritative. Volkogonov concludes:

> Stalin was not the 'gifted military leader' that hundreds of books, films, poems and studies had portrayed him to be….[he] was an armchair general, with a practical, 'strong-willed', but evil brain, who entered into the 'secrets' of the art of warfare at the cost of bloody experiments….he had no professional military knowledge. Military science was unknown to him….His highly amateurish and incompetent military leadership, especially during the first year and a half of the war, manifested itself in catastrophic losses in terms of *matériel* and manpower. But the Soviet people were able to withstand this, not *because* of Stalin's genius but *in spite of it*….As Supreme Commander of the armed forces, Stalin led them to victory, but at the cost of unimaginable losses.[34]

Volkogonov is not alone in his largely negative evaluation of Stalin as warlord. Moshe Lewin is particularly damning in his critique, insisting that, although Stalin learnt from some of his errors, basically:

> the man and his system continued their routine: a relentless pressure to engage in [military] offensives without time to prepare them, identification

of retreat with treason....crude, voluntaristic and repressive methods, the tendency to explain failure by sabotage and the incredible cruelty in treating the supposed culprits....The Commander-in-Chief suspected and fought his own no less fiercely than he fought the enemy.

Displaying 'personal inhumanity', he amassed total power in his hands and effectively paralysed the efficient functioning of government as the other leaders could show no initiative or independence, fearing his retribution.[35] The German expert, Bernd Bonwetsch, is less scathing but likewise sees precious little glory in Stalin's military capacities, emphasising that he 'never hesitated to sacrifice his men' and hence 'the victory had been achieved with genuine Stalinist methods.'[36]

Other analysts, however, are more even-handed in their judgements. Typical of this more judicious approach is that of John Barber and Mark Harrison, who argue cautiously that:

some credit for the Soviet Union's ultimate victory undoubtedly belongs to Stalin....[who] gradually mastered complex areas of strategy and logistics....Whatever the means employed, he ensured the unity of the Soviet government and its total commitment to defeating Nazism. Stalin's contribution to Soviet victory may have been less than his propagandists claimed, but it was substantial none the less.[37]

Albert Seaton also compares Stalin favourably to his great rival Hitler, asserting that 'he must be allowed credit for the amazing [Red Army] successes of 1944', which are 'among the most outstanding in the world's military history.'[38] Finally, we would do well to bear in mind Richard Overy's insightful observation that Stalin is an easy figure to hate but hard to comprehend and locate in a broader perspective:

the concentration of fire on the dictator not only makes it difficult to understand how a man so apparently corrupt and brutalized could have led his country to victory at all, but also fails to take account of the wider system in which Stalin was lodged. The war effort was not the product of one man, nor could it be made to bend entirely to his will. The role of the Party in sustaining popular mobilization, of the apparatus of terror under the grotesque Beria or of the Red Army itself....is as much a part of the history of the war as Stalin's personal dictatorship.[39]

One might add to this list the actions and experiences of millions of ordinary Soviet soldiers and civilians, men and women, who endured the most

barbaric war in modern times and whose suffering and toil are truly incon-
ceivable for later generations. As several historians have emphasised, this
was a 'people's war' as much as 'Stalin's war' and it could not have been
won without the genuine commitment, sacrifice and widespread popular
determination to destroy fascism.[40]

It is necessary now to flesh out Stalin's military contribution to the war. It
would scarcely be an exaggeration to say that no wartime leader, including
Hitler, exerted a more decisive day-to-day influence over their country's fate
than Stalin. Despite the fact that he only once visited the front, he regularly
intervened in the detailed planning and monitoring of campaigns, he
trusted no one and routinely sacked and replaced military commanders,
he often overruled professional advice from his generals, and hence made
many inordinately costly mistakes and, totally in character, he continued to
use crass repression as punishment for perceived 'cowardice', 'failures' and
'treason'. Although some purged Red Army officers were released because
their expertise was desperately needed at the fronts, not a few others were
executed on his orders, especially in the early crisis months of the conflict.[41]
His miscalculations and misjudgements were legion, sometimes bordering
on the fatal. For instance, his insistence, against the warnings of his military
chiefs, that the Germans would concentrate their forces to the south for an
attack on the Ukraine and that therefore the bulk of the Red Army should
be deployed in these areas left the western front and the approaches to
Moscow dangerously under-protected. It was a wilful decision that almost
cost the Soviet Union the war. Barber and Harrison among others have
identified Stalin's 'obsession with counterattacking at the earliest opportunity, his slowness in adopting a strategy of defence in depth, his extreme reluctance to allow Soviet troops to retreat, however hopeless their position,
[and] his support for military formations of highly questionable value, such
as light cavalry divisions'. Above all, Stalin's 'expenditure of military and
civilian lives in pursuit of victory was, from beginning to end, profligate,
and was one of the main reasons for the enormous Soviet losses.'[42] One
example among many will suffice. In the late summer of 1941, Stalin refused
to sanction a coordinated retreat of Red Army forces from Kiev, angrily rejecting Zhukov's pleas that withdrawal was necessary to avoid a disastrous
encirclement. The result was the capture of between 450,000 and 600,000
Soviet soldiers.

Stalin's negative impact on the Soviet war effort and morale does not end
here. Throughout the conflict he insisted on overall political-civilian control
of the armed forces, which meant that until October 1942 'political commissars', such as the detested Lev Mekhlis, effectively shared command of

the fronts with the generals, meddling in their duties and often overriding their expert judgement. Hence, these Stalin-appointees, later dubbed 'military illiterates', seriously undermined the professional confidence of the Red Army leaders, paralysed their independence of will, and all too often considered setbacks and defeats to be the work of 'enemies of the people' and 'traitors'. There is no doubt that in this they reflected the opinions of the main 'military illiterate' in the Kremlin. Most controversially, it is reported that in October 1941 Stalin sought to sign a peace accord with Hitler that would have ceded the Baltic republics, Moldavia and large parts of Belorussia and the Ukraine to the Nazis. The story is murky, possibly apocryphal, and it is hard to imagine that the offer was genuine. More likely it was designed as a delaying tactic to confuse the Germans at a crucial time during their assault on Moscow. Nevertheless, it is taken seriously by many historians and if true reveals the panic that swept through the Soviet elite in the days when the *Wehrmacht* seemed certain to capture the Russian capital.

Despite all these instances of gross incompetence, crass interference and arrogant behaviour, the Red Army *won the war* under Stalin's leadership. Clearly, Soviet survival and eventual victory depended on multiple factors, many extraneous to Stalin. Aside from the oft-cited bitter Russian winter of 1941 for which the German armies were totally ill-prepared, an obvious case in point is the Nazis' ideologically motivated inhuman treatment of the Slavic peoples and Jews in the occupied regions. Without this barbarity, it is possible that many Ukrainian and other non-Russian peasants would have supported German 'liberation' from the communist yoke. Another external input is the impressive economic, technical, military and food aid supplied to the USSR by the Western Allies under the terms of the Lend Lease Act. Although the Soviets at times denigrated this vital contribution, it has been calculated that as much as 10 per cent of Russia's wartime economic needs was furnished by Lend Lease, most of it after the Battle of Stalingrad.[43] However, most experts today conclude that it was the effectiveness of the *Soviet* armed forces and the truly epic *domestic* economic, organisational and military effort that made the decisive difference in the 'war of the century'. The Red Army spawned military commanders, most notably Marshals Zhukov and Vasilevskii, of world rank and soldiers and partisans who, for whatever reason be it national, ideological or personal, fought to the death to defend their country. The party-state bureaucracies gave birth to countless administrators who successfully improvised their way through the web of decrees from Moscow. Above all, by 1943 the Soviet command economy (that is, in practice largely women workers) was producing more guns, tanks and aircraft than its overstretched German counterpart. Thus, both the structural and human determinants of Soviet success should never be overlooked. Where does Stalin come in to the equation? How precisely did he stamp his mark on these developments?

Stalin may have been overweeningly self-important and self-confident, but gradually in the course of the war he proved capable of listening to, and acting on, the expert opinion and reports of his generals. What is more, he let it be known that he respected decisive well-informed commanders who were prepared to stand up to him, even on occasion argue with him. In short, 'Stalin at last confronted his own inadequacy as Supreme Commander.' He curtailed the powers of the political overseers of the Red Army and permitted the General Staff a far greater say in the planning and management of all aspects of the war effort.[44] He was still overall Supremo, but 'the difference lay in Stalin's attitude....He allowed the [military] staff to suggest operations; he came to insist that front commanders should be consulted for their views first....He liked to be told the truth, however unpalatable. He took advice and bowed to others' judgement.'[45] This deference to military professionalism showed a highly unusual degree of flexibility, even humility, on Stalin's part. He was also capable of striking symbolic, even brave, gestures, such as his last-minute decision to remain in panic-stricken Moscow in mid-October 1941. With the capital seemingly about to fall to the Germans, with the evacuation of the Soviet government to the Volga city of Kuibyshev (now Samara) already in motion and with his railway transport primed for the trip east, a rattled but resilient Stalin vowed that Moscow would not be defeated. This act and his overtly Russocentric patriotic speeches on 6 and 7 November helped calm the population and provided a much needed sense of psychological stability and historical continuity. Even his notorious Order 227 of 28 July 1942 ('Not a Step Back!'), which promulgated summary execution for army deserters, 'panickers' and 'cowards', genuinely inspired millions of soldiers to fight to the end regardless of the callous repression and punishments in the rear.[46] Red Army troops may not have gone to their deaths crying 'for the Motherland, for Stalin!', but it appears that Stalin to a large extent came to symbolise the patriotic cause. Nowhere was this more evident than in the epic battles for Stalingrad from August 1942 to February 1943. It is fair to say that Stalin, together with Zhukov and Vasilevskii, were the main architects of this historic triumph which turned the war on the Eastern front.

Finally in this section it is necessary to examine the role and significance of the 'mythic Stalin'; not the 'real boss' with all his blemishes, inadequacies and human frailties, but the Stalin portrayed in the omnipresent Soviet propaganda. Two aspects of Stalin's wartime cult are particularly striking.

Firstly, it tended to fluctuate according to military fortunes. With the Red Army in retreat and suffering defeat after defeat in the dark days of August to October 1941 and again from May 1942 to early 1943 Stalin's image and appeals to his leadership appeared less and less frequently in the press. He apparently had no wish to be identified with failure. But after his decision to remain in the Soviet capital in October 1941 and with the subsequent Red Army triumph in the Battle of Moscow in December, the Stalin cult was revived and after Stalingrad it took on new dimensions. His name was closely and immediately linked with all battlefield victories: 'the military genius of Stalin'. These accolades peaked after the war in June 1945, when an ostensibly reluctant and modest Stalin was honoured with the ultimate title 'Generalissimo'.

Secondly, the wartime cultic Stalin was less a party ideological boss than a national military leader. 'Soviet patriotism' took precedence over Marxism-Leninism as the prime mass mobilising force. The latter never disappeared, but it took a backstage role as in the typical slogan: 'Comrade Stalin calls on the people to rise to the defence of the motherland'. Moreover, in their search for a 'usable past' party propagandists strove to instil in the people a love of Mother *Russia* (as opposed to the Soviet Union), its language, literature, history and the soil itself and Stalin, by invoking the memory of 'our great ancestors' and heroic Tsarist generals, consolidated these primordial themes.[47] Not all Soviet citizens, notably many non-Russians, were galvanised by this overt Russocentrism or mesmerised by the cult. But as one expert has concluded, given the string of Soviet victories from early 1943 and Stalin's personification with these triumphs, 'it is not hard to see why in the war years the Stalin cult took root in popular consciousness and became a mass phenomenon.'[48] Like Churchill in Britain, Stalin represented for millions of Soviet combatants resoluteness, iron will and above all hope. Stalin's impact on the home front was equally decisive.

Stalin and the Home Front

Two contradictory elements characterise Stalinist domestic policies during the war: on the one hand, continued fearsome repression of real and perceived 'enemies' and on the other, selective concessions to different strata of Soviet society designed to rally popular support for the war effort. Vera Dunham has aptly summarised Stalin's wartime rule as 'a combination of permissiveness with drastic punitive measures or, rather, it introduced some permissive elements into a basically draconian practice.'[49] The mass arrests and executions associated with the Great Terror abated after autumn 1938, but they did not stop entirely; far from it. The new head of the NKVD, Lavrentii Beria, oversaw a purge of the secret police itself, rooting out hundreds of over-zealous 'Ezhovites'. Ezhov himself resigned on 23 November 1938, was reportedly accused of 'groundless repression of the Soviet people', was arrested personally by Beria in April 1939 and shot on 4 February 1940. He was not the only leading communist to be executed in 1939–40.[50] However, the main victims of Stalinist terror in the immediate pre-war period were the recently incorporated Polish, west Ukrainian, west Belorussian and Baltic peoples, hundreds of thousands of whom were deported in successive waves in 1940 and 1941 to camps and 'special settlements' deep in the Soviet hinterlands. The most notorious barbarity was the NKVD massacre of almost 4,500 Polish army officers in the Katyn forest in the spring of 1940. In total over 21,000 were shot at several different sites.[51] The likely reason for the cold-blooded slaughter was that Stalin and Beria considered the officers 'bourgeois counter-revolutionaries' who posed an ideological and security risk to the Soviet regime. For fifty years the Soviet government maintained the pretence that the Nazis were responsible. Only in the era of Gorbachev's *glasnost'* did the truth emerge.

Internal state coercion and violence continued throughout the war. In particular, Stalin used the struggle to target entire peoples accused, on the basis of very little evidence, of collaborating with the Nazi invaders. The first to suffer in the autumn of 1941 were the Volga Germans, approximately 450,000 of whom were herded off to western Siberia and Central Asia. Then in 1943–4 the Chechens, Ingushi, Crimean Tartars, Kalmyks and several other Caucasian ethnic minorities, well over a million people in total, were deported *en masse* from their homelands to Kazakhstan and Central Asia. Approximately 250,000 died in transit or in terrible hardship at their inhospitable destinations.[52] Conditions in the labour camps were also dire during the war. The number of Gulag inmates may have decreased between 1941–5 as many were released to fight the Germans, but the living and working environment of those who remained was nothing short of atrocious. Famine, epidemics, overcrowding, summary shootings and inhuman exploitation were commonplace. For instance, in 1942 the Gulag Administration registered 249,000 deaths (eighteen per cent of the camp population) and in 1943 167,000 deaths (seventeen per cent).[53] The 'myth' of the Battle of Stalingrad and the euphoria of total victory in May 1945 have tended to obscure the horrendous suffering perpetrated by the regime on millions of Soviet citizens during World War II. It was not about to end as we shall discover in the final chapter.

However, undue repression was tempered by pragmatic concession. In the course of the war, the Soviet state softened its position towards the Russian Orthodox Church, permitted certain economic liberalisations in town and countryside, relaxed its attitudes towards the cultural and technical intelligentsia, loosened the mechanisms of tight control over its own vast *nomenklatura* and oversaw a blossoming of folk and popular culture. This tentative moderation was not the result of a single decision taken by Stalin or any other leader, and neither did it represent an unmitigated shift in the regime's attitude to Soviet citizenry. At all times an underlying mistrust remained just below the surface. Moreover, many of these concessions were doubtless made reluctantly or under the extreme duress of war. Many tacitly recognised pre-existing realities on the ground or were responses to pressures 'from below'. Nevertheless, they were highly significant both for the war effort and for potential post-war developments. They seemed to indicate a changing relationship between state and society, raising hopes and aspirations among millions of Soviets that once the fighting was finally over civic reconciliation and reform would be the order of the day.

Symptomatic of the wartime 'thaw' was an extraordinary event that took place in early September 1943: Stalin summoned Metropolitan Sergei, Acting Patriarch of the Orthodox Church, to his Kremlin office and at the end of a lengthy audience proceeded to offer him an unprecedented deal. The Church had made collections and donations for the military campaigns and had undoubtedly contributed to mobilising the people behind the Red Army. Partly in recognition of this support, Stalin proposed a limited rehabilitation of the Church – the reopening of buildings for worship, the revival of the Holy Synod and the granting of a spiritual, if not political and social, role in public affairs – in return for which the Church would acknowledge the legitimacy of the Soviet regime and refrain from criticising its policies. The Stalinist state also set ideological purity aside in some of its dealings with the long-suffering peasantry. Life on the collective farms during the war was unremittingly hard and in general rural labourers, the majority of whom were the old, the infirm, women and children, ate less than industrial workers. Nevertheless, the authorities 'suspended [their] hostility to private production and the market, turned a blind eye to the peasants' informal and theoretically illegal economic activity, and so enabled most of them to stay, however precariously, above subsistence level.'[54] The partial revival of private trade and increased emphasis on private plot cultivation benefited many town inhabitants too as they were able to buy, at a price, scarce foodstuffs at the semi-legal markets that sprang up on the outskirts of urban areas.

Intellectuals, 'technocrats' and many regional party-state officials and enterprise managers likewise enjoyed a measure of independence and respite after the battering of the Great Terror. Naturally, the horrendous wartime conditions affected all sections of society and censorship remained, but the Soviet 'middle classes' were rewarded for their efforts by a greater degree of cultural, academic and institutional autonomy than at any time since the NEP in the 1920s. With central control and interference at the local level weakened as a result of wartime exigencies, provincial bureaucrats, industrial 'captains' and the scientific and cultural elites became more accustomed to relying on their own initiative and hence their self-confidence grew. The war also witnessed a flowering of diverse popular and folk culture. All mediums were used to rally the people, raise the morale of soldiers and citizens, and indeed inculcate hatred of the German enemy: films, novels, poems, songs, plays and performance art. Not all of this output was mobilised from above; a certain spontaneity was perforce permitted.[55] As the victorious Red Army bludgeoned its way towards Berlin and the war drew to a close, the question was: after the fighting was over would Stalin continue to countenance an attenuation of his dictatorial rule or would he revert to authoritarian 'normality'?

Chapter 6: Statesman

Stalin emerged from the immense stresses and strains of the 'Great Patriotic War' immeasurably strengthened. Proclaimed as the indefatigable infallible 'Generalissimo' who had ensured victory over the barbarian Teutonic hordes, he enjoyed, arguably for the first time, buoyant levels of popular support. The regime had proven its ability to survive the supreme challenge of Hitler's 'war of annihilation', the most destructive in history. The imperative to expel the invader had forged a certain national unity between people and government and in this sense the successful prosecution of the war more than any other single factor legitimised the Stalinist system and Stalin himself as undisputed *vozhd'*. The dilemma facing the triumphant leadership after May 1945 was how best to reconstruct the shattered Soviet economy and society, while safeguarding the sole socialist bastion in an unpredictable international climate. In theory at least, the relatively moderate wartime policies could have been continued both at home and abroad and it is possible that some in the party-state elites favoured measured reform. For Stalin, however, this was anathema and soon the regime reverted to increased repression and state intervention, severely testing its citizens' new-found loyalty and tentative trust. On the domestic front, the period 1945–53 is normally designated as the era of 'High Stalinism', a stiflingly bureaucratised, centralised and personalised form of rule in which political and social stability, cultural uniformity and rapid economic recovery were the order of the day after the turmoil of war. On the diplomatic scene, these years witnessed the gradual degeneration of East-West relations into what became known as the Cold War. The USSR was transformed into the second global superpower, its military and industrial might eventually rivalling that of the USA. A Soviet dominated socialist bloc was created in the lands of Central and Eastern Europe. Communism, strange as it may seem to a twenty-first century audience, appeared to be the wave of the future, not only in Europe, but in Asia and beyond.

These developments raise important and perplexing questions: how did an aging and ailing Stalin attempt to consolidate his dictatorial grip on the Soviet political structures?; how, if at all, did his relations with colleagues in the ruling circle change?; did he become a totally capricious paranoiac tyrant, or did his actions reveal a consistent wider political logic?; how should Stalin's forays into various intellectual fields be evaluated and why are they significant?; what are the interlinkages between domestic and foreign policies?; how far should Stalin be held responsible for the 'Soviet-isation' of Eastern Europe and the outbreak of the Cold War?; was he primarily motivated by *realpolitik* – an inward-looking pragmatic defence of the territories of the USSR – or by ideology – a revolutionary Marxist expansion of the borders of socialism?; how successful was his diplomacy in securing the integrity of the Soviet state?; should he be considered a master statesman or was he a dangerous dilettante whose actions brought the world close to atomic destruction? The focus here is clearly on the final years of Stalin's rule, but I shall also examine his pre-war dominance of the Communist International (Comintern) as an example of his regular involvement in foreign affairs.

Stalin's Power under 'High Stalinism'

Compared to the 1920s and 1930s, the late Stalinist era remains under-re-searched. Several important texts had been published before the partial opening of the archives, but it is only really since the early 1990s that a number of specialist accounts have appeared and the theme is attracting much attention from younger scholars. The post-war years saw a rapid end to the relatively liberalised policies of the war as the regime resorted to the tried-and-tested methods of repression and strict party-state control. Widespread popular aspirations for a more relaxed political system, civic reconciliation and better standards of living were soon dashed. Conditions in the factories in the late 1940s generally worsened, inflation reduced real wages in 1950 to 1940 levels, life on the reimposed collective farms was as tough as ever, and the wartime reinvigoration of the Orthodox Church was suspended.[1] These outcomes reflected partly the desperate state of the Soviet economy and agri-culture after the annihilation of the war, partly the leadership's re-emphasis on heavy industry and the cumbersome command-administrative mechanism, but also Stalin's fears that meaningful concessions and reforms would threaten the system and his power within it. He was particularly concerned that Red Army officers and veterans returning from the more advanced countries of Europe could contaminate Soviet society with notions of 'the good life' and, with his keen sense of history, he apparently regarded them as potential 'Decembrists' (army officers who had attempted to overthrow Tsar Alexander I in 1825 after the Napoleonic Wars).

Crucially, 'High Stalinism' witnessed yet more mass arrests (though far fewer executions), a baleful rise of anti-semitism, and the apotheosis of the appeal to 'Soviet patriotism' and 'anti-cosmopolitanism' as a source of legitimacy. From the summer of 1946, tight cultural and ideological regimentation was introduced to muzzle and discipline a restive intelligentsia. This campaign is normally associated with Stalin's ideological chief, Andrei Zhdanov, after whom it is named (the 'Zhdanovshchina'), but recently it has been established that the whole affair was instigated and promoted by Stalin. Although there were no 'objective' rivals to his leadership, no consistent factions in the party hierarchies that could oppose him, and no one dared undertake any major domestic or foreign policy innovations independently of him, Stalin felt compelled to launch on-going struggles to maintain his personal hegemony in a precarious environment. We might speculate that he *never* felt safe, especially as his health began to fail him. Did he imagine a long line of successors ready to hasten his demise? Before tackling these issues, it is necessary to set the historical context by tracing the devastating effects of war on the Soviet state, society and economy.

At a most elementary level, the demographic legacy of World War II was absolutely catastrophic. Scholars still dispute the exact statistics, but the best estimate is that, in stark contrast to the figure of seven million announced by Stalin in 1946, no fewer than 26.6 million Soviets perished during the war, approximately 70 per cent of whom were men. The majority of these were from the younger generation, the most fit and capable. In terms of overall population, in 1946 women outnumbered men by 96.2 million to 74.4 million. The socio-economic and psychological consequences of this imbalance were profound and long-lasting. Hundreds of thousands of illegitimate children were born every year after 1945, almost a million in 1949 alone. War invalids and veterans crowded the urban areas looking for work. Hunger reigned, culminating in yet another dreadful, but little-known, famine in 1946–7. Entire towns and villages had been razed to the ground, factories uprooted, countless bridges destroyed, livestock severely depleted. An official commission calculated that total wartime material losses amounted to 2,569 billion roubles.[2] The pressure on overstretched state resources was intense and with the American refusal to extend Lend Lease provisions after the fighting, the USSR was left largely to its own devices to overcome these horrendous conditions. Suffice it to say that by the end of the 1940s the Soviet economy had been essentially rebuilt from scratch at the cost of yet more immense human suffering.

In the realm of politics, it is commonly held that in the final eight years of his rule an ill and exhausted Stalin increasingly displayed despotic tendencies, was prone to petty Byzantine intrigues and pathological fears, acted out irrational fantasies and odd flights of fancy, fell prey to gross anti-semitic attitudes, and appeared detached from reality, eventually showing signs of marked mental deterioration, even derangement. There is certainly more than a grain of truth in this portrayal. Stalin suffered from arthritis, rheumatism and high blood pressure and many of his biographers, possibly following Khrushchev's negative evaluation of his boss, have noted the vain, capricious and temperamental nature of his behaviour: how late-night boozy gatherings at his country *dacha* punctuated with films, music, dancing and the occasional puerile game often became the scene of top-level decision-making[3]; how he petulantly demoted loyal acolytes, like Malenkov and Marshal Zhukov, who had aroused the dictator's jealousy and ire by apparently claiming to be the 'victor over Germany'; how he terrorised close colleagues and tested the fealty of erstwhile friends by arresting their relatives (Molotov's wife, Polina Zhemchuzhina, being the highest placed victim); how he later publicly attacked Molotov and Mikoian and tried to exclude them from his 'inner circle'; how he concocted mysterious, almost unfathomable, vendettas against perceived rivals, such as the 'Leningrad Affair' in 1949, which culminated in the execution of powerful local bosses Nikolai Voznesenskii and Aleksei Kuznetsov,[4] and the so-called 'Mingrelian Affair' of 1951, which was aimed at weakening Beria's position; how he presided over a considerable expansion of the Gulag camp and colony population from approximately 1.5 million in 1945 to a high of 2.5 million in the early 1950s, and this despite the fact that slave labour had proven economically unsound and wasteful of state resources[5]; and how he acted illogically, spasmodically, often seemingly distracted and losing interest in pet schemes.

A reprehensible feature of Stalin's mentality after the Second World War was his recourse to anti-semitism, which became pronounced after 1948. It may well be true, as Robert Service has stated in his recent biography, that '[Stalin's] campaign against "rootless cosmopolitanism" cannot be automatically attributed to hatred of Jews as Jews....his motives were of Realpolitik rather than visceral prejudice'.[6] Nevertheless, already in 1948–9 hundreds of Jewish intellectuals had been arrested, at least one of whom, the world renowned actor and theatre director Solomon Mikhoels, was murdered almost certainly on Stalin's orders. As a leading scholar has written: 'Jews were systematically removed from all positions of authority in the arts and the media, in journalism and publishing, and in medicine and many other professions.'[7] The campaigns reached a peak in the summer of 1952 with the secret trial of the members of the Jewish Anti-Fascist Committee, thirteen of whom were executed.[8] Some historians have argued, on the basis of unconfirmed evidence, that the ailing Stalin was at this time preparing the exposure of a wide-scale 'Judeo-Zionist conspiracy', which was to conclude with the mass deportation of Soviet Jews to Birobidzhan, a barren region in Far Eastern Siberia. This now appears unlikely, but certainly several high-ranking Jewish doctors were arrested and accused, among other things, of complicity in the deaths of two Soviet luminaries. Their trial, it seems, was set for the end of March 1953, but Stalin's timely demise on 5 March put an end to their ordeal and brought to a close the era of mass repression in the USSR. His successors, notably Khrushchev, but also initially Beria, renounced terror, released large numbers of Gulag prisoners and attempted, not altogether systematically, to 'de-Stalinise' Soviet politics and society.

In contrast to this standard 'paranoid Stalin' interpretation, the latest archival research has offered a more nuanced, though no less controversial, understanding of the elite politics of the post-war era. Yoram Gorlizki and Oleg Khlevniuk have endeavoured to reconceptualise Stalin's methods of rule, suggesting that from 1945 virtually until his death his behaviour, while displaying 'high drama' and obsession, followed a clear interlocking political logic. In part, it was the rationale of a ceaseless drive to preserve his dictatorial rule by means of periodically harassing, humiliating and demoting his top aides, even the physical elimination of a few perceived 'enemies'. In this, Gorlizki's and Khlevniuk's analysis differs little from the 'orthodox' assessments outlined above. But they also insist that Stalin's machinations concealed a broader ideologically-driven logic of consolidating a 'separate, respected, and powerful socialist system.' According to Gorlizki and Khlevniuk:

In order to press home his country's claims as a global power and to put it on a level economic and military footing with the West, Stalin vested authority in committees, elevated younger specialists, and initiated key institutional innovations. No matter how perverse they may have appeared, Stalin's actions did not contradict his wider political objectives.

This combination of traditional autocracy with modern features of governance they term 'neo-patrimonialism', signifying an uneasy marriage of highly personalised, occasionally brutal, authority at the apex of power with more rational and predictable forms of administration and decision-making at lower levels via expert commissions and committees often staffed by a younger generation of officials. This institutionalised regularised pattern of administration was most evident in the cabinet, the Council of Ministers, to which Stalin delegated much responsibility. Indeed, as in the pre-war decade he seems to have left the detailed running of the government and economy largely to subordinates, although when deemed necessary he could, and did, decisively intervene. Gorlizki and Khlevniuk also maintain that the year 1949 marked an important watershed in Stalin's relations with his leading courtiers. After the Voznesenskii and Kuznetsov affair, his underlings recognised that personal intrigues among themselves could swerve out of control with deadly outcomes. They therefore refrained from attacking each other and tentatively developed an embryonic form of the 'collective leadership' that would prevail after Stalin's death. In this way they sought to contain and deflect the tyrant's wrath, while continuing to curry his favour.[9]

The overall image of Stalin under 'High Stalinism' is of a man who obstinately and tenaciously clung to the reins of power, even as his mental and physical capacities began to desert him by the early 1950s. He controlled the main levers of decision-making and, crucially, continued to dominate the secret police apparatus until his last days. He countenanced no contradiction. He remained vindictive, suspicious and murderously dangerous. He was morbidly fearful of his own frailties, loneliness and finality, terrified of becoming irrelevant to the system he had created, even dimly aware of his own impotency.[10] Yet his many plots and conspiracies right up to the end were carefully conceived and finely constructed. According to two experts: 'They were not the product of blind hatred or thuggish rage. Their characteristic shape points to an intellect capable of a high order of abstraction and geometrical ratiocination. The shape was teleological and always had political intent. This, as much as his cruelty, was fundamental to Stalin's makeup.'[11] Furthermore, if we believe Gorlizki and Khlevniuk, Stalin was not solely motivated by power lust and paranoia. He retained a deep ideological commitment to the building of a modern strong communist utopia, both in the USSR and in the newly-established 'socialist commonwealth', and was aware that in order to achieve this lofty goal the promotion of younger talent and streamlined forms of administration were required. The Stalin who emerges is more complex, but certainly no less a tyrant. He was also a leader with intellectual pretensions.

Stalin as Intellectual

It is remarkable that at a time when the world was plunged into turmoil by Cold War 'hotspots' like the Berlin Blockade (June 1948 to May 1949) and the Korean War (1950–3), Stalin found the space and energy to intervene directly in the ideological, cultural and scientific life of the Soviet Union, most notably in the fields of genetics, linguistics and political economy. What does his involvement in seemingly arcane academic disputes tell us? For a start, it challenges the notion that Stalin was mentally incapacitated in these years. No doubt he was less attuned and quick-witted than in his prime, but he remained alert, read voraciously and widely, and even penned the occasional lengthy treatise. Secondly, it suggests that he had lost none of his drive to tame the autonomous urges of the Soviet intelligentsia, and, finally, it illustrates the striking interconnection of domestic and foreign policy under late Stalinism. In an atmosphere of rising Cold War tensions abroad, Stalin's inclinations to 'Soviet patriotism' at home, bordering on xenophobia, became hypertrophied and he constantly berated the cultural and academic elites for their kowtowing and grovelling before 'bourgeois' western trends and achievements. Such attitudes, he believed, threatened the integrity of the state and instilled passivity in the masses. What was needed was pride in *Soviet* achievements and intellectual prowess.

Above all, these exclusivist 'nationalist' sentiments alien to Marxism reveal the consolidation of a strong hybrid element in Stalin's ideology, the origins of which can be found in his pre-revolutionary experiences and in his recourse to 'national Bolshevism' and 'Russocentrism' from the mid-to-late 1930s. They are indicative of the confusing and complicated ideological terrain of post-war Stalinism. Nevertheless, I would maintain that his decisive interventions in the scholarly debates of the late 1940s and early 1950s show that he continued to treat questions of theory very seriously and that his underlying worldview continued to be Marxist oriented.[12] This was his self-perception and that of his public persona. He could allow no internal contradiction in his thought or in Soviet ideology: the USSR was now a *socialist*, not a Tsarist or bourgeois, fatherland, its guiding philosophy was Marxism-Leninism animated by an unremitting hostility to capitalist exploitation and property relations, and this superior state and socio-economic formation had to be defended by all means and at all costs, including appeals to Russian nationalism. Precisely because 'he recognised that in some respects the legitimacy of the system relied on the coherency of its ideology',[13] Stalin felt compelled to intercede in the academic and scientific fields, since no area of inquiry was 'apolitical'. The belief was that Soviet science and Marxism, marching in step, would establish absolute human truths about the material world thus proving the intellectual and ideological supremacy of Marxism-Leninism over its 'degenerate' western rivals, and in so doing serve the productive needs of the ordinary people, strengthen the popular base of the Soviet state, and sustain Stalin's authority and cultic image as the embodiment of communism.

Donning the mantle of intellectual, Stalin ostensibly granted the cultural and scientific communities a measure of professional autonomy by encouraging open discussion and disagreement: 'It is universally recognized that no science can develop and flourish without battles of opinion, without freedom of criticism.'[14] Stalin may not have been completely disingenuous here, but ultimately it was his intention to pronounce theoretical orthodoxy in any field. The example of linguistics is instructive. In the summer of 1950 Stalin wrote his penultimate major work, *Marxism and Problems of Linguistics*. In it he debunked the tenets of the pre-eminent Soviet linguist, Nikolai Marr, who in the 1920s had conceived the Marxist premise that languages evolved along class-specific lines in relation to the changing modes of production. Marr's ideas had remained dominant in Soviet linguistics since his death in 1934. But by the late 1940s such notions ran counter to Stalin's renewed emphasis on the importance of national traditions and interests. Therefore, he firmly rejected the proposition that the contemporary Russian language was a bourgeois phenomenon forged under capitalism. Its roots went back centuries, proof of its longevity, vitality and resilience. Notwithstanding Stalin's stress on the special nature of the Russian language and the related issue of Russian nationhood, I agree with Robert Service's judgement:

> [Stalin's] fascination with the 'Russian question' did not exclude a concern with communism and globalism. Stalin in fact asserted that eventually national languages would disappear as socialism covered the world....The widely held notion that Stalin's ideology had turned into an undiluted nationalism cannot be substantiated....his current zeal to play up Russia's virtues did not put an end to his Marxist belief that the ultimate stage in world history would bring about a society of post-national globalism.[15]

Another important conclusion to be drawn from Stalin's intellectual forays is that although his intention was to resolve the ideological crisis, in this case in Soviet linguistics, by a definitive statement of Marxist orthodoxy, his mediations produced as much confusion as clarity. Or at least this is the argument of Ethan Pollock, an American specialist in post-war Soviet ideological disputes. Pollock insists that Stalin's interventions and the linguistics discussion in general 'far from settled disputes about language in the USSR....Stalin's decisive role only deepened the quagmire.' Academics and ordinary citizens, a few mildly critical of Stalin's views, continued diplomatically to debate the issue and ask for elucidation on key points.[16] Evidently, even the *vozhd'* could not totally foreclose a 'battle of opinion'.

Stalin and the Comintern

Experts on Stalin have tended to focus on his domestic policies, downplaying his active involvement in Soviet foreign affairs. But Stalin's abiding legacy for many Russians today is his statesmanship, his creation and consolidation of an imposing Soviet state at home and a mighty empire abroad. Soviet superpower status was laid under Stalin and this remains a source of genuine pride for those Russians humiliated by the collapse of their once globally respected country. In the next two sections I assess Stalin's influence, firstly, on the Comintern and, secondly, on the early evolution of the Cold War with particular reference to the 'Sovietisation' of Central and Eastern Europe after 1945.

Stalin's controversial role in the international communist movement is often under-explored, even ignored, by both western and Russian biographers.[17] I have always found this perplexing because his aims, motivations and actions had a truly profound impact on communist parties worldwide from the 1920s through to his death, and well beyond. We saw in chapter four how many thousands of loyal foreign Stalinists were brutally repressed in the USSR in the late 1930s, and during the Spanish Civil War Stalin's long arm extended to decimating large numbers of Catalan 'Trotskyites' and anarchists. But Stalin's authority, mainly pernicious, went far beyond the Terror. He introduced the bitter Soviet inner-party struggles of the 1920s into the Comintern, resulting in demotions, expulsions and the general weakening of many communist parties; he did much to shape the German communists' disastrous response to the Nazi threat thereby, so it is often argued, actively contributing to Hitler's *machtergreifung*; he delineated the changing relationships between communists and social democrats, invariably exacerbating tensions between them; and he determined the attitude of foreign communists to the outbreak of war in September 1939, causing major rifts in several parties.

These were crucial interventions with long-lasting ramifications. In short, a significant aspect of Stalin's statesmanship relates to his activities in the international communist movement as well as in conventional foreign diplomacy. Indeed, for Stalin the two – revolutionary prospects and the defence of Soviet state interests – were inextricably interwoven and mutually reinforcing.

Ever since the great debates in the mid-1920s with Trotsky over 'permanent revolution' versus 'socialism in one country', Stalin has frequently been seen as the gravedigger of world revolution and a traitor to the Leninist cause of revolutionary internationalism, solely motivated by the construction of socialism in the USSR. It is certainly true that Stalin held the Communist International in fairly low esteem and regarded the defence of the USSR as the prime duty of foreign communists. As he pointedly announced as early as August 1927:

> An *internationalist* is one who is ready to defend the U.S.S.R. without reservation, without wavering, unconditionally; for the U.S.S.R. is the base of the world revolutionary movement, and this revolutionary movement cannot be defended and promoted unless the U.S.S.R. is defended. For whoever thinks of defending the world revolutionary movement apart from, or against, the U.S.S.R., goes against the revolution and must inevitably slide into the camp of the enemies of the revolution.[18]

However, Stalin never publicly renounced the Leninist doctrine of world revolution and his private communications from the 1920s reveal his deep concern for what Lars Lih has termed the 'amalgamation of state and revolutionary interests'. Stalin believed that a tough diplomatic line with capitalist governments and their 'lackeys' in the colonies would rebound to the benefit of both the Soviet state and the international revolution. Witness his uncharacteristic enthusiasm in October 1929, when he declared in a letter to Molotov that 'it's time to think about *organizing* an uprising by a *revolutionary* movement in Manchuria.'[19] Nothing came of this dare-devil idea, but the evidence indicates that Stalin, supposedly the arch enemy of internationalist fervour, did retain, at least in the 1920s, a sensitivity to revolutionary prospects and sought to combine statist pragmatism with orthodox Marxist-Leninist theory.

Not surprisingly given the complexity of these issues, historians' estimations of Stalin's role in, and dominance over, the Comintern and the international communist movement vary markedly. The lack of any consensus is evident from the following two quotations, the first from Franz Borkenau, a German ex-communist writing in 1938, the second from E. H. Carr, the British expert on the Comintern writing in 1982. Borkenau states categorically that during the early 1930s, 'Stalin kept an iron control over all details of Comintern work, and both the policy and the lists of parliamentary candidates of the communist parties were rigidly controlled by Moscow'.[20] Carr begs to differ, arguing that 'Stalin, heavily engaged elsewhere, was not tempted to concern himself with the petty disputes of an institution he had always despised.' Thus, 'it would be misleading to depict Comintern and its component parties in the early nineteen-thirties as a monolithic structure responding blindly to the dictates of a single supreme authority.'[21] It would be hard to imagine a more unequivocal clash of opinion. But which interpretation is closer to reality?

Stalin's control over the central Comintern apparatus in Moscow is incontrovertible. But the problem lies in the exact definition of the term 'control'. It is open to debate. We can agree that Stalin was the ultimate boss in that he personally approved any major change of 'line', but how that new line was actually put into practice depended partly on the Comintern's Executive Committee (ECCI), and not all Comintern leaders were completely docile 'yesmen', and partly on the national parties, which operated in diverse local conditions. Perhaps the real source of Stalin's power lay in the fact that he was the only person who had intimate knowledge of all three main policy areas – domestic, diplomatic and Comintern. His position at the pinnacle of a vast bureaucratic information and intelligence system enabled him to coordinate strategies and rather cynically to manipulate the Comintern leaders and, indeed, the entire international communist movement. The ultra-leftist postulates of the 'Third Period' of Comintern history (1928–34), in which social democrats were castigated as 'social fascists' and the prime enemy of the communists, are a perfect example of this manipulation. Stalin, unlike many foreign party members and bosses, hardly believed in the revolutionary diagnosis of this 'line', but it suited his purposes to advocate it with dire results in Germany where the communists' sustained attack on the social democrats facilitated Hitler's rise to power.

Borkenau's line of reasoning encapsulates, indeed did much to establish, the standard image of Stalin and the Comintern in the 1930s. In the late 1980s and beyond it was largely resubstantiated by Soviet historians with access to the Comintern Archives in Moscow. It cannot be dismissed lightly. Stalin's pivotal role in Comintern affairs from 1923–4 has been established beyond all doubt. As discussed above, by late 1929 he had become *primus inter pares* in the Russian party leadership, a position which gave his words and policies even greater weight. It was at this time too that Stalin's 'cult of personality' began to assume prominence. It would not be long before communists the world over would be paying homage to the 'Great Leader'. More specifically, there can be no question that with the purge of the 'Bukharinite rightists' in 1928–9, Stalin's hold over the Comintern central apparatus and national party leaderships was immeasurably strengthened. 'His' men were now at the helm and through them he preserved a strict ideological and organisational grip on the international movement. The training of loyal Stalinist cadres finely attuned to the interests of the Soviet state became one of the main tasks of the Comintern, and from Moscow's point of view one its greatest long-term achievements. However, should the 'obedient Stalinist' of today turn out to be the 'heretic' of tomorrow, then ways were found of removing the trouble-maker. The successive campaigns against unruly leaders in the German, French, Czechoslovak and Polish parties in the years 1931–3 are prime examples of Stalin's determination to construct a highly disciplined set of Bolshevik cadres in the national 'sections' of the Comintern.

On the basis of painstaking work in the Comintern Archives, the Russian expert, Fridrikh Firsov, has confirmed the 'Borkenau line', if we may call it that. He maintains that 'Stalin, personally, and through Molotov, Kaganovich and Zhdanov, controlled the most important sectors of the Comintern's activities.'[22] As a concrete example, Firsov describes what one suspects was a typical episode in the life of the International. On the eve of the Thirteenth ECCI Plenum, due to open in Moscow in November 1933, Osip Piatnitskii, an eminent Comintern functionary, became concerned about the theses to be adopted at the meeting. Firsov writes:

> On 21 November, Piatnitskii, having found out that Stalin had refused to read the draft theses because 'they are too long', sent him a short-ened version with the request 'to read this summary and inform us if the theses' line is correct or if not how it should be reworked. We cannot open the plenum without your instructions on the theses.' On 14 December Piatnitskii sent Stalin, Molotov and Kaganovich the reso-lutions and theses of the plenum, which were ready to go to press. He asked them to look them over and tell him 'which changes should be introduced into the theses and resolutions'.[23]

It seems that a missive or telephone call sufficed for Stalin and his closest colleagues not only to approve, but formulate the lamentable decisions of the Thirteenth Plenum, which, at a time of ferocious Nazi repression, prophesied 'a new round of revolution and wars', continued to employ the tendentious term 'social fascist', and emphasised the struggle for a 'Soviet government' as the only way out of the capitalist crisis.[24] There was no mention of a broad united front against fascism or transitional democratic demands.

This is not the sole example of Stalin's personal intervention in the framing of Comintern policy. It was he who in 1928 disassociated Soviet institutions and leaders from public involvement in the activities of the International in order 'not to give our enemies any cause to assert the inter-linking of Soviet power with the Comintern'[25]; it was he who on several occasions in 1930 and 1931 inserted anti-social democratic diatribes into ECCI resolutions; it was he who in July 1931 insisted on the German communists' participation in the Nazi-sponsored referendum against the Prussian social democratic government; it was his famous 'Letter' to the journal *Proletarskaia revoliutsiia* in October 1931 that served as a sharp reminder of the dangers of flirtations with social democracy; it was he who in the spring of 1933, that is *after* Hitler's accession to power, instructed the ECCI to step up the campaign against the Second International and the German social democrats; it was he who as late as July 1934 defended the basic correctness of the 'social fascist' theory; and it was he who appears to have personally selected the Russian party delegates to the Seventh, and final, Comintern World Congress in the summer of 1935.[26] Stalin's burning hostility to social democracy shines through and it was this animosity which, according to Firsov, 'precluded any possibility of establishing contact between communist and social democratic....parties for the purpose of creating a united workers' front against the fascist offensive.'[27]

Does this fascination with Stalin mean that Carr's less personalised view is insupportable? Clearly, his claim that the Comintern was not a monolithic structure is debatable. It was a highly bureaucratised organisation and once Stalin had spoken, the ECCI and party leaderships jumped to attention. Where he is on more solid ground is in his depiction of Stalin as 'an absentee director who occasionally turns up unexpectedly and demands that props be removed or the odd actor....replaced, and then disappears, leaving others to cope with the mess.'[28] Stalin, weighed down with the massive burdens of rapid industrialisation and the on-going agricultural crisis, had neither the time nor the inclination to indulge in day-to-day supervision of the ECCI. Borkenau's claim that Stalin controlled 'all details' of the Comintern's work is thus an exaggeration. The result, if we believe Carr, was a kind of vacuum at the heart of the Comintern, which encouraged caution, confusion and indecision, but which also gave the leadership a certain leeway in interpreting orders from above. The fact that firm directives were not always forthcoming only added to the vacillation and fostered subtle divisions among the Comintern hierarchy. This image of an aloof Stalin, unable or unwilling to exert sustained continuing control, reinforces recent western research on Soviet domestic history in the 1930s, much of which, as we have seen, has challenged the totalitarian paradigm of Stalin's rule.

The picture of the 'absentee director' could profitably be taken further in an analysis of Stalin's influence on the conception of the 'Third Period' line. Is it possible that in 1928–9, Stalin, rather than initiating the 'left turn', actually appropriated and sanctioned the uncompromising positions of others, 'hawks' such as Molotov and the German party leader Ernst Thälmann? This appears to be the case with the 'social fascist' slogan, which almost definitely did not originate with Stalin, but which was canonised by him in the course of 1929. Perhaps he countenanced the radical rhetoric 'only because he attributed very little practical significance to whatever the Comintern did in those years'?[29] Perhaps, as Sheila Fitzpatrick has argued in relation to the contemporaneous cultural revolution in the USSR, Stalin accepted a predefined and pre-existing hard-line platform once he had resolved to move against his Politburo colleagues?[30] Miloš Hájek, a leading Czech Comintern specialist, has asserted that the 'class against class' policy 'arose autonomously....Stalin decided to support it only when strong and vital elements in the European communist parties upheld it.'[31]

Like so much in Comintern history, there are no definitive answers to these problems. The received wisdom that Stalin decided everything probably needs revising. He was a more distant ruler than this interpretation would allow. It is feasible, moreover, that the details of the Third Period line were elaborated by others, both within the Comintern hierarchy and the national parties. But it would be a brave historian who denied that Stalin maintained a decisive influence over the determination of the general strategies, and, crucially, pronounced them irrevocable and universal. When he decided to speak, his word was gospel. It is clear that no major policy innovation was possible without his direct intervention or sanction, and nor was any change in the composition of communist party leaderships.

In conclusion to this section, it can be argued that the main features of Stalinism in the Communist International were a strictly centralised form of decision-making which ultimately rested on the cult of the 'infallible leader'; a dogmatic stultified Marxism, but one which employed the rhetoric of mass democracy and legitimation; a repressive, and eventually arbitrary terroristic, regime that removed all real or imaginary opponents; and by the end of the 1930s the primacy of *realpolitik* over revolutionary ideology and of Soviet state interests over those of the international movement, nowhere better manifested than in the Nazi-Soviet Pact of August 1939. Perhaps the best way of understanding the international communist movement under Stalin is to recognise that he helped to create a stiflingly bureaucratised Comintern apparatus and highly centralised communist parties pledged primarily to the defence of the USSR. As such, by insisting on monolithic ideological orthodoxy and by launching mass repression, Stalin did much to discredit the ideal of socialism among broad strata of European workers and intellectuals not only in the 1930s, but well beyond. Hence from this perspective, Stalin's actions in the Comintern ultimately did little to further the Marxist cause to which he was deeply committed. However, viewed through the spectacles of Soviet statesmanship, the assessment is less damning. The anti-fascist struggles of the 1930s and the wartime resistance efforts of communist partisans significantly raised the worldwide prestige of communism and its embodiment, the USSR. The Stalinised Comintern also helped lay the foundations of post-war communist expansion in Central and Eastern Europe by consolidating disciplined parties led by an efficient, highly trained and fiercely loyal band of cadres capable of administering the new 'People's Democracies'. It is to Stalin's deeds during the early years of the Cold War that we now turn.

Stalin and the Cold War

The widely held notion that Stalin rarely concerned himself with international affairs is inaccurate. Even in the pre-war decades, Stalin's letters to Molotov and Kaganovich reveal a constant interest in, and knowledge of, foreign policy. Many of the Politburo's top secret 'special files' relate to events in both Europe and Asia, underlining the basic fact that the USSR spanned two massive continents. The rise of a militaristic Japan in the Far East was as much a worry to the Stalinist leaders as the emergence of Hitlerite Germany. Stalin's involvement in diplomacy became even more pronounced after the war as the Soviet Union acquired global superpower status, an 'empire' in Eastern Europe and, by the early 1950s, an atomic arsenal rivalling that of the USA. In the new post-war balance of power, Stalin's attributes as statesman mattered literally to millions worldwide and were to be tested to the limits.[32]

Two leading authorities on this theme, Vladislav Zubok and Constantine Pleshakov, have argued that a 'revolutionary-imperial paradigm' best characterises the principles of Soviet foreign policy under Stalin (and his successors). It represents 'a strange amalgam of ideological proselytism and geopolitical pragmatism....[a] combination of traditional Russian messianism and Marxist ideology'.[33] For Stalin, international statecraft was not simply a Bismarckian tool of *realpolitik* to be manipulated to protect and strengthen the Soviet state. It was certainly this in part, but it was also a means to promote a longer-term revolutionary expansion of communism, what one scholar has called Stalin's 'revolution by degrees'.[34] In this sense, contrary to those who detect little or no ideological content in Stalin's strategies, I would note his commitment to a crude Marxist-Leninist doctrine of anti-capitalism, anti-imperialism and anti-pacifism. This does not mean that he was a war-monger hell-bent on global domination, as so many in the West believed after 1945. Rather, it signifies a profound embedded mistrust of all capitalist leaders and regimes and an un-shakable conviction in the ultimate historic triumph of a superior ideology and state formation, communism, over capitalist exploitation and its bour-geois civilisation. The difficulty for the historian is how to interpret and delineate the shifting symbiosis between ideology and *realpolitik*, between revolutionary inputs and pragmatic statism. Stalin, I suspect, saw no such dichotomy: what was good for the Soviet state was good for the world revolu-tion. An examination of Stalin's actions in Europe after the war will elucidate this hypothesis.

Western historiography of the origins of the Cold War has followed a fa-miliar pattern: an 'orthodox' interpretation was established in the 1950s, which was then contested by a 'revisionist' school from the 1960s, which was in turn superseded by a 'neo-revisionist' consensus beginning in the 1970s, which is now being challenged by a 'post-neo-revisionist' cohort. According to 'orthodox' scholars, prime responsibility for the outbreak of the Cold War lies with Stalin, because of his aggressive expansionist designs in Eastern Europe, China, Korea and elsewhere. It is argued that he reneged on the Yalta agreements for free elections in Poland, conspired immediately after 1945 to 'Sovietise' the other countries of Central and Eastern Europe, in-cluding the Soviet zone of occupation in Germany, interfered in the domes-tic affairs of democratic European states, notably France, Italy and Greece, via his direct control over the respective communist parties, provided mili-tary assistance to the Chinese communists in their civil war with the pro-western Nationalists, and incited the North Koreans to invade the South in 1950, thus precipitating a near catastrophic confrontation with the USA. This image of Stalin as renegade statesman out for world dominion helped lay the foundations of the Cold War. From the 1960s onwards, the 'revision-ists' countered by claiming that Stalin's actions in the period 1945–50 were largely cautious, defensive and reactive to American expansion, economic hegemony and overwhelming military superiority. The 'revisionists' main-tained that, rather than having a preconceived plan to incorporate the countries of Eastern Europe into a Soviet dominated communist bloc, Stalin from 1947 was responding to aggressive US signals, such as the Truman Doctrine and the Marshall Plan, and was primarily concerned with Soviet state security. The 'neo-revisionist' interpretation emphasised that monocausal explanations for the degeneration of East-West relations were inadequate. Mistakes, misunderstandings and misperceptions were evident on *both* sides, contributing to the gradual breakdown in relations among the 'Big Three'. The 'post-neo-revisionists', basing their ideas partly on new Soviet archival sources, come close to vindicating the original 'orthodox' conclusion that Stalin was the guilty partner.

The first thing to be established is that Stalin was *the* dominant figure in Soviet foreign policy formation in these years. Molotov, as Foreign Minister, deferred to his boss in all significant, and not a few minor, matters. When he showed any spark of independence Stalin severely wrapped his knuckles.[35] It appears that all major strategic decisions were taken on Stalin's own initiative: the 'Sovietisation' of Eastern Europe, the expulsion of Tito's Yugoslavia from the communist bloc, the imposition of the Berlin Blockade, the show trials of East European communists (including many Jews), and the sanctioning of the North Korean invasion of South Korea were all ultimately Stalin's deeds. That said, he had no such control over the responses and reactions of his western protagonists and hence the results of his policies were unpredictable and not always commensurate with expectations. Secondly, Stalin's designs were not unchanging; he adapted them, sometimes subtly, sometimes in quite major ways, to changing circumstances and pressures. In Eastern Europe he operated a differentiated strategy depending on the country and the international conjuncture. Thirdly, he was not at all times implacably hostile to the Western Allies and it is quite probable that he hoped for some mode of cooperation with them after the victory over the Nazis, if only to ensure US assistance in rebuilding the shattered Soviet economy and western support for his territorial and reparations claims. It is no surprise that Molotov later said: 'It was to our benefit to stay allied with America. It was important.'[36]

The bottom line for Stalin's diplomacy was state security. The USSR had been invaded three times since 1914 through its western borders and he was absolutely adamant that this would not be repeated. Hence, the creation of a *cordon sanitaire* was imperative, a Soviet sphere of influence in large swathes of Central and Eastern Europe. The means to achieve this security was through revolutionary transformations combined with the military might and presence of the Red Army in the liberated parts of the continent. In the years 1944–7 this meant that neighbouring countries had to have either essentially one-party communist regimes (Romania, Bulgaria) or coalition governments 'friendly' to the Soviet Union (Czechoslovakia, Hungary). Stalin had to be cautious. He was in no hurry to bring Prague and Budapest under the Soviet wing. In October 1944, he told Hungarian communist leaders in Moscow that it could take up to fifteen years before their country would be socialist.[37] Poland was a special case; for Stalin it was the key to Soviet security. Stalin was prepared to bide his time here too given western interests, but he was determined to 'Sovietise' the Poles relatively rapidly, even if it signified tearing up the Yalta accords. In Finland, Stalin accepted a compromise solution: a western democratic structure, but leaning towards Moscow. As for defeated Germany, Stalin did not wish to see a permanently divided country and apparently retained hopes for a united 'socialist Germany'. Indeed, he followed the western lead in the creation of sovereign states, West and then East Germany.

Stalin's European foreign policy in the crucial years 1944–7 attempted to reconcile two ultimately incompatible goals: territorial and politico-ideological aggrandisement on his western borders and continued collaboration with his erstwhile Western Allies. In this his approach was eminently Leninist and dialectical. He sought to negotiate and deal with the USA and Great Britain in order to exacerbate their mutual contradictions and differences, to diminish capitalist influence in Europe and promote Soviet-style socialism. It was a judicious mixture of Zubok and Pleshakov's 'revolutionary-imperial paradigm', but it did not fully succeed. This was because firstly the Western Allies remained solidly united, unyielding to Soviet pressure, and secondly because the East European communists were generally not as popular as they and Moscow imagined. Only in Czechoslovakia and Yugoslavia were they genuinely mass parties. Therefore, from the summer of 1947 Stalin adopted a more offensive posture, including the formation of the Communist Information Bureau (Cominform) predicated on the notion that the world was now divided into 'two camps', the takeover of power in Hungary and Czechoslovakia, the intensification of Stalinist measures of control in the other countries of the region, and the testing of western resolve by risky episodes such as the Berlin Blockade, one of his greatest miscalculations, and the launching of the Korean War in 1950.

How best to evaluate Stalin's post-war statesmanship? The opinion of many experts is essentially negative. Vojtech Mastny talks of his 'illusions and wishful thinking', his 'chronic error of judgment', his 'bungling' and many 'blunders', which by the early 1950s meant that 'Soviet foreign policy all but came to a standstill.'[38] This is a damning assessment partially shared by Zubok and Pleshakov. They invoke Stalin's 'poor diplomacy' as an important contributory factor in the 'conflagration of the Cold War'. As examples they cite his failures and setbacks in Iran, Turkey, Yugoslavia and, most significantly, a divided and resurgent Germany.[39] Even Caroline Kennedy-Pipe in her less censorious approach refers to Stalin's 'somewhat contradictory' German strategy and 'the complicated legacy' that he left his successors.[40] Perhaps the most telling critique comes from the American specialist John L. Gaddis, who concludes that 'the states [Stalin] seized, the boundary concessions he insisted upon, and the sphere of influence he imposed provided no lasting security for the Soviet Union: just the opposite.'[41]

However, historians, including those mentioned above, do not deal in categorical imperatives of 'total success' and 'outright failure'. Surely, Stalin's international policies left a deeply ambiguous legacy. From a more positive perspective, it seems clear that Stalin and his top advisers knew the limits of their ambitions and powers. Stalin was not some reckless megalomaniac out for world domination and, regardless of his Marxist-Leninist conviction in the inevitability of war, he had no wish to embroil the planet in another Armageddon, a conflict the exhausted USSR was in no position to prosecute in the mid-to-late 1940s. This relative restraint and coolheaded realism ensured that the Cold War would remain 'cold'. It does not mean, however, that the threat he posed to the west was non-existent. Stalin did not simply respond *ad hoc* to western pressures and initiatives. He had broader strategies, some of which can be construed as aggressive and also largely successful, at least in the short to medium term. In particular, the establishment of a 'Soviet Empire' stretching from the Baltic to the Adriatic must have been deeply satisfactory to Stalin, both geopolitically and ideologically. Indeed, a 'Sovietised' socialist Eastern Europe was, according to Eduard Marks:

> the ultimate aim of his policies....an aim deeply rooted in his regime's ideology and his personal beliefs. From his Marxist-Leninist perspective, moreover, it was obviously more prudent that the military security of the USSR should ultimately be entrusted to a glacis of socialized states in Eastern Europe than to agreements with capitalist states that he viewed as intrinsically predatory potential enemies.[42]

Stalin's diplomacy also enjoyed more than a modicum of success in the Far East. In 1945, the Soviet Union gained territories such as the Kurile Islands and Sakhalin from defeated Japan and secured control over Outer Mongolia, Manchuria and the important naval bases of Dairen and Port

Arthur. In October 1949 the Chinese Communist Party under Mao Zedong came to power, fuelling western fears that Moscow sought to conquer the world. However, from Stalin's point of view a huge communist China represented a double-edged sword not least because Mao could not be so easily manipulated as the East European 'mini Stalins'. Indeed, Sino-Soviet relations in this period (and beyond) were generally fraught. The situation on the USSR's southern peripheries was also not so comforting as the Generalissimo's manoeuvres in Turkey and Iran in 1945–6 had been rebuffed. In the vital realm of military security, Stalin's endeavours were likewise mixed. On the one hand, the Red Army remained the largest conventional fighting force on the continent, the imposition of a communist Poland had strengthened the Soviet Union's exposed western borders and, crucially, the USSR acquired the atomic bomb in 1949 ending America's monopoly. But the creation of NATO in the same year, western rearmament of their zones in Germany, and the stalemate in Korea were worrying developments and did not bode well for future Soviet security.

Stalin's 'revolutionary-imperial' strategies had left his successors to deal with a restive empire in Eastern Europe, an unfinished conflict in Korea, a wary ally in China, and, most importantly, a staunchly uncooperative, antagonistic and awesomely powerful Western coalition. Stalin, though, would certainly not have seen it in these terms. He had modernised the Soviet military arsenal, pacified the perennially volatile lands of Eastern Europe, extended the boundaries of the 'socialist peace-loving camp' and hence improved the security of the USSR. As Molotov, his life-long crony, intimated many years after the event:

> Stalin led the cause for the downfall of imperialism and the advent of communism....we had to consolidate our conquests. We made our own socialist Germany out of our part of Germany, and restored order in Czechoslovakia, Poland, Hungary, and Yugoslavia, where the situations were fluid. *To squeeze out the capitalist order.* This was the cold war.[43]

Stalin and the 'Paradigm of Death'

Controversy and obfuscation attend Stalin even in death. Why was the terminally ill 'boss' left without medical care for many hours? Did he die naturally or was he murdered by one or more of his associates? There is much speculation that Beria had Stalin poisoned or fatally injected and it is true that there was good reason for any one of his terrified underlings to remove him.

Foul play cannot be ruled out completely.[44] But the available evidence is fairly conclusive: Stalin was not killed by Beria or anyone else; he died of a massive cerebral haemorrhage. Even after interviews with several eye-witnesses, the publication of the memoirs of various participants and the declassification of the top secret medical report compiled by the doctors who tended the dying Stalin, the course of events is still very hazy and details impossible to verify with any certainty.

That said, Stalin's last few days can be reconstructed roughly as follows.[45] On 28 February 1953 Stalin, together with a select list of comrades, held his customary late night soirée at his Blizhniaia *dacha* on the outskirts of Moscow. The party broke up around 4.00am, Stalin apparently showing no sign of ill health. Sometime on 1 March, he suffered a debilitating stroke which paralysed the right side of his body. For several hours he lay painfully in his study before his minders finally summoned up the temerity to enter unbidden at about 10.30pm. They found their boss barely conscious on the floor in a pool of urine. Mysteriously, doctors were not immediately informed either by his alarmed staff, or the Minister of State Security, or his top aides, Beria, Malenkov, Khrushchev and Bulganin, who arrived at the scene in the early hours of 2 March. It was not until 7.00am that morning that physicians first examined the patient, a delay of up to twenty four hours since the stroke. It is quite plausible that this procrastination was a deliberate attempt to hasten Stalin's demise on the part of his scheming subordinates; it is also possible that they were afraid of calling for the doctors lest Stalin recover naturally. Stalin's disdain for the medical profession was legendary. For the next three days the doctors prescribed leeches, various injections and enemas, but to no avail. It was clear to them that the 'Leader' was in his death-throes. Now and then he regained a measure of consciousness, but the end came at 9.50pm (several accounts say 9.50*am*) on 5 March. The great 'Father of the Peoples' was no more and his anxious faction-ridden successors had to somehow oversee the transition to a stable post-Stalin era.

Genuine grief, apprehension and confusion affected millions of Soviet citizens on hearing the news of Stalin's decease. Many were trampled to death in the overcrowded streets of Moscow on the day of his funeral, 9 March. For many others it was a profound release and was greeted with a silent sense of satisfaction. Stalin's legacy for the USSR and the world will be briefly discussed in the conclusion, but I want to finish this chapter by contemplating 'the paradigm of death' that, arguably, had haunted Stalin for decades.[46] This discussion enters the realm of conjecture, but it seems fitting to end this book with an inquiry into the impact of death and suffering on Dzhugashvili-Koba-Stalin. From a relatively early age, Stalin's private and professional life had been punctuated, one might even say shaped, by the demise, often violent, of key figures: he was not yet thirty when his first wife died, an event which, according to most accounts, had a deep effect on him; not a few of his comrades fell to Tsarist bullets in the pre-revolutionary struggles; overwork and 'White Terror' claimed the lives of several Old Bolshevik colleagues during the Civil War; most significantly, Lenin's prolonged illness and premature death in 1924 not only opened the way for Stalin's dominance over the party, but must also have been a psychological trauma and an enormous drain on his physical and emotional resources.

It can be speculated that this 'paradigm of death' remained in Stalin's consciousness throughout the 1930s: the devastating suicide of his second wife in November 1932 was a cataclysmic event which strengthened Stalin's natural introspection, spiritual desolation and vindictiveness; barely two years later Kirov was assassinated in Leningrad (it has never been proved that Stalin ordered his death); Kuibyshev, a long-time associate, died in 1935 and Stalin's old sparring partner 'Sergo' Ordzhonikidze committed suicide in 1937, admittedly after a fierce row with the 'boss'. Indeed, high level suicides became a common feature under Stalin and he was totally disparaging of them, viewing them as an 'un-Bolshevik' act and a personal attack on him, his policies and the entire party 'line'. After the war, another close colleague, Zhdanov, died in suspicious circumstances. For many years, in all likelihood, he had been wary of his creeping ailments (he even gave up smoking in 1952); hence the long trips for medical treatment in the warm south. It is evident that by the late 1940s and early 1950s the knowledge of his own death constantly accompanied Stalin, ultimately manifested in the grotesque 'Doctors' Plot'.

The consequences of Stalin's 'paradigm of death' can only be surmised. One important aspect is that, as a Bolshevik who had not succumbed to suicide, assassination or early death, Stalin was able to project a public mantle of a 'living martyr and martyr survivor', an image that contributed to his cultic status.[47] But more fundamental perhaps was his fear of becoming a victim of terrorism, a fear which called for unprecedented security measures and which figured prominently in the charges levelled against the accused dignitaries in the Show Trials of the 1930s. Personal fear and the Terror were in this way interconnected. Stalin could never feel entirely safe and at the end he was cut off, his psyche destroyed, a victim indeed of his own conspiratorial system.

Conclusion

Stalin: Revolutionary in an Era of War

By way of conclusion I will address three major themes: the centrality of war and revolution for Stalin and Stalinism, the recent debate on the 'boss' as a 'weak dictator', and Stalin's historical legacy for his immediate successors and for the longer term evolution and ultimate collapse of the USSR.

Stalin and the 'War-Revolution Model'

In the Introduction to this book, I outlined my idea that Stalin's thought and actions could best be encapsulated in a 'war-revolution model'. I have not belaboured this notion in the main text, more often than not addressing it implicitly. This is because, firstly, I am aware that 'one size does not fit all': the model does not pretend to explain every aspect of Stalin's mentality, activities and policies. Indeed, contradictory tendencies are all too evident, notably the 'Great Retreat' of the 1930s as a conservative reversal of revolutionary communist socio-cultural policies and values, and the reliance on Russocentrism and nationalist rhetoric beginning in the mid-1930s, escalating during World War II and culminating in the era of 'High Stalinism'. Both concepts belie the image of Stalin as committed Marxist revolutionary, but both I think need to be qualified as I attempted to do in chapter three. Furthermore, I am wary of the applicability of 'master narratives', which by their very nature tend to simplify what are massively complex historical developments. A perfect example would be the 'totalitarian paradigm' that dominated much of western 'Sovietology' and continues to exert a big influence today on popular discourses. While certainly not entirely 'wrong', the totalitarian argument restricted our understanding of Soviet history by positing an essentially uni-dimensional 'from above' methodology which insufficiently recognised that the 'Great Dictator' had constraints on his power, had to interact with colleagues, subordinates and society as a whole, and was thus not able to control everything in his vast domain, let alone in the outside world. 'Life is messy' and not even the best laid plans always work out as intended.

Before making explicit why I think the 'war-revolution model' is useful and how it relates directly to Stalin's dictatorship, it would be worthwhile to recap the essence of the 'Russian experience' in the first half of the twentieth century. It makes for sober reading indeed. In the space of a mere fifty years Russia/Soviet Union endured five wars (Russo-Japanese, World War I, Civil War, World War II and the Cold War) and four revolutions (1905–06, February and October 1917 and Stalin's 'revolution from above'). In addition, the Great Terror of 1937–8 shook the social foundations of the country. The Soviet people only knew two relatively 'normal' phases in this period: the New Economic Policy (1921–8) and the moderate interlude of 1934–6. The total number of deaths attributable to these vast human transformations and upheavals, if we include the famine of 1932–3, comes in my rough estimation to about forty million, the majority (circa 27 million) during the 'Great Patriotic War'.

I cite these traumatic experiences and horrendous figures not primarily to indict communism or Stalinism – that has been done many times[1] – but rather to make two interrelated points. Firstly, Stalin's and the Bolsheviks' worldview, mentality and often their specific policies were shaped by conditions of war, real or potential, and revolution. The revolutionary regime itself had been born in the midst of 'total war', a conjuncture that 'substantially lessened traditional constraints on state power and greatly heightened the willingness of Party leaders to deploy massive coercion in their bid to move history forward to communism.'[2] Ideologically too, Bolshevism was predicated on the notion of the 'inevitability of war', which in turn engendered profound fears of counter-revolution based on internal instability and external threat. Stalinism was a particularly potent, militarised and repressive response to these perceived moments of crisis; it was the product of what Chris Ward has called the 'politics of permanent emergency'.[3] Secondly, Soviet society was deeply divided and rarely, if ever, at peace with itself: class-based hatreds and conflicts, urban-rural tensions, multi-ethnic animosities, the lack of political and social 'trust' between rulers and ruled, and weak civil society relations meant that the state, regardless of ideology, was bound to play a hegemonic role. In this highly inauspicious internal and external climate in a country with long porous borders and a largely authoritarian political culture, the emergence of a democratic *Rechtsstaat* was unlikely to say the least. Even in our own era the transition to democracy under Yeltsin and Putin has been fraught with difficulties. To be sure, Lenin, Stalin and other Bolshevik leaders mightily contributed to the hostilities and violence by their 'statist' extremism, profound intolerance of opposition and rhetoric of 'class war'. Stalin, especially, stamped his ugly personality on Soviet state and society. But whoever ruled Russia, it seems to me, would have found western-style liberal democracy a dangerous luxury.

More specifically, I have identified five factors in each part of the 'war-revolution' equation that impacted directly on Stalin's political and personal evolution.

War:

1. *World War I and the Russian Civil War:* the brutalisation of politics, the Bolsheviks' 'siege mentality' and the creation of a 'Stalin clan' form the backdrop to his rise to prominence in the Party. More broadly, the impulse to state management of societies engendered by the First World War is reflected and augmented in the authoritarian policies of the Bolshevik government.

2. *War Scares and capitalist encirclement:* Stalin's theory of 'socialism in one country' can be interpreted as a response to war threats and geopolitical isolation. In turn, his 'revolution from above' and absolute insistence on rapid industrialisation were partly determined by the War Scare of 1927, and the Great Terror was predicated on a perceived 'fifth column' in conditions of continuing 'capitalist encirclement'.

3. *World War II:* the 'Great Patriotic War' was not only a desperate defence of the 'motherland', but also a catalyst of 'revolution from abroad', the Sovietisation of Eastern Europe and hence the spread of socialism. Domestically, the victorious outcome of the war legitimised Stalin's rule and arguably made him a 'popular dictator'.

4. *Cold War:* rising post-war international tensions between East and West contributed to crackdowns at home on the Church, Jews, intellectuals and other social strata and a return to repression and mass arrests.

5. *'Inevitable War':* the Marxist-Leninist theory of the 'clash of civilisations' underlay Stalin's policies. He was haunted by the idea of an anti-Soviet imperialist coalition waging war on the 'socialist' USSR and his prime foreign policy aim was both to delay, and prepare for, the 'inevitable war'.

Revolution:

1. *Marxist revolutionary ideology:* early in his political career Stalin became convinced of the necessity of violent class war and developed an acute hatred of 'bourgeois civilisation', which could only be swept away by full-scale revolution.

2. *Bolshevik Revolution*: the Revolution was highly significant for Stalin's rise to prominence in the Communist Party, even though he played a relatively minor role in the events of 1917. Subsequently, the absolute imperative to secure the Revolution from its multifarious internal and external enemies helps to explain the gradual evolution of 'Stalinism'.

3. *'Revolution from Above'*: Stalin's socio-economic revolution *par excellence* represented a massive upheaval in millions of Soviets' lives; an attempt, however distorted and brutal, to 'construct socialism'.

4. *Ideologised foreign policy:* Stalin's diplomacy remained partly informed by ideological goals and premises – a gut hostility to the capitalist Great Powers and, in the 1920s at least, a sensitivity to revolutionary strivings abroad, though increasingly *realpolitik*, national security interests and a traditional 'balance of power' diplomacy came to the fore.

5. *Fear of counter-revolutionary forces:* Stalin actions reflected his belief in the existence of a broad anti-Soviet foreign alliance combined with a domestic 'fifth column' of 'spies' and 'enemies' in and outside the party. This formed the basis and rationale of the Great Terror, which also included an impulse to 'revolutionise' and 'homogenise' Soviet society by eliminating 'socially harmful elements' and 'unfit human weeds'.

Linking both components is Stalin's militarised conception of the Communist Party as an '*Order of Knights of the Sword*....the officer corps and general staff of the proletariat.'[4] In 1934, the arch-Stalinist Kaganovich put it even more succinctly, depicting the Party as 'an army of revolutionary warriors'.[5]

My fundamental point, and one that I have emphasised several times in this volume, is that Stalin's power was not wielded simply to enhance his own position as dictator. He was not, I think, motivated solely or, dare I say it, even mainly by power lust, deep-seated paranoia and personal evilness. These phenomena were undoubtedly present, but Stalin was guided rather by a toxic mixture of ideology and practical defence of revolutionary gains in an unpredictable world that constantly threatened war, crises and counter-revolution. Not that he was some fearful totally cowed 'little man'. His speeches, letters and other private and public communications reveal an underlying confidence in his and the Soviet state's ability to overcome their rivals. His deep Marxist conviction told him that capitalism would be defeated and that socialism and ultimately communism were the bright future of humanity. Relying to a large extent on Lenin's ideas, Stalin's innovation was that whole strata of society *and* loyal communists, if not willing to tread this deterministic road, should be coerced into his model of socialism. This in turn meant that awesome state power would be deployed in a colossal feat of social engineering.

Stalin: A 'Weak Dictator'?

In recent years several western historians, evaluating the nature and scale of Stalin's power, have suggested that in some important ways he may be considered a 'weak dictator', similar to Hans Mommsen's characterisation of Hitler.[6] It is argued that, although Stalin stood at the apex of a huge power structure and was central to all major domestic and foreign policy decisions including the Terror, he was forever conscious that his decrees and directives were being ignored, diluted or otherwise subverted by provincial party-state bureaucrats. Furthermore, large strata of society from industrial workers to collectivised peasants resented Stalinist policies that lowered standards of living and raised work norms. Finally, Stalin feared that this internal resistance and disaffection might ally itself with his defeated political opponents and foreign enemies. While I do not reject these examples (indeed I have borrowed some of them in my section 'Limits of Tyranny' in chapter four), I think it would be more accurate to speak, as Moshe Lewin does, of Stalin as an 'insecure' rather than a 'weak' despot.[7] Clearly, it depends on the definition of the term 'weak'. An individual who can send tens of thousands to their untimely death by a stroke of the pen, who can unilaterally decide governmental and state policy (large and small), who can subjugate all others in the leading cohort, who can manufacture and control a vast mythic cult of his own personality, who can impress, if he so chooses, his views on the cultural and intellectual life of the country, and who can uproot the lives of millions of citizens by vast socio-economic transformations cannot, in my estimation, be judged 'weak'. In this sense Stalin's power was probably unrivalled in modern history. If Stalin was 'weak', it would be horrendous to contemplate a 'strong' dictator! All this is not to say that he was some omnipotent, omnipresent, omniscient being. Such notions are alien to historical analysis and are totally unsustainable.

A related, though highly problematic, issue is: was Stalin a 'successful dictator'? The late Dmitrii Volkogonov succinctly summarised these debates in the subtitle of his massive biography, *Stalin: Triumph and Tragedy*. Again, the 'answer' rests with the definition of 'success' and this can change depending on whose perspective we adopt to assess 'success'. From an anti-Marxist viewpoint, Stalin's rule, and communism more generally, was terroristic, morally perverted, and by seeking fundamentally to alter human nature ultimately doomed to failure. More sympathetic western observers have maintained that, despite the carnage of the Great Terror, the Stalinist system modernised the socio-economic and military capabilities of the USSR and hence laid the foundations for victory in the supreme test of World War II. For 'Soviet patriots', of whom there appear to be many even in today's Russia, Stalin was a consummate statesman who, from a largely agrarian slumbering giant in the 1920s, created an orderly egalitarian military-industrial superpower supported by a 'socialist commonwealth' in Eastern Europe compared to which contemporary 'democratic' Russia is weak, crime-ridden and socially inequitable. We might speculate that Stalin himself would have seen his achievements in these terms. In my opinion, Stalinist 'triumphs' do not outweigh the 'tragedies'. Leaving aside moral concerns, the barbarities, lawlessness and vast human suffering of the 1930s cannot be justified. The ideologically-driven campaign of forced collectivisation, for instance, did not contribute to Soviet economic stability and productivity. Socialised agriculture remained *the* weak link in the Soviet economy right through to the 1980s and early 1990s.

Rather than a categorical judgement of 'success' or 'failure', itself a dubious undertaking, another way of evaluating Stalin's policies might be to ponder the alternatives to Stalinism. Which other route to 'socialist modernity' could have been chosen? Would other Bolshevik leaders, when faced with the awesome dilemmas of the late 1920s and 1930s, have adopted similar policies to the 'boss'? These are, of course, counter-factual questions. We will never know which line of development Lenin would have pursued had he lived, nor Trotsky or Bukharin had they won the power struggles. Would they have herded the peasantry into collective farms at gunpoint? Would they have insisted on exporting grain in the face of looming famine? Would they have launched the Great Terror against a host of 'enemies', communists included? Quite likely not; Stalin's 'evil', if you will, shines through here. But what would the anti-Stalinist Oppositions have done about widespread peasant recalcitrance given their ideological conviction that collectivised agriculture was superior to private? Would Bukharin and his co-'rightists' have persuaded the peasants to join the collectives voluntarily? Would Trotsky, given his commitment to rapid industrialisation, have permitted long-term small-scale agriculture based on peasant private holdings? What can be said with certainty is that

there were no easy solutions to Russia's historic 'backwardness' and in circumstances of 'capitalist encirclement' and constant war scares it is more than
possible that some form of state-sponsored coercion was inevitable if the
utopian communist dream was to be fulfilled. After all, Lenin and other
Bolshevik leaders did not shirk from violence and terror in 1918–20. Stalin's
was a particularly ruthless and heartless route, and the level of violence
was gratuitous. But it seems fanciful to suggest that in the highly pressurised
world of the 1930s a Trotsky or Bukharin would have discovered a humane
consensual path to communism.

Stalin's Legacy

No study of Stalin and Stalinism can ignore the legacy that the 'boss' left his
successors and how this legacy contributed to the eventual downfall of the
'Soviet experiment'. Still today a fine summary of the problems that Stalin be-
queathed to his heirs can be found in Alec Nove's *Stalinism and After*, first published in 1975.[8] Nove outlines four main areas: foreign policy and the Cold
War, terror, the economy and the political system. In the international arena,
Stalin had overseen a period of intense East-West tensions, epitomised by the
on-going Korean War and the threat of nuclear Armageddon. The notion of
'the inevitable war' had to be rethought. At home, it was clear to all his successors that the level of terror and repression had to be reduced. It was, above all,
counter-productive, stifling all initiative and creativity and paralysing people,
themselves included, by an all-pervasive fear. The number of labour camp
inmates was unacceptably high. The Stalinist 'command economy' prioritised
certain branches of heavy industry, was over-centralised, resistant to innovation and in many ways inefficient and wasteful of natural and human resources. Living standards, particularly among collective farmers, were low and
consumer goods in short supply. Agricultural production and yields were invariably poor. All these issues, and many more, demanded serious attention
after 5 March 1953.

The crucial dilemma, however, was political: 'how far could any relaxation
go without endangering the Soviet state, the monopoly of power of the
Party, the many vested interests associated in that monopoly?'[9] If the authorities gave an inch would the masses take a mile? Would reform, if undertaken, spiral out of control? In addition, procedures had to be found to
select a new leadership and the rules and regulations regarding the convening of party congresses and Central Committee plena had to be formalised
and revitalised. A modicum of democratisation was in order. This is not the

place to discuss post-Stalin developments in any detail. Suffice it to say that by 1956 Nikita Khrushchev had emerged as Stalin's unlikely successor and he and his supporters embarked on a tentative 'de-Stalinisation', a western term never used in the USSR. This 'thaw' entailed improving the living standards, housing and diets of the Soviet population, returning to 'democratic Leninist norms' in party life, reforming aspects of the command economy, especially in agriculture, seeking 'peaceful coexistence' with the West, and, above all, ending mass terror, releasing the majority of Gulag prisoners and curbing the powers of the secret police. In 1954 the newly created KGB (Committee of State Security) was brought under party tutelage and never again became a 'state within a state'. Khrushchev also bravely addressed the vexed 'Stalin question'. He denounced specific Stalinist crimes in his pivotal 'secret speech' to the Twentieth Party Congress in February 1956, attacking Stalin's 'cult of personality' and causing tremors throughout the communist world. In 1961 Khrushchev went further in his exposure of Stalin's despotism. The dictator's body was removed from its resting place in the revered Lenin Mausoleum and reburied in the Kremlin wall.

The Brezhnevite regime that replaced Khrushchev after October 1964 preferred, if possible, to ignore Stalin altogether. His legacy was too explosive: if Stalin, as a self-proclaimed Marxist-Leninist, had committed numerous crimes, then does this not signify that Marxism-Leninism is a criminal ideology and state form? What if millions of Soviet citizens asked themselves this question? Hence, under Brezhnev from the mid-1960s to the early 1980s a curtain of silence more or less descended on key moments of the Soviet past. This situation was reversed spectacularly under Mikhail Gorbachev, party leader from March 1985 to December 1991. In November 1987 Gorbachev announced in his spirit of *glasnost'* (openness) that all the 'blank spots' in Soviet history should be publicly discussed. This was almost *carte blanche* for an avalanche of criticism and soul-searching which ended up with overt scepticism not only towards Stalinism, but also Leninism, Marxism and the 'holy of holies', the Bolshevik Revolution, typified by a book I bought in Moscow in the summer of 1991 entitled *October 1917: The Greatest Event of the Century or a Social Catastrophe?* A few months later the USSR was no more and the Communist Party had been outlawed by Boris Yeltsin, President of the new Russian Federation.

What was the relationship between Stalin's legacy and this unhappy denouement for the Soviet Communist Party? Did Stalinism sow the seeds of the collapse of the USSR? The connections are multiple and I do not have space to examine them all. Let me concentrate on one important link: the socio-economic contradictions of Stalinism and post-Stalinism.[10] Stalin's 'revolution from above', which was designed to 'build socialism' and create a mighty Soviet state, unleashed contradictory longer-term socio-economic developments that ultimately contributed to the demise of that mighty state. The Stalinist command economy was based on nineteenth-century macro-models of industrialisation and modernisation: coal, iron, steel, machine building and metallurgy. It found it increasingly difficult to adapt to the 'scientific-technological revolution' of the second half of the twentieth century: the era of the microchip, computer technology, robotics and consumer society. Socially, as more and more Soviet citizens benefited from higher education, urbanisation, upward social mobility and measured prosperity – all trends set in motion by Stalin's revolution – so their aspirations, expectations and hopes for a better life grew concomitantly. But the top-heavy, bureaucratic, wasteful and rigid structures of the neo-Stalinist economy struggled to meet the social aspirations and consumer orientations of the burgeoning Soviet 'middle classes'. The result was a gradual disillusionment with 'socialism', a cynicism towards ideological mobilisation and thus ultimately a political threat to the regime itself.

Stalin, as a revolutionary, devoted his life to creating a Marxian socialist/communist utopia in an era stamped by civil war, internal class wars, war scares, looming foreign threats, the awesome reality of world war and potential post-war atomic oblivion. Paradoxically, many of his policies turned out to be the grave-digger of that utopia.

Notes

Introduction

1. The following texts are a representative sample of recent English language assessments of Stalin and Stalinism, many based on published and unpublished archival materials accessible since the late 1980s and early 1990s: R. C. Tucker, *Stalin in Power: The Revolution from Above, 1928–1941* (New York, 1990); A. Bullock, *Hitler and Stalin: Parallel Lives* (London, 1991); D. Volkogonov, *Stalin: Triumph and Tragedy* (London, 1991); R. Conquest, *Stalin: Breaker of Nations* (London, 1993); C. Ward, *Stalin's Russia* (London, 1993; 2nd edn 1999); E. Radzinsky, *Stalin* (London, 1997); I. Kershaw and M. Lewin (eds), *Stalinism and Nazism: Dictatorships in Comparison* (Cambridge, 1997); C. Ward (ed.), *The Stalinist Dictatorship* (London, 1998); E. Mawdsley, *The Stalin Years: The Soviet Union, 1929–1953* (Manchester, 1998; 2nd edn 2003); P. Boobbyer, *The Stalin Era* (London, 2000); R. Brackman, *The Secret File of Joseph Stalin: A Hidden Life* (London, 2001); M. McCauley, *Stalin and Stalinism*, 3rd edn (London, 2003); C. Read (ed.), *The Stalin Years: A Reader* (Basingstoke, 2003); M. Kun, *Stalin: An Unknown Portrait* (Budapest, 2003); S. Sebag Montefiore, *Stalin: The Court of the Red Tsar* (London, 2003); Z. Medvedev and R. Medvedev, *The Unknown Stalin* (London, 2003); E. A. Rees (ed.), *The Nature of Stalin's Dictatorship: The Politburo, 1928–1953* (Basingstoke, 2004); D. Rayfield, *Stalin and his Hangmen: An Authoritative Portrait of a Tyrant and Those Who Served Him* (London, 2004); R. Overy, *The Dictators: Hitler's Germany, Stalin's Russia* (London, 2004); R. Service, *Stalin: A Biography* (London, 2004). Aside from the translated volumes by Volkogonov and Radzinsky cited above, there are few full-scale studies of Stalin in Russian. Recent volumes include: B. V. Sokolov, *Stalin. Vlast' i*

krov' (Moscow, 2004); V. M. Soima, *Zapreshchennyi Stalin* (Moscow, 2005); and Iu. N. Zhukov, *Stalin: tainy vlasti* (Moscow, 2005). However, by far the most convincing work is done by Oleg Khlevniuk, but his approach is not biographical. See his *Politbiuro. Mekhanizmy politicheskoi vlasti v 1930-e gody* (Moscow, 1996); *1937-i: Stalin, NKVD i sovetskoe obshchestvo* (Moscow, 1992); and the translated work, *In Stalin's Shadow: The Career of 'Sergo' Ordzhonikidze* (New York, 1995).

2. E. H. Carr, *Socialism in One Country 1924–1926*, vol. 1 (Harmondsworth, 1970), p. 192.

3. On this, see P. Pomper, 'Historians and Individual Agency', *History and Theory*, vol. 35 (1996), pp. 281–308.

4. See S. Courtois et al., *The Black Book of Communism: Crimes, Terror, Repression* (Cambridge: MA, 1999), p. 4.

5. See, for example, I. Kershaw and M. Lewin, 'Introduction: The Regimes and Their Dictators: Perspectives of Comparison', in Kershaw and Lewin (eds), *Stalinism and Nazism*, p. 8; and C. S. Maier, *The Unmasterable Past: History, Holocaust, and German National Identity* (Cambridge: MA, 1988), pp. 71–84.

6. J. C. Scott, *Seeing Like a State: How Certain Schemes to Improve the Human Condition Have Failed* (New Haven and London, 1998).

7. On these ideas, see A. J. Rieber, 'Stalin, Man of the Borderlands', *American Historical Review*, vol. 106 (2001), pp. 1651–91.

8. A. Cooke, *Letter from America*, BBC News website, 23 June 2003, p. 5.

9. D. L. Hoffmann and Y. Kotsonis (eds), *Russian Modernity: Politics, Knowledge, Practices* (Basingstoke, 2000).

10. G. Boffa, *The Stalin Phenomenon* (Ithaca, 1992).

11. L. Lih et al. (eds), *Stalin's Letters to Molotov, 1925–1936* (New Haven and London, 1995), pp. 1–63.

12. R. G. Suny, 'Stalin and his Stalinism: power and authority in the Soviet Union, 1930–53', in Kershaw and Lewin (eds), *Stalinism and Nazism*, pp. 26–52.

13. R. C. Tucker, 'Stalin and Stalinism: Sources and Outcomes', in M. Hildermeier and E. Müller-Luckner (eds), *Stalinismus vor dem Zweiten Weltkrieg: Neue Wege der Forschung* (Munich, 1998), pp. 1–16; also Tucker, *Stalin in Power*.

14. D. Brandenberger, *National Bolshevism: Stalinist Mass Culture and the Formation of Modern Russian National Identity, 1931–1956* (Cambridge: MA, 2002).

15. E. van Ree, *The Political Thought of Joseph Stalin: A Study in Twentieth-Century Revolutionary Patriotism* (London, 2002).

16. E. A. Rees, *Political Thought from Machiavelli to Stalin: Revolutionary Machiavellism* (Basingstoke, 2004).
17. T. McDaniel, *The Agony of the Russian Idea* (Princeton, 1996).
18. For an important volume that emphasises the centrality of war to the experience of modern Russia, see S. Pons and A. Romano (eds), *Russia in the Age of Wars, 1914–1945* (Milan, 2000).
19. On the impact of 'total war' in an 'age of catastrophe', see E. Hobsbawm, *Age of Extremes: The Short Twentieth Century, 1914–1991* (London, 1994).
20. P. Holquist, '"Information is the Alpha and Omega of Our Work": Bolshevik Surveillance in its Pan-European Context', *Journal of Modern History*, vol. 69 (1997), pp. 415–50.
21. van Ree, *The Political Thought of Joseph Stalin*; see also C. Read, *The Making and Breaking of the Soviet System* (Basingstoke, 2001).
22. Lih et al. (eds), *Stalin's Letters*, p. 36.
23. See M. Lewin, 'Stalin in the Mirror of the Other', in Kershaw and Lewin (eds), *Stalinism and Nazism*, pp. 120–5.
24. This is essentially the interpretation of the new book by Rayfield, *Stalin and his Hangmen*; see also A. Antonov-Ovseyenko, *The Time of Stalin: Portrait of a Tyranny* (New York, 1983).
25. The 'bureaucratic mediocrity' assessment is forcibly espoused in L. Trotsky, *Stalin*, 2 vols (London, 1969). For Sukhanov's 'grey blur' reference, see R. Conquest, *Stalin: Breaker of Nations* (London, 1993), pp. 60–1. For the 'weak dictator' debates, see J. Harris, 'Was Stalin a Weak Dictator?', *Journal of Modern History*, vol. 75 (2003), pp. 375–86.
26. Sebag Montefiore, *Stalin*, pp. 3–4.
27. Service, *Stalin*, pp. 3–12.
28. Overy, *The Dictators*, pp. 5–13, quote at p. 13.
29. N. M. Naimark, 'Cold War Studies and New Archival Materials on Stalin', *Russian Review*, vol. 61 (2002), pp. 1–15.
30. F. Chuev, *Tak govoril Kaganovich* (Moscow, 1992), p. 154.
31. For details, see Rieber, 'Stalin, Man of the Borderlands', pp. 1661–3. The assassination of Stalin's close associate, Sergei Kirov, in December 1934 only compounded matters.

Chapter 1: Revolutionary

1. Archival records have been discovered that indicate that Stalin was born over a year earlier than his 'official' birth date, 21 December 1879. See E. Radzinsky, *Stalin* (London, 1997), pp. 11–12; M. Kun, *Stalin. An*

Unknown Portrait (Budapest, 2003), pp. 8–10; and D. Rayfield, *Stalin and his Hangmen: An Authoritative Portrait of a Tyrant and Those Who Served Him* (London, 2004), pp. 4–5. However, another document clearly shows December 1879 as his date of birth. See Kun, *Stalin*, p. 60 and A. J. Rieber, 'Stalin, Man of the Borderlands', *American Historical Review*, vol. 106 (2001), p. 1659.

2. I have based the following account of Stalin's formative years in Georgia on these sources: R. H. McNeal, *Stalin: Man and Ruler* (Basingstoke, 1988); R. C. Tucker, *Stalin as Revolutionary, 1879–1929: A Study in History and Personality* (New York, 1974); P. Pomper, *Lenin, Trotsky, and Stalin: The Intelligentsia and Power* (New York, 1990); I. Deutscher, *Stalin: A Political Biography*, revised edn (Harmondsworth, 1976); Kun, *Stalin*; R. Conquest, *Stalin: Breaker of Nations* (London, 1993); Rayfield, *Stalin and his Hangmen*; E. E. Smith, *The Young Stalin: The Early Years of an Elusive Revolutionary* (London, 1968). The most detailed Russian source is now A. V. Ostrovskii, *Kto stoial za spinoi Stalina?* (St. Petersburg, 2002).

3. S. Beria, *Beria: My Father. Inside Stalin's Kremlin* (London, 2001), p. 143; Rayfield, *Stalin and his Hangmen*, p. 20.

4. These were Stalin's words given in an interview with Emil Ludwig in December 1931. See J. V. Stalin, *Works*, vol. 13 (Moscow, 1955), pp. 115–16.

5. Pomper, *Lenin, Trotsky, and Stalin*, p. 154.

6. The most recent study of Lenin and his ideas is C. Read, *Lenin: A Revolutionary Life* (London, 2005). *What is to be Done?* is analysed in detail on pp. 52–9.

7. Cited in Kun, *Stalin*, p. 54.

8. J. V. Stalin, *Works*, vol. 2 (Moscow, 1953), p. 52.

9. Cited in Tucker, *Stalin as Revolutionary*, p. 140.

10. R. Brackman, *The Secret File of Joseph Stalin: A Hidden Life* (London, 2001).

11. Kun, *Stalin*, pp. 74–84, quote at p. 75 (emphasis in the original).

12. These words, attributed to Stalin by one of his friends Iosif Iremashvili, are cited in Pomper, *Lenin, Trotsky, and Stalin*, p. 171. A photo of Ekaterina's funeral shows a distraught Stalin. See Kun, *Stalin*, p. 407.

13. The first, third and fourth quotations are cited from E. van Ree, 'Stalin's Bolshevism: The First Decade', *International Review of Social History*, vol. 39 (1994), pp. 368–9. The second is from J. V. Stalin, *Works*, vol. 1 (Moscow, 1952), p. 78 (emphasis in the original).

14. E. van Ree, *The Political Thought of Joseph Stalin: A Study in Twentieth-Century Revolutionary Patriotism* (London, 2002), pp. 5–6.

15. Tucker, *Stalin as Revolutionary*, pp. 115–21.

16. Rieber, 'Stalin, Man of the Borderlands', pp. 1651–91, quote from p. 1690; see also A. J. Rieber, 'Stalin as Georgian: the formative years' in S. Davies and J. Harris (eds), *Stalin: A New History* (forthcoming: Cambridge, 2005); and A. J. Rieber, 'The Marginality of Totalitarianism', in Lord Dahrendorf et al. (eds), *The Paradoxes of Unintended Consequences* (Budapest, 2000), pp. 265–84.

17. This paragraph is based on R. G. Suny, 'Beyond Psychohistory: The Young Stalin in Georgia', *Slavic Review*, vol. 50 (1991), pp. 48–58 and R. G. Suny, 'A Journeyman for the Revolution: Stalin and the Labour Movement in Baku, June 1907–May 1908', *Soviet Studies*, vol. 23 (1971–2), pp. 373–94.

18. J. V. Stalin, *Works*, vol. 8 (Moscow, 1954), p. 183.

19. Deutscher, *Stalin*, p. 111. Stalin's first published article in Russian appeared in 1907. He never published in Georgian after this time.

20. Rieber, 'Stalin, Man of the Borderlands', p. 1677.

21. Tucker, *Stalin as Revolutionary*, pp. 197–8 and 133–7.

22 Stalin, *Works*, vol. 1, pp. 96–132.

23. J. V. Stalin, *Works*, vol. 6 (Moscow, 1953), p. 56.

24. Cited from archival sources in van Ree, 'Stalin's Bolshevism', pp. 375 and 379.

25. Tucker, *Stalin as Revolutionary*, p. 150.

26. V. I. Lenin, *Collected Works*, 4th edn, vol. 35 (Moscow, 1966), p. 84.

27. Stalin, *Works*, vol. 2, pp. 300–81, quotations on pp. 307 and 375 (emphasis in the original).

28. V. I. Lenin, *Polnoe sobranie sochinenii*, 5th edn, vol. 49 (Moscow, 1964), p. 161.

29. R. M. Slusser, *Stalin in October: The Man who Missed the Revolution* (Baltimore, 1987).

30. E. van Ree, 'Stalin's Bolshevism: The Year of the Revolution', *Revolutionary Russia*, vol. 13 (2000), pp. 29–54.

31. For Stalin's activities in 1917 I have relied on McNeal, *Stalin*, pp. 27–40, and Tucker, *Stalin as Revolutionary*, pp. 163–80.

32. Tucker, *Stalin as Revolutionary*, pp. 178–9 and 182–3.

33. For more detailed discussions of the highly complex nationality issue, see J. Smith, *The Bolsheviks and the National Question, 1917–1923* (Basingstoke, 1999); T. Martin, *The Affirmative Action Empire: Nations and Nationalism in the Soviet Union, 1923–1939* (Ithaca, 2001); R. G. Suny, *The Revenge of the Past: Nationalism, Revolution, and the Collapse of the Soviet Union* (Stanford, 1993); and Rieber, 'Stalin, Man of the Borderlands'.

34. J. V. Stalin, *Works*, vol. 4 (Moscow, 1953), pp. 77 and 372.

35. *The Bolsheviks and the October Revolution: Central Committee Minutes of the Russian Social–Democratic Labour Party (bolsheviks) August 1917–February 1918* (London, 1974), p. 177.
36. M. Lewin, 'Stalin in the Mirror of the Other' in M. Lewin, *Russia/ USSR/Russia: The Drive and Drift of a Superstate* (New York, 1995), p. 214. For a fine collection of essays on the Civil War, see D. P. Koenker, W. G. Rosenberg and R. G. Suny (eds), *Party, State, and Society in the Russian Civil War: Explorations in Social History* (Bloomington, 1989). It should be noted that the Bolsheviks took the name 'Russian Communist Party (Bolsheviks)' in March 1918. In the same month the seat of government and capital moved from Petrograd to Moscow.
37. S. Alliluyeva, *Twenty Letters to a Friend* (London, 1967) and *Only One Year* (London, 1969).
38. For details of Stalin and Allilueva's unsettled relationship and Nadezhda's suicide, see S. Sebag Montefiore, *Stalin: The Court of the Red Tsar* (London, 2003), pp. 1–90.
39. 'Dnevnik Marii Anisimovny Svanidze' in Iu. G. Murin (ed.), *Iosif Stalin v obiatiiakh semi: Iz lichnogo arkhiva* (Moscow, 1993), p. 177.
40. R. Richardson, *The Long Shadow: Inside Stalin's Family* (London, 1993), pp. 129–30.
41. Stalin, *Works*, vol. 4, pp. 130 and 271.
42. Conquest, *Stalin*, pp. 81 and 85.
43. McNeal, *Stalin*, pp. 55–8.
44. Tucker, *Stalin as Revolutionary*, p. 206.
45. McNeal, *Stalin*, pp. 50 and 63.
46. T. H. Rigby, *Political Elites in the USSR: Central Leaders and Local Cadres from Lenin to Gorbachev* (Aldershot, 1990), p. 127; see also, T. H. Rigby, 'Early Provincial Cliques and the Rise of Stalin', *Soviet Studies*, vol. 33 (1981), pp. 3–28; and A. Graziosi, 'G. L. Piatakov: A Mirror of Soviet History', *Harvard Ukrainian Studies*, vol. 16 (1992), pp. 127–32.

Chapter 2: Oligarch

1. L. Lih et al. (eds), *Stalin's Letters to Molotov, 1925–1936* (New Haven and London, 1995); V. Vilkova, *The Struggle for Power: Russia in 1923* (Amherst, 1996); A. V. Kvashonkin et al. (eds), *Bolshevistskoe rukovodstvo. Perepiska, 1912–1927* (Moscow, 1996); A. V. Kvashonkin et al. (eds), *Sovetskoe rukovodstvo. Perepiska, 1928–1941* (Moscow, 1999).

2. For a fine collection of essays on the NEP period, see S. Fitzpatrick, A. Rabinowitch and R. Stites (eds), *Russia in the Era of NEP: Explorations in Soviet Society and Culture* (Bloomington, 1991).

3. R. Service, *Stalin: A Biography* (London, 2004), pp. 189–90; also A. Ulam, *Stalin: The Man and his Era* (London, 1974), pp. 207–9.

4. Founded in March 1919, the Communist International (Comintern) was originally designed by its Bolshevik creators to foment worldwide socialist revolution.

5. R. H. McNeal, *Stalin: Man and Ruler* (London, 1989), p. 82.

6. E. G. Gimpel'son, *Novaia ekonomicheskaia politika Lenina i Stalina. Problemy i uroki (1920-e gody XX veka)* (Moscow, 2004), p. 78.

7. G. Gill, *The Origins of the Stalinist Political System* (Cambridge, 1990), pp. 140–3, 158, 162, 166–7 and 174. A similar interpretation can be found in O. G. Nazarov, *Stalin i bor'ba za liderstvo v bol'shevistskoi partii v usloviiakh Nepa* (Moscow, 2000), pp. 196–8.

8. J. Harris, 'Stalin as General Secretary: the appointments process and the nature of Stalin's power', in S. Davies and J. Harris (eds), *Stalin: A New History* (forthcoming: Cambridge, 2005).

9. Gill, *Origins*, p. 167.

10. For details, see J. Smith, *The Bolsheviks and the National Question, 1917–1923* (Basingstoke, 1998), pp. 172–212. For other examples of Stalin's critical attitude towards Lenin in late 1922, see A. Iu. Vatlin, 'Iosif Stalin na puti k absoliutnoi vlasti: novye dokumenty iz moskovskikh arkhivov' (unpublished ms), pp. 5–6.

11. See M. Lewin, *Lenin's Last Struggle* (London, 1973) and more emphatically M. Lewin, *The Soviet Century* (London, 2005), pp. 14–31 and 145.

12. V. I. Lenin, *Collected Works*, 4th edn, vol. 36 (Moscow, 1966), pp. 594–6; see also Y. Buranov, *Lenin's Will: Falsified and Forbidden* (New York, 1994).

13. This is confirmed by Stalin's correspondence with his co-factionalists. See Lih et al. (eds), *Stalin's Letters to Molotov*; and Kvashonkin et al. (eds), *Bolshevistskoe rukovodstvo*.

14. Vatlin, 'Iosif Stalin', p. 6.

15. See E. van Ree, 'Stalin's Organic Theory of the Party', *Russian Review*, vol. 52 (1993), pp. 43–57; also Nazarov, *Stalin i bor'ba za liderstvo*, p. 196.

16. Paraphrased from Stalin's archival files in Harris, 'Stalin as General Secretary' (forthcoming).

17. Cited in E. H. Carr, *Socialism in One Country, 1924–1926*, vol. 1 (Harmondsworth, 1970), p. 191.

18. Lih et al. (eds), *Stalin's Letters to Molotov*, p. 26.

19. The classic account is R. V. Daniels, *The Conscience of the Revolution: Communist Opposition in Soviet Russia* (New York, 1969).

20. This summary of Trotsky's critique and failings is based on I. D. Thatcher, *Trotsky* (London, 2003), pp. 124–6.

21. Lih et al. (eds), *Stalin's Letters to Molotov*, p. 5.

22. Cited from the German Foreign Ministry archive by M. Reiman, *The Birth of Stalinism: The USSR on the Eve of the 'Second Revolution'* (London, 1987), p. 35. To the best of my knowledge, this document has not been published in Russian.

23. *Izvestiia TsK KPSS*, no. 4 (1991), p. 198.

24. Lih et al. (eds), *Stalin's Letters to Molotov*, pp. 24–7 and 115–17.

25. RGASPI, f. 17, op. 85, del. 505, l. 29. We know that Stalin sometimes read these letters, or at least summaries of them, because on occasion he would write 'To the Archive' on them. A few letters were even passed on to the secret police because of their 'anti-Soviet character'.

26. Cited in Daniels, *The Conscience of the Revolution*, p. 316.

27. For a detailed analysis of the Stalin-Bukharin struggles, see S. F. Cohen, *Bukharin and the Bolshevik Revolution: A Political Biography, 1888–1938* (New York, 1975), pp. 270–336; also Reiman, *The Birth of Stalinism*, pp. 85–101.

28. R. V. Daniels (ed.), *A Documentary History of Communism*, vol. 1 (London, 1987), p. 207; and Cohen, *Bukharin and the Bolshevik Revolution*, p. 291.

29. A. Iu. Vatlin, 'Goriachaia osen' dvadtsat' vos'mogo. (K voprosu o stalin-izatsii Kominterna)', in A. V. Afanas'ev (ed.), *Oni ne molchali* (Moscow, 1991), p. 103.

30. N. I. Bukharin, *Problemy teorii i praktiki sotsializma* (Moscow, 1989), pp. 298–9 (emphasis in the original).

31. The following section is based on K. McDermott and J. Agnew, *The Comintern: A History of International Communism from Lenin to Stalin* (Basingstoke, 1996), pp. 68–90.

32. RGASPI, f. 495, op. 6, d. 8, l. 20.

33. Gill, *Origins*, p. 135.

34. *International Press Correspondence*, vol. 8 (13 August 1928), p. 874 (emphasis in the original).

35. A. Nove, *An Economic History of the USSR, 1917–1991*, 3rd edn (London, 1992), p. 62.

36. R. G. Suny, *The Soviet Experiment: Russia, the USSR, and the Successor States* (New York, 1998), p. 151.

37. R. Himmer, 'The Transition from War Communism to the New Economic Policy: An Analysis of Stalin's Views', *Russian Review*, vol. 53 (1994), pp. 515–29, quotation on p. 517.

38. The section on NEP debates, including quotations, is based on Nove, *An Economic History of the USSR*, pp. 118–26.

39. J. V. Stalin, *Works*, vol. 6 (Moscow, 1953), pp. 386–7 and 391.

40. Cited in R. C. Tucker, *Stalin as Revolutionary, 1879–1929: A Study in History and Personality* (New York, 1974), p. 384 (emphasis in the original).

41. See E. van Ree, *The Political Thought of Joseph Stalin: A Study in Twentieth-Century Revolutionary Patriotism* (London, 2002), pp. 92–3.

42. See L. H. Siegelbaum, *Soviet State and Society between Revolutions, 1918–1929* (Cambridge, 1992), p. 181; and J. Hatch, 'The "Lenin Levy" and the Social Origins of Stalinism: Workers and the Communist Party in Moscow, 1921–1928', *Slavic Review*, vol. 48 (1989), pp. 558–77.

43. C. Ward, *Stalin's Russia*, 2nd edn (London, 1999), p. 36.

44. R. K. Balandin and S. Mironov, *Zagovory i bor'ba za vlast' ot Lenina do Khrushcheva* (Moscow, 2003), p. 116.

45. J. V. Stalin, *Works*, vol. 7 (Moscow, 1954), pp. 267–8.

46. For examples of Stalin's use of the chilling term *otsechenie*, see F. I. Firsov, 'Stalin i Komintern' (part 1), *Voprosy istorii*, no. 8 (1989), p. 10.

47. The following discussion is based on the excellent critique of the historiographical debates in Ward, *Stalin's Russia*, pp. 18–37.

48. For fascinating pen portraits of Trotsky, Zinoviev, Kamenev, Bukharin and Stalin, see Carr, *Socialism in One Country*, vol. 1, pp. 151–202.

49. See C. Merridale, 'The Making of a Moderate Bolshevik: an Introduction to L. B. Kamenev's Political Biography' in J. Cooper, M. Perrie and E. A. Rees (eds), *Soviet History, 1917–53: Essays in Honour of R. W. Davies* (Basingstoke, 1995), pp. 22–41.

50. The major study remains Cohen, *Bukharin and the Bolshevik Revolution*.

51. However, in the same speech in April 1924 Trotsky asserted that 'even the Party itself can make occasional mistakes.' Cited in R. V. Daniels, *Trotsky, Stalin, and Socialism*, (Boulder, 1991), p. 101.

52. L. Trotsky, *Stalin: An Appraisal of the Man and his Influence*, vol. 2 (London, 1969), p. 215.

53. Ward, *Stalin's Russia*, p. 25. In this quotation Ward is summarising the views of other scholars.

54. Ward, *Stalin's Russia*, pp. 36–7.

Chapter 3: Moderniser

1. J. Stalin, *Problems of Leninism* (Moscow, 1953), p. 458.

2. These conclusions are based on J. Hughes, *Stalin, Siberia and the Crisis of the New Economic Policy* (Cambridge, 1991), pp. 3–4.

3. Stalin, *Problems of Leninism*, pp. 414–18.

4. For a vivid and moving account of one urban Bolshevik 'collectiviser', see L. Kopelev, *The Education of a True Believer* (London, 1981).

5. Hughes, *Stalin, Siberia*, p. 211.

6. A. Romano, 'Permanent War Scare: Mobilisation, Militarisation and the Peasant War', in S. Pons and A. Romano (eds), *Russia in the Age of Wars, 1914–1945* (Milan, 2000), pp. 103–19.

7. Stalin's letter, admittedly from a later period (May 1933), to the famous author Mikhail Sholokhov reveals his thinking about the 'war of starvation' directed by the 'esteemed grain growers' against Soviet power. See D. P. Koenker and R. D. Bachman (eds), *Revelations from the Russian Archives. Documents in English Translation* (Washington D. C., 1997), pp. 397–8.

8. Stalin, *Problems of Leninism*, pp. 419–25.

9. For details on the implementation of collectivisation and 'dekulakisation', see R. W. Davies, *The Socialist Offensive: The Collectivisation of Soviet Agriculture, 1929–1930* (London, 1980) and L. Viola, *The Best Sons of the Fatherland: Workers in the Vanguard of Soviet Collectivization* (New York, 1987).

10. These statistics are taken from Romano, 'Permanent War Scare', pp. 108–9.

11. These figures are taken from L. Viola, *Peasant Rebels under Stalin: Collectivization and the Culture of Peasant Resistance* (New York, 1996), pp. 135–40 and Romano, 'Permanent War Scare', p. 109. S. Fitzpatrick, *Stalin's Peasants: Resistance and Survival in the Russian Village after Collectivization* (New York, 1994) suggests peasant resistance was less serious.

12. R. W. Davies, *Soviet Economic Development from Lenin to Khrushchev* (Cambridge, 1998), p. 45.

13. R. Conquest, *The Harvest of Sorrow: Soviet Collectivisation and the Terror-Famine*, reprint edn (London, 2002), pp. vii, 3–7, 217–24, 301–3 and 328–30. This volume was first published in 1986.

14. In a letter to Kaganovich and Molotov dated 18 June 1932 reproduced in R. W. Davies et al. (eds), *The Stalin-Kaganovich Correspondence, 1931–36* (New Haven and London, 2003), p. 138.

15. R. W. Davies and S. G. Wheatcroft, *The Years of Hunger: Soviet Agriculture, 1931–1933* (Basingstoke, 2004), pp. xiv, 182–5, 412–5 and 441. For a survivor's graphic description of the horrors of the famine, see M. Dolot, *Execution by Hunger: The Hidden Holocaust* (New York, 1985).

16. C. Ward, *Stalin's Russia*, 2nd edn (London, 1999), p. 102.

17. For numerous examples, see Davies et al. (eds), *The Stalin-Kaganovich Correspondence.*

18. RGASPI, f. 17, op. 163, d. 828, l. 29.

19. RGASPI, f. 17, op. 162, d. 11, l. 46.

20. Stalin, *Problems of Leninism*, pp. 455–6.

21. Davies, *Soviet Economic Development*, pp. 43–59 and 82. See also R. W. Davies, M. Harrison and S. G. Wheatcroft (eds), *The Economic Transformation of the Soviet Union, 1913–1945* (Cambridge, 1994); and V. Andrle, *A Social History of Twentieth-Century Russia* (London, 1994).

22. For a detailed account of the construction of Magnitogorsk, see S. Kotkin, *Magnetic Mountain: Stalinism as a Civilization* (Berkeley, 1995).

23. W. Z. Goldman, *Women at the Gates: Gender and Industry in Stalin's Russia* (Cambridge, 2002), p. 269; also M. Ilič, *Women Workers in the Soviet Interwar Economy: From 'Protection' to 'Equality'* (Basingstoke, 1999); and G. W. Lapidus, *Women in Soviet Society: Equality, Development, and Social Change* (Berkeley, 1978).

24. For fascinating insights into Stalin's advocacy of the consumer, food and luxury goods industries, see J. Gronow, *Caviar with Champagne: Common Luxury and the Ideals of the Good Life in Stalin's Russia* (Oxford, 2003). The quotation is in Stalin, *Problems of Leninism*, p. 670.

25. Stalin, *Problems of Leninism*, pp. 617–18.

26. On '*Homo Sovieticus*' the survivor, see S. Fitzpatrick, *Everyday Stalinism. Ordinary Life in Extraordinary Times: Soviet Russia in the 1930s* (New York, 1999), pp. 1–3, 226–7.

27. L. Trotsky, *The Revolution Betrayed* (New York, 1970).

28. S. Fitzpatrick, *The Russian Revolution*, 2nd edn (Oxford, 1994), p. 141.

29. Cited in E. van Ree, *The Political Thought of Joseph Stalin: A Study in Twentieth-Century Revolutionary Patriotism* (London, 2002), p. 174.

30. On the *vydvizhentsy*, see S. Fitzpatrick, *The Cultural Front: Power and Culture in Revolutionary Russia* (Ithaca, 1992), pp. 149–82.

31. N. S. Timasheff, *The Great Retreat: The Growth and Decline of Communism in Russia*, reprint edn (New York, 1972 [first edn 1946]).

32. Stalin, *Problems of Leninism*, pp. 459–82.

33. van Ree, *The Political Thought of Joseph Stalin*, p. 171.

34. D. L. Hoffmann, *Stalinist Values: The Cultural Norms of Soviet Modernity, 1917–1941* (Ithaca, 2003), pp. 3–4 and 7–10.

35. J. Stalin, *Marxism and the National and Colonial Question* (London, 1941), p. 210. Stalin later changed 'proletarian' to 'socialist'.

36. R. G. Suny, *The Revenge of the Past: Nationalism, Revolution, and the Collapse of the Soviet Union* (Stanford, 1993), pp. 102–6; for a massively detailed

account, see T. Martin, *The Affirmative Action Empire: Nations and Nationalism in the Soviet Union, 1923–1939* (Ithaca, 2001).

37. Davies et al. (eds), *The Stalin-Kaganovich Correspondence*, p. 180 (emphasis in the original).

38. T. Martin, 'An Affirmative Action Empire: The Soviet Union as the Highest Form of Imperialism', in R. G. Suny and T. Martin (eds), *A State of Nations: Empire and Nation-Making in the Age of Lenin and Stalin* (New York, 2001), pp. 67–90.

39. For the diverse response of the Soviet people to Stalinist propaganda, see S. Davies, *Popular Opinion in Stalin's Russia: Terror, Propaganda and Dissent, 1934–1941* (Cambridge, 1997).

40. E. A. Rees, 'Stalin and Russian Nationalism', in G. Hosking and R. Service (eds), *Russian Nationalism Past and Present* (Basingstoke, 1998), pp. 102–3; for a slightly different interpretation which emphasises Stalin's 'russocentrism', see D. Brandenberger, *National Bolshevism: Stalinist Mass Culture and the Formation of Modern Russian National Identity, 1931–1956* (Cambridge: MA, 2002).

41. D. L. Hoffmann, 'European Modernity and Soviet Socialism', in D. L. Hoffmann and Y. Kotsonis (eds), *Russian Modernity: Politics, Knowledge, Practices* (Basingstoke, 2000), pp. 245–60, quotation on p. 245.

42. T. Martin, 'Modernization or Neo-traditionalism? Ascribed Nationality and Soviet Primordialism', in Hoffmann and Kotsonis (eds), *Russian Modernity*, pp. 161–82, quotations on pp. 175–6.

43. R. Service, *Stalin: A Biography* (London, 2004), p. 309.

44. D. L. Hoffmann (ed.), *Stalinism* (Oxford, 2003), p. 109.

45. For a detailed analysis of the *Lady Macbeth* affair, see Fitzpatrick, *The Cultural Front*, pp. 183–215.

46. E. Hobsbawm and T. Ranger (eds), *The Invention of Tradition* (Cambridge, 1983).

Chapter 4: Dictator

1. Cited from A. G. Latyshev, 'Riadom so Stalinym', *Sovershenno sekretno*, no. 12 (1990), p. 19. A slightly different translation is available in I. Banac (ed.), *The Diary of Georgi Dimitrov, 1933–1949* (New Haven and London, 2003), p. 65.

2. This reading of developments is inspired by L. Viola, 'Introduction', in L. Viola (ed.), *Contending with Stalinism: Soviet Power and Popular Resistance in the 1930s* (Ithaca, 2002), pp. 1–16.

3. For details, see O. Khlevniuk, *In Stalin's Shadow: The Career of 'Sergo' Ordzhonikidze* (Armonk, 1995); and A. Graziosi, 'G. L. Piatakov: A Mirror of Soviet History', *Harvard Ukrainian Studies*, vol. 16 (1992), pp. 132–3. For Molotov on Kaganovich, see *Sto sorok besed s Molotovym: Iz dnevnika F. Chueva* (Moscow, 1991), p. 319.

4. R. W. Davies, M. Ilič and O. Khlevnyuk, 'The Politburo and Economic Policy-making', in E. A. Rees (ed.), *The Nature of Stalin's Dictatorship: The Politburo, 1924–1953* (Basingstoke, 2004), p. 109.

5. Calculated from S. G Wheatcroft, 'From Team-Stalin to Degenerate Tyranny', in Rees (ed.), *The Nature*, p. 84.

6. Davies, Ilič and Khlevnyuk, 'The Politburo', pp. 108–31, quotations on pp. 110 and 121.

7. R. W. Davies, O. V. Khlevniuk and E. A. Rees (eds), *The Stalin-Kaganovich Correspondence, 1931–36* (New Haven and London, 2003), p. 15.

8. Davies, Ilič and Khlevnyuk, 'The Politburo', p. 110.

9. RGASPI, f. 81, op. 3, d. 100, l. 7.

10. For details, see J. Howlett, O. Khlevniuk, L. Kosheleva and L. Rogovaia, *The CPSU's Top Bodies under Stalin: Their Operational Records and Structure of Command* (Toronto, 1996).

11. See N. E. Rosenfeldt, 'The Importance of the Secret Apparatus of the Soviet Communist Party during the Stalin Era', in N. E. Rosenfeldt, B. Jensen and E. Kulavig (eds), *Mechanisms of Power in the Soviet Union* (Basingstoke, 2000), pp. 40–70 quotation on p. 61; and N. E. Rosenfeldt, *Knowledge and Power: The Role of Stalin's Secret Chancellery in the Soviet System of Government* (Copenhagen, 1978).

12. Wheatcroft, 'From Team-Stalin', pp. 79–107, quotation on p. 90.

13. T. H. Rigby, 'Was Stalin a Disloyal Patron?', *Soviet Studies*, vol. 38 (1986), pp. 311–24.

14. Wheatcroft, 'From Team-Stalin', p. 104. A similar interpretation can be found in J. Arch Getty, 'Stalin as Prime Minister: power and the Politburo', in S. Davies and J. Harris (eds), *Stalin: A New History* (forthcoming: Cambridge, 2005).

15. In the years 1931–6 Stalin regularly took two to three month 'holidays', in itself a remarkable fact. For the dates of these vacations, see Davies et al. (eds), *Stalin-Kaganovich*, pp. 37, 104, 186, 236, 289 and 316; see also L. Lih, O. Naumov and O. Khlevniuk (eds), *Stalin's Letters to Molotov, 1925–1936* (New Haven and London, 1995).

16. K. Simonov, *Glazami cheloveka moego pokoleniia: Razmyshleniia o I. V. Staline* (Moscow, 1990), pp. 378–9.

17. See E. van Ree, *The Political Thought of Joseph Stalin: A Study in Twentieth-Century Revolutionary Patriotism* (London, 2002), pp. 114–25.

18. F. I. Firsov, 'Stalin i Komintern' (part 1), *Voprosy istorii*, no. 8 (1989), p. 10.
19. Lih et al. (eds), *Stalin's Letters to Molotov*, p. 200.
20. RGASPI, f. 81, op. 3, d. 99, ll. 109, 111 and 122 (emphasis in the original). For details on 'economic crimes' in the Soviet countryside and urban areas, see O. V. Khlevniuk, *Politbiuro. Mekhanizmy politicheskoi vlasti v 1930-e gody* (Moscow, 1996), pp. 56–8.
21. RGASPI, f. 17, op. 2, d. 354, ch. 2, ll. 42–3.
22. RGASPI, f. 81, op. 3, d. 100, l. 158.
23. Lih et al. (eds), *Stalin's Letters to Molotov*, p. 210.
24. RGASPI, f. 81, op. 3, d. 99, l. 16.
25. RGASPI, f. 81, op. 3, d. 99, ll. 35–6 (emphasis in the original).
26. Rukhimovich was expelled from the Central Committee and arrested as an 'enemy of the people' following a resolution at the CC plenum in December 1937. See D. Volkogonov, *Stalin: Triumph and Tragedy* (London, 1991), p. 309.
27. RGASPI, f. 81, op. 3, d. 99, ll. 42–3.
28. Cited in O. V. Khlevniuk, *1937-i: Stalin, NKVD i sovetskoe obshchestvo* (Moscow, 1992), p. 77.
29. R. C. Tucker, *Stalin in Power: The Revolution from Above, 1928–1941* (New York, 1990), p. 444.
30. The fierce polemics engendered by the totalitarian-revisionist controversy can be found in S. Fitzpatrick, 'New Perspectives on Stalinism', *Russian Review*, vol. 45 (1986), pp. 357–73, the discussions that followed at pp. 375–413, and in *Russian Review*, vol. 46 (1987), pp. 375–431.
31. The classical work on Stalinist terror from the totalitarian perspective is R. Conquest, *The Great Terror: Stalin's Purges of the Thirties* (Harmondsworth, 1971), up-dated as *The Great Terror: A Reassessment* (London, 1990). Other important works that stress Stalin's dominant role in the Terror are R. A. Medvedev, *Let History Judge: The Origins and Consequences of Stalinism*, 2nd edn (Oxford, 1989); Tucker, *Stalin in Power*; and R. Service, *Stalin: A Biography* (London, 2004). The prime examples of 'revisionist' work are J. Arch Getty, *Origins of the Great Purges: The Soviet Communist Party Reconsidered, 1933–1938* (Cambridge, 1985); G. T. Rittersporn, *Stalinist Simplifications and Soviet Complications: Social Tensions and Political Conflicts in the USSR, 1933–1953* (Chur, 1991); J. Arch Getty and R. A. Manning (eds), *Stalinist Terror: New Perspectives* (Cambridge, 1993); and R. W. Thurston, *Life and Terror in Stalin's Russia, 1934–1941* (New Haven and London, 1996).
32. For details, see *Reabilitatsiia. Politicheskie protsessy 30–50-kh godov* (Moscow, 1991).

33. For details, see *Trud*, 4 June 1992; *Moskovskie novosti*, no. 25, 21 June 1992; J. A. Getty and O. V. Naumov, *The Road to Terror: Stalin and the Self-Destruction of the Bolsheviks, 1932–1939* (New Haven and London, 1999), pp. 444–51 and 454–62; O. Suvenirov, *Tragediia RKKA 1937–1938* (Moscow, 1998); O. V. Khlevniuk, *The History of the Gulag: From Collectivization to the Great Terror* (New Haven and London, 2004), pp. 190–1; and also the startling telegram correspondence between A. A. Andreev, Secretary of the Central Committee, and Stalin in RGASPI, f. 73, op. 2, d. 19 and d. 20, some of which is published in A. V. Kvashonkin et al. (eds), *Sovetskoe rukovodstvo. Perepiska, 1928–1941* (Moscow, 1999), pp. 364–7, 371–5, 377–80, 383–9, 393–7. A particularly rich collection of documents can be found in V. N. Khaustov, V. P. Naumov and N. S. Plotnikova (eds), *Lubianka. Stalin i glavnoe upravlenie gosbezopastnosti NKVD 1937–1938* (Moscow, 2004).

34. Cited in R. W. Davies, *Soviet History in the Gorbachev Revolution* (Basingstoke, 1989), p. 67.

35. Getty and Naumov, *The Road to Terror*, pp. xiii and 451; see also J. A. Getty, 'Afraid of Their Shadows: The Bolshevik Recourse to Terror, 1932–1938', in M. Hildermeier with E. Müller-Luckner (eds), *Stalinismus vor dem Zweiten Weltkrieg: Neue Wege der Forschung* (Munich, 1998), pp. 169–91; and J. A. Getty, '"Excesses are not permitted": Mass Terror and Stalinist Governance in the Late 1930s', *Russian Review*, vol. 61 (2002), pp. 113–38.

36. This is the interpretation of the Russian expert, Oleg Khlevniuk, in his numerous works on the subject. See for example, 'The Objectives of the Great Terror, 1937–1938', in J. Cooper, M. Perrie and E. A. Rees (eds), *Soviet History, 1917–1953: Essays in Honour of R. W. Davies* (Basingstoke, 1995), pp. 158–76.

37. M. Ellman, 'The Soviet 1937 Provincial Show Trials: Carnival or Terror?', *Europe-Asia Studies*, vol. 53 (2001), p. 1225.

38. D. J. Nordlander, review of Getty and Naumov, *The Road to Terror* in *Europe-Asia Studies*, vol. 52 (2000), pp. 769–71; see also E. A. Rees' review of the same volume, 'The Great Terror: Suicide or Murder?', *Russian Review*, vol. 59 (2000), pp. 446–50.

39. P. M. Hagenloh, '"Socially Harmful Elements" and the Great Terror', in S. Fitzpatrick (ed.), *Stalinism: New Directions* (London, 2000), pp. 286–308, quotation on pp. 286–7.

40. D. Shearer, 'Social Disorder, Mass Repression and the NKVD during the 1930s', in B. McLoughlin and K. McDermott (eds), *Stalin's Terror: High Politics and Mass Repression in the Soviet Union* (Basingstoke, 2003),

pp. 85–117; see also D. R. Shearer, 'Crime and Social Disorder in Stalin's Russia: A Reassessment of the Great Retreat and the Origins of Mass Repression', *Cahiers du Monde russe*, vol. 39 (1998), pp. 119–48.

41. A. Weiner, 'Nature and Nurture in a Socialist Utopia: Delineating the Soviet Socio-Ethnic Body in the Age of Socialism', in D. L. Hoffmann (ed.), *Stalinism* (Oxford, 2003), pp. 244–7.

42. For the English text of Order No. 00447, see Getty and Naumov, *The Road to Terror*, pp. 473–80.

43. M. Iunge (Junge) and R. Binner, *Kak terror stal 'bol'shim': Sekretnyi prikaz no. 00447 i tekhnologiia ego ispolneniia* (Moscow, 2003), p. 136.

44. These figures are taken from Iunge and Binner, *Kak terror stal 'bol'shim'*, p. 136. J. Arch Getty gives a total of 194,000 Gulag sentences. See his '"Excesses are not permitted"', p. 117.

45. The evolution of Stalinist national policies can be found in T. Martin, 'The Origins of Soviet Ethnic Cleansing', *Journal of Modern History*, vol. 70 (1998), pp. 813–61.

46. N. Petrov and A. Roginskii, 'The "Polish Operation" of the NKVD, 1937–8', in McLoughlin and McDermott (eds), *Stalin's Terror*, pp. 153–72; see also J. Morris, 'The Polish Terror: Spy Mania and Ethnic Cleansing in the Great Terror', *Europe-Asia Studies*, vol. 56 (2004), pp. 751–66.

47. W. J. Chase, *Enemies within the Gates?: The Comintern and the Stalinist Repression, 1934–1939* (New Haven and London, 2001); see also K. McDermott and J. Agnew, *The Comintern: A History of International Communism from Lenin to Stalin* (Basingstoke, 1996), pp. 142–57.

48. I am indebted to Barry McLoughlin for the idea of 'intentional' and 'functional' victims.

49. I. Kershaw and M. Lewin, 'The Regimes and Their Dictators: Perspectives of Comparison', in I. Kershaw and M. Lewin (eds), *Stalinism and Nazism: Dictatorships in Comparison* (Cambridge, 1997), p. 8.

50. I. Halfin, *Terror in My Soul: Communist Autobiographies on Trial* (Cambridge: MA, 2003), pp. 2–5. For a similar approach, see B. Studer, B. Unfried and I. Hermann (eds), *Parler de Soi sous Staline: La Construction identitaire dans le communisme des années trente* (Paris, 2002) and B. Studer and H. Haumann (eds), *Stalinistische Subjekte/Stalinist Subjects/Sujets staliniens: Individuum und System in der Sowjetunion und der Komintern, 1929–1953* (forthcoming, Zurich, 2005).

51. *The Land of Socialism Today and Tomorrow: Reports and Speeches at the Eighteenth Congress of the Communist Party of the Soviet Union* (Moscow, 1939), p. 41.

52. G. Gill, *The Origins of the Stalinist Political System* (Cambridge, 1990), p. 279.

53. See O. V. Khlevniuk, 'The Reasons for the "Great Terror": The Foreign-Political Aspect', in S. Pons and A. Romano (eds), *Russia in the Age of Wars, 1914–1945* (Milan, 2000), pp. 159–69.

54. A. Resis (ed.), *Molotov Remembers: Inside Kremlin Politics* (Chicago, 1993), p. 254.

55. *Voprosy istorii*, no. 2 (1994), p. 21 (my emphasis).

56. *Voprosy istorii*, no. 3 (1995), p. 6.

57. Cited in *Istoricheskii arkhiv*, no. 1 (1992), p. 119.

58. Rosenfeldt, 'The Importance of the Secret Apparatus', p. 43.

59. For this interpretation, see Getty and Naumov, *The Road to Terror*, pp. 468–9.

60. Interesting local and regional studies of the Terror include: S. Fitzpatrick, 'How the Mice Buried the Cat. Scenes from the Great Purges in the Russian Provinces', *Russian Review*, vol. 52 (1993), pp. 299–320; S. Kotkin, *Magnetic Mountain: Stalinism as a Civilization* (Berkeley, 1995), pp. 280–354; J. R. Harris, 'The Purging of Local Cliques in the Urals Region, 1936–7', in Fitzpatrick (ed.), *Stalinism*, pp. 262–85; and O. Hlevnjuk, 'Les mécanismes de la "Grande Terreur" des années 1937–1938 au Turkménistan', *Cahiers du Monde russe*, vol. 39 (1998), pp. 197–208.

61. See H. Hudson Jnr, *Blueprints and Blood: The Stalinization of Soviet Architecture, 1917–1937* (Princeton, 1994), pp. 147–65; S. Reid, 'Socialist Realism in the Stalinist Terror: The *Industry of Socialism* Art Exhibition, 1935–41', *Russian Review*, vol. 60 (2001), pp. 153–84; and C. Brooke, 'Soviet Musicians and the Great Terror', *Europe-Asia Studies*, vol. 54 (2002), pp. 397–413.

62. S. Davies, '"Us" against "Them": Social Identity in Soviet Russia, 1934–41', in Fitzpatrick (ed.), *Stalinism*, pp. 47–70.

63. See G. T. Rittersporn, 'The Omnipresent Conspiracy: On Soviet Imagery of Politics and Social Relations in the 1930s', in Getty and Manning (eds), *Stalinist Terror*, pp. 99–115.

64. See Thurston, *Life and Terror in Stalin's Russia*, pp. 199–226.

65. See B. McLoughlin, 'Mass Operations of the NKVD, 1937–8: A Survey', in McLoughlin and McDermott (eds), *Stalin's Terror*, pp. 118–52.

66. Figures are cited from 'O sud'be chlenov i kandidatov v chleny TsK VKP(b), izbrannogo XVII s''ezdom partii', *Izvestiia TsK KPSS*, no. 12 (1989), pp. 82–113; N. Werth, 'A State against Its People: Violence, Repression, and Terror in the Soviet Union', in S. Courtois et al. (eds),

The Black Book of Communism: Crimes, Terror, Repression (Cambridge: MA, 1999), p. 192; Getty and Naumov, *The Road to Terror*, pp. 590–1; and Khlevniuk, *The History of the Gulag*, pp. 288–90.

67. On conditions in the Gulag, see A. Applebaum, *Gulag. A History of the Soviet Labour Camps* (London, 2003).

68. Davies et al. (eds), *Stalin-Kaganovich*, p. xiii.

69. *Istochnik*, no. 3 (1994), p. 79.

70. M. Lewin, *Russia/USSR/Russia: The Drive and Drift of a Superstate* (New York, 1995), pp. 204–6.

71. See S. Davies, *Popular Opinion in Stalin's Russia: Terror, Propaganda and Dissent, 1934–1941* (Cambridge, 1997).

72. On strikes and workers' protest, see J. J. Rossman, 'The Teikovo Cotton Workers' Strike of April 1932: Class, Gender and Identity Politics in Stalin's Russia', *Russian Review*, vol. 56 (1997), pp. 44–69.

73. On banditry in Western Siberia and elsewhere, see Shearer, 'Crime and Social Disorder in Stalin's Russia'.

74. On gender non-conformity, see D. Healey, *Homosexual Desire in Revolutionary Russia: The Regulation of Sexual and Gender Dissent* (Chicago, 2001).

75. On the 'shadow economy', see E. A. Osokina, 'Economic Disobedience under Stalin', in Viola (ed.), *Contending with Stalinism*, pp. 170–200.

76. See S. Fitzpatrick, *Everyday Stalinism. Ordinary Life in Extraordinary Times: Soviet Russia in the 1930s* (Oxford, 1999).

77. Cited in S. Talbott (ed.), *Khrushchev Remembers* (Boston, 1971), p. 329.

78. Lewin, *Russia/USSR/Russia*, p. 90.

79. V. Volkov, 'The Concept of *Kul'turnost*': Notes on the Stalinist Civilizing Process', in Fitzpatrick (ed.), *Stalinism*, p. 211.

80. E. A. Rees, 'Leader Cults: Varieties, Preconditions and Functions' in B. Apor, J. C. Behrends, P. Jones and E. A. Rees (eds), *The Leader Cult in Communist Dictatorships: Stalin and the Eastern Bloc* (Basingstoke, 2004), p. 22.

81. D. L. Hoffmann, *Stalinist Values: The Cultural Norms of Soviet Modernity* (Ithaca, 2003), p. 156.

82. For a non-totalitarian perspective on Stalin's charisma, see J. Brooks, *Thank You, Comrade Stalin!: Soviet Public Culture from Revolution to Cold War* (Princeton, 2000), pp. 59–77.

83. Tucker, *Stalin in Power*, p. 3; see also R. C. Tucker, 'The Rise of Stalin's Personality Cult', *American Historical Review*, vol. 84 (1979), pp. 347–66.

84. RGASPI, f. 558, op. 1, d. 5324, l. 33. For other examples, see f. 558, op. 1, d. 3118, l. 1 and f. 558, op. 1, d. 4572, l. 1.

85. S. Davies, 'Stalin and the Making of the Leader Cult in the 1930s', in Apor et al. (eds), *The Leader Cult*, pp. 29–46. For a post-communist Russian interpretation of the cult, see L. Maksimenkov, 'Kul't. Zametki o slovakh-simvolakh v sovetskom politicheskom kul'ture', *Svobodnaia mysl'*, no. 11 (1993), pp. 26–43.
86. 'Dnevnik Marii Anisimovny Svanidze' in Iu. G. Murin (ed.), *Iosif Stalin v ob''iatiiakh sem'i: Iz lichnogo arkhiva* (Moscow, 1993), pp. 176–7.
87. See B. Ennker, 'The Stalin Cult, Bolshevik Rule and Kremlin Interaction in the 1930s', in Apor et al. (eds), *The Leader Cult*, pp. 83–101.
88. RGASPI, f. 667, op. 1, d. 17, ll. 5–6.
89. Davies, *Popular Opinion in Stalin's Russia*, p. 154.
90. Gill, *Origins*, p. 293.

Chapter 5: Warlord

1. Cited in D. Volkogonov, *Stalin: Triumph and Tragedy* (London, 1991), p. 410.
2. Figures from R. Overy, *The Dictators: Hitler's Germany and Stalin's Russia* (London, 2004), pp. 493 and 496. The statistics, as ever, are contested and it should be noted that other sources give lower figures.
3. S. Pons, 'The Papers on Foreign and International Policy in the Russian Archives: The Stalin Years', *Cahiers du Monde russe*, vol. 40 (1999), p. 245.
4. For a judicious assessment of Soviet foreign policy in the 1920s, see G. Gorodetsky, 'The Formulation of Soviet Foreign Policy: Ideology and *Realpolitik*' in G. Gorodetsky (ed.), *Soviet Foreign Policy, 1917–1991: A Retrospective* (London, 1994), pp. 30–44.
5. L. T. Lih et al. (eds), *Stalin's Letters to Molotov, 1925–1936* (New Haven and London, 1995), pp. 178 and 232 (emphasis in the original).
6. The classic account of Soviet foreign policy in this period is J. Haslam, *The Soviet Union and the Struggle for Collective Security in Europe, 1933–39* (London, 1984).
7. R. C. Tucker, 'The Emergence of Stalin's Foreign Policy', *Slavic Review*, vol. 36 (1977), pp. 563–89.
8. See T. J. Uldricks, 'Soviet Security Policy in the 1930s', in Gorodetsky (ed.), *Soviet Foreign Policy*, pp. 65–74; and G. Roberts, *The Soviet Union and the Origins of the Second World War: Russo-German Relations and the Road to War, 1933–1941* (Basingstoke, 1995).
9. J. Stalin, *Problems of Leninism* (Moscow, 1953), pp. 592–3.

10. The following account is based on Roberts, *The Soviet Union*, pp. 62–91; for a different reading, see Tucker, *Stalin in Power*, pp. 592–8.

11. Cited in I. Banac (ed.), *The Diary of Georgi Dimitrov, 1933–1949* (New Haven and London, 2003), p. 115.

12. J. T. Gross, *Revolution from Abroad: The Soviet Conquest of Poland's Western Ukraine and Western Belorussia* (Princeton, 1988).

13. Cited in Banac (ed.), *The Diary of Georgi Dimitrov*, p. 116.

14. Cited in G. Gorodetsky, *Grand Delusion: Stalin and the German Invasion of Russia* (New Haven and London, 1999), p. 9.

15. For a judicious critique of Suvorov's work and the debates unleashed by it, see T. J. Uldricks, 'The Icebreaker Controversy: Did Stalin Plan to Attack Hitler?', *Slavic Review*, vol. 58 (1999), pp. 626–43; the views of post-Soviet historians can be found in G. A. Bordiugov (ed.), *Gotovil li Stalin nastupitel'nuiu voinu protiv Gitlera?* (Moscow, 1995).

16. E. Mawdsley, 'Crossing the Rubicon: Soviet Plans for Offensive War in 1940–1941', *International History Review*, vol. 25 (2003), pp. 818–65, quotations on pp. 820, 850 and 852–4.

17. For an opposing view that sees Stalin embarking on an ideologically-driven war of revolutionary conquest, see R. C. Raack, *Stalin's Drive to the West, 1939–1945: The Origins of the Cold War* (Stanford, 1995); E. Topitsch, *Stalin's War: A Radical New Theory of the Origins of the Second World War* (London, 1987) and A. L. Weeks, *Stalin's Other War: Soviet Grand Strategy, 1939–1941* (Lanham, 2002).

18. A. Resis (ed.), *Molotov Remembers: Inside Kremlin Politics* (Chicago, 1993), p. 31.

19. On Stalin's attitudes to security intelligence, see C. Andrew and J. Elkner, 'Stalin and Foreign Intelligence', in H. Shukman (ed.), *Redefining Stalinism* (London, 2003), pp. 69–94.

20. On Stalin's dilemmas and gross misconceptions, see Gorodetsky, *Grand Delusion* and S. Pons, *Stalin and the Inevitable War, 1934–1941* (London, 2002).

21. The following account of post-invasion events is based on Z. and R. Medvedev, *The Unknown Stalin* (London, 2003), pp. 230–4; R. Service, *Stalin: A Biography* (London, 2004), pp. 412–5; and R. Overy, *Russia's War* (Harmondsworth, 1997) pp. 73–9.

22. A. I. Mikoian, *Tak bylo. Razmyshleniia o minuvshem* (Moscow, 1999), p. 391.

23. Banac (ed.), *The Diary of Georgi Dimitrov*, p. 166.

24. Resis (ed.), *Molotov Remembers*, p. 38.

25. For the shifting popular attitudes in Moscow in the first year of the war, see M. Gorinov, 'Dynamics of the Mood of Muscovites, 22 June

1941–May 1942', in K. McDermott and J. Morison (eds), *Politics and Society under the Bolsheviks* (Basingstoke, 1999), pp. 199–244.

26. J. Stalin, *The Great Patriotic War of the Soviet Union*, reprint edn (New York, 1969), pp. 9–17.

27 D. R. Stone, *Hammer and Rifle: The Militarization of the Soviet Union, 1926–1933* (Lawrence, 2000), p. 158.

28. L. Samuelson, *Plans for Stalin's War Machine: Tukhachevskii and Military-Economic Planning, 1925–1941* (Basingstoke, 2000), pp. 198–9.

29. M. Harrison, '"Barbarossa": The Soviet Response, 1941', in B. Wegner (ed.), *From Peace to War: Germany, Soviet Russia and the World, 1939–1941* (Oxford, 1997), p. 433.

30. For a summary of recent Russian historiography on the military purges (and also the Nazi-Soviet Pact, June 1941 and World War II), see A. L. Litvin, *Writing History in Twentieth-Century Russia: A View from Within* (Basingstoke, 2001), pp. 98–101, 105–13 and 130–1.

31. Figures from Overy, *The Dictators*, p. 477; and B. Bonwetsch, 'The Purge of the Military and the Red Army's Operational Capability during the "Great Patriotic War"', in Wegner (ed.), *From Peace to War*, pp. 396–8.

32. See R. Reese, *Stalin's Reluctant Soldiers: A Social History of the Red Army, 1925–1941* (Lawrence, 1996).

33. Overy, *The Dictators*, p. 478.

34. D. A. Volkogonov, 'Stalin as Supreme Commander', in Wegner (ed.), *From Peace to War*, pp. 463–4 and 477 (emphasis in the original); see also Volkogonov, *Stalin*, pp. 451–93.

35. M. Lewin, 'Stalin in the Mirror of the Other', in I. Kershaw and M. Lewin (eds), *Stalin and Nazism: Dictatorships in Comparison* (Cambridge, 1997), pp. 125–31, quotations on pp. 127 and 128.

36. B. Bonwetsch, 'Stalin, the Red Army, and the "Great Patriotic War"', in Kershaw and Lewin (eds), *Stalinism and Nazism*, pp. 185–207, quotations on pp. 206 and 207.

37. J. Barber and M. Harrison, *The Soviet Home Front, 1941–1945: A Social and Economic History of the USSR in World War II* (London, 1991), p. 55.

38. A. Seaton, *Stalin as Warlord* (London, 1976), pp. 271–2.

39. Overy, *Russia's War*, pp. xv–xvi.

40. See R. W. Thurston and B. Bonwetsch (eds), *The People's War: Responses to World War II in the Soviet Union* (Urbana, 2000); also C. Ward, *Stalin's Russia*, 2nd edn (London, 1999), pp. 221–3; and Barber and Harrison, *The Soviet Home Front*, pp. 210–11.

41. For details on Stalin's early interventions, see J. Erickson, *The Road to Stalingrad* (London, 1985), pp. 240–54.

42. Barber and Harrison, *The Soviet Home Front*, pp. 53–4.

43. G. Roberts, *Victory at Stalingrad* (London, 2002), p. 117.

44. For an interesting Brezhnev era account by a high-ranking General Staff officer, see S. M. Shtemenko, *The Soviet General Staff at War, 1941–1945* (Moscow, 1975).

45. Overy, *Russia's War*, pp. 187–8.

46. A full translation of Order 227 can be found in Roberts, *Victory at Stalingrad*, pp. 203–10.

47. On Russocentric propaganda during the war and its popular reception, see D. Brandenberger, *National Bolshevism: Stalinist Mass Culture and the Formation of Modern Russian National Identity, 1931–1956* (Cambridge: MA, 2002), pp. 115–80.

48. J. Barber, 'The Image of Stalin in Soviet Propaganda and Public Opinion during World War 2', in J. Garrard and C. Garrard (eds), *World War 2 and the Soviet People* (Basingstoke, 1993), p. 48.

49. V. S. Dunham, *In Stalin's Time: Middleclass Values in Soviet Fiction*, enlarged edn (Durham and London, 1990), p. 7.

50. On post-Ezhov, wartime and post-war repression, see M. Parrish, *The Lesser Terror: Soviet State Security, 1939–1953* (Westport, 1996); and from a different perspective A. Weiner, *Making Sense of War: The Second World War and the Fate of the Bolshevik Revolution* (Princeton, 2001).

51. The most recent treatment is G. Sanford, *Katyn and the Soviet Massacre of 1940: Truth, Justice and Memory* (forthcoming: London, 2005).

52. See V. Tolz, 'New Information about the Deportation of Ethnic Groups in the USSR during World War 2', in Garrard and Garrard (eds), *World War 2 and the Soviet People*, pp. 161–79; and N. Naimark, *Fires of Hatred: Ethnic Cleansing in Twentieth-Century Europe* (Cambridge: MA, 2001), pp. 85–107.

53. N. Werth, 'A State against Its People: Violence, Repression, and Terror in the Soviet Union', in S. Courtois et al. (eds), *The Black Book of Communism: Crimes, Terror, Repression* (Cambridge: MA, 1999), p. 226; see also E. Bacon, *The Gulag at War: Stalin's Forced Labour System in the Light of the Archives* (Basingstoke, 1994).

54. Barber and Harrison, *The Soviet Home Front*, p. 102.

55. See R. Stites, *Russian Popular Culture: Entertainment and Society since 1900* (Cambridge, 1992), pp. 98–116; and R. Stites (ed.), *Culture and Entertainment in Wartime Russia* (Bloomington, 1995).

Chapter 6: Statesman

1. For a detailed, yet succinct, account of post-war reconstruction, see S. Fitzpatrick, 'Postwar Soviet Society: the "Return to Normalcy",

1945–1953' in S. J. Linz (ed.), *The Impact of World War II on the Soviet Union* (Totowa, 1985), pp. 129–56.

2. All figures are from E. Zubkova, *Russia after the War: Hopes, Illusions, and Disappointments, 1945–1957* (Armonk, 1998), pp. 20–1.

3. See M. Djilas, *Conversations with Stalin* (Harmondsworth, 1969) and S. Sebag Montefiore, *Stalin: The Court of the Red Tsar* (London, 2003).

4. The mysterious 'Leningrad Affair' continues to be the source of great debate among historians. See D. Brandenberger, 'Stalin, the Leningrad Affair, and the Limits of Postwar Russocentrism', *Russian Review*, vol. 63 (2004), pp. 241–57 and the exchanges in *Russian Review*, vol. 64 (2005), pp. 90–7.

5. These are official NKVD statistics and hence should be treated with caution. Cited in J. A. Getty, G. T. Rittersporn and V. N. Zemskov, 'Victims of the Soviet Penal System in the Pre-war Years: A First Approach on the Basis of Archival Evidence', *American Historical Review*, vol. 98 (1993), p. 1040. The figures do not include 'special settlers' in exile, of whom there were an estimated 2.5 million in 1950. See O. Khlevnyuk, 'The Economy of the OGPU, NKVD, and MVD of the USSR, 1930–1953: The Scale, Structure, and Trends of Development', in P. R. Gregory and V. Lazarev (eds), *The Economics of Forced Labour: The Soviet Gulag* (Stanford, 2003), p. 60.

6. R. Service, *Stalin: A Biography* (London, 2004), p. 568.

7. N. Werth, 'A State against Its People: Violence, Repression, and Terror in the Soviet Union', in S. Courtois et al. (eds), *The Black Book of Communism: Crimes, Terror, and Repression* (Cambridge: MA, 1999), p. 245.

8. J. Rubinstein and V. P. Naumov (eds), *Stalin's Secret Pogrom: The Postwar Inquisition of the Soviet Jewish Anti-Fascist Committee* (New Haven and London, 2002); G. Kostyrchenko, *Out of the Red Shadows: Anti-semitism in Stalin's Russia* (New York, 1995).

9. Y. Gorlizki and O. Khlevniuk, *Cold Peace: Stalin and the Soviet Ruling Circle, 1945–1953* (Oxford, 2004), quotation on p. 3.

10. His daughter eluded to her father's inability to either destroy or control 'the frightful system that had grown up around him like a huge honeycomb'. See S. Alliluyeva, *Twenty Letters to a Friend* (Harmondsworth, 1967), p. 183. For an interesting post-Soviet account of the late Stalin years, see N. V. Romanovsky, *Russia (USSR) under High Stalinism: The Last Phase of Stalin's Rule, 1945–1953* (New Delhi, 1995).

11. J. Brent and V. P. Naumov, *Stalin's Last Crime: The Plot against the Jewish Doctors, 1948–1953* (New York, 2003), p. 334.

12. For an erudite opposing view, see D. Brandenberger, *National Bolshevism: Stalinist Mass Culture and the Formation of Modern Russian National Identity, 1931–1956* (Cambridge: MA, 2002).

13. E. Pollock, 'Stalin as the Coryphaeus of science: ideology and knowledge in the postwar years', in S. Davies and J. Harris (eds), *Stalin: A New History* (forthcoming: Cambridge, 2005).

14. Cited in A. Kojevnikov, 'Games of Stalinist Democracy: Ideological discussions in Soviet sciences, 1947–52', in S. Fitzpatrick (ed.), *Stalinism: New Directions* (London, 2000), p. 161.

15. Service, *Stalin*, p. 565.

16. Pollock, 'Stalin as the Coryphaeus of science' (forthcoming).

17. D. Volkogonov, *Stalin: Triumph and Tragedy* (London, 1991); R. Conquest, *Stalin: Breaker of Nations* (London, 1993); E. Radzinsky, *Stalin* (London, 1997) and Service, *Stalin* make no substantial reference to Stalin's actions in the Comintern.

18. J. V. Stalin, *Works*, vol. 10 (Moscow, 1954), pp. 53–4 (emphasis in the original).

19. L. Lih et al. (eds), *Stalin's Letters to Molotov, 1925–1936* (New Haven and London, 1995), pp. 33–5 and 182 (emphasis in the original).

20. F. Borkenau, *World Communism: A History of the Communist International*, reprint edn (Ann Arbor, 1971), pp. 351–2.

21. E. H. Carr, *The Twilight of Comintern, 1930–1935* (London, 1982), pp. 5 and 6.

22. F. Firsov, 'The VKP(b) and the Communist International', unpublished manuscript, n.p.

23. F. I. Firsov, 'Stalin i Komintern' (part 2), *Voprosy istorii*, no. 9 (1989), pp. 10–11, citing the former Central Party Archive.

24. *Theses and Decisions: Thirteenth Plenum of the E.C.C.I.* (New York, 1934), pp. 3, 5 and 19.

25. RGASPI, f. 17, op. 162, d. 6, l. 70.

26. RGASPI, f. 17, op. 120, d. 203, ll. 1–6.

27. Firsov, 'Stalin i Komintern', (part 2), pp. 7–12.

28. The quotation is from J. Haslam's review of Carr's work in *Historical Journal*, vol. 26 (1983), p. 1026.

29. I. Deutscher, *Stalin: A Political Biography*, revised edn (Harmondsworth, 1976), p. 400.

30. S. Fitzpatrick, *The Cultural Front: Power and Culture in Revolutionary Russia* (Ithaca, 1992), pp. 113–14.

31. M. Hájek, *Jednotná fronta. K politické orientaci Komunistické internacionály v letech 1921–1935* (Prague, 1969), p. 162.

32. I have based my discussions of Stalin's post-war diplomacy on the follow-ing sources: V. Zubok and C. Pleshakov, *Inside the Kremlin's Cold War: From Stalin to Khrushchev* (Cambridge: MA, 1996); V. Mastny, *The Cold War and Soviet Insecurity: The Stalin Years* (Oxford, 1996); and C. Kennedy-Pipe, *Stalin's Cold War: Soviet Strategies in Europe, 1943 to 1956* (Manchester, 1995). Numerous translated documents and relevant arti-cles can be found in the Bulletins and Working Papers of the Cold War International History Project, available on-line at http://cwihp.si.edu

33. Zubok and Pleshakov, *Inside the Kremlin's Cold War*, p. 4.

34. E. Mark, 'Revolution by Degrees: Stalin's National Front Strategy for Europe, 1941–1947', Cold War International History Project, *Working Paper No. 31* (Washington D. C., 2001).

35. See N. Naimark, 'Cold War Studies and New Archival Materials on Stalin', *Russian Review*, vol. 61 (2002), pp. 1–15.

36. A. Resis (ed.), *Molotov Remembers: Inside Kremlin Politics* (Chicago, 1993), p. 51; see also the summary of Stalin's strategies in 1943–5 in Mastny, *The Cold War and Soviet Insecurity*, pp. 17–22.

37. Mark, 'Revolution by Degrees', p. 9.

38. Mastny, *The Cold War and Soviet Insecurity*, p. 193.

39. Zubok and Pleshakov, *Inside the Kremlin's Cold War*, pp. 46–7.

40. Kennedy-Pipe, *Stalin's Cold War*, pp. 138 and 163.

41. J. L. Gaddis, *We Now Know: Rethinking Cold War History* (Oxford, 1998), p. 20.

42. Mark, 'Revolution by Degrees', p. 20.

43. Resis (ed.), *Molotov Remembers*, pp. 59 and 63 (my emphasis).

44. The competing theories of Stalin's death (or murder) were the subject of a rather sensationalist BBC2 *Timewatch* programme in March 2005.

45. My account of Stalin's death is based on Service, *Stalin*, pp. 582–8; Brent and Naumov, *Stalin's Last Crime*, pp. 312–22; Z. Medvedev and R. Medvedev, *The Unknown Stalin* (London, 2003), pp. 1–33; Radzinsky, *Stalin*, pp. 549–60; Alliluyeva, *Twenty Letters*, pp. 12–21; and S. Talbott (ed.), *Khrushchev Remembers* (Boston, 1971), pp. 340–5. Unsurprisingly, Khrushchev's rendition is self-serving and inaccurate in certain details, as is Alliluyeva's.

46. I am indebted to Aleksandr Vatlin for the idea of Stalin's 'paradigm of death'. By concentrating on Stalin's experiences of death and suffering, I in no way seek to demean the memory of the millions of innocents who died and suffered under him.

47. See M. G. Smith, 'Stalin's Martyrs: The Tragic Romance of the Russian Revolution' in H. Shukman (ed.), *Redefining Stalinism* (London, 2003), pp. 95–126.

Conclusion

1. Most notably and controversially in S. Courtois et al., *The Black Book of Communism: Crimes, Terror, Repression* (Cambridge: MA, 1999); and also M. Malia, *The Soviet Tragedy: A History of Socialism in Russia, 1917–1991* (New York, 1994).
2. D. L. Hoffmann, *Stalinist Values: The Cultural Norms of Soviet Modernity, 1917–1941* (Ithaca, 2003), p. 186.
3. C. Ward, *Stalin's Russia*, 2nd edn (London, 1999), p. 37.
4. J. V. Stalin, *Works*, vol. 5 (Moscow, 1953), p. 73 (emphasis in the original).
5. Cited in S. Fitzpatrick, *Everyday Stalinism. Ordinary Life in Extraordinary Times: Soviet Russia in the 1930s* (New York, 1999), p. 17.
6. J. Harris, 'Was Stalin a Weak Dictator?', *Journal of Modern History*, vol. 75 (2003), pp. 375–86; also R. W. Thurston, *Life and Terror in Stalin's Russia, 1934–1941* (New Haven and London, 1996).
7. M. Lewin, *Russia/USSR/Russia: The Drive and Drift of a Superstate* (New York, 1995), pp. 88–90.
8. A. Nove, *Stalinism and After*, 2nd edn (London, 1986), pp. 121–4.
9. Nove, *Stalinism and After*, p. 122.
10. I have based this analysis on M. Lewin, *The Gorbachev Phenomenon: A Historical Interpretation* (London, 1988).

Bibliography

Archives

Russian State Archive of Socio-Political History (RGASPI), Moscow (former Central Party Archive)

fond 17, *opis'* 2	Central Committee Plena
fond 17, *opis'* 85	Secret Department of the Central Committee
fond 17, *opis'* 120	Organisational Bureau and Secretariat of the Central Committee
fond 17, *opis'* 162	'Special Files' (*osobye papki*) of the Politburo
fond 17, *opis'* 163	Politburo protocols
fond 73, *opisi* 1–2	Andreev files
fond 74, *opisi* 1–2	Voroshilov files
fond 81, *opisi* 1–3	Kaganovich files
fond 82, *opisi* 1–2	Molotov files
fond 495, *opis'* 6	Small Commission of the Executive Committee of the Communist International
fond 558, *opisi* 1–11	Stalin files
fond 667, *opis'* 1	Enukidze files

Published Primary Sources

Adibekov, G. M. et al. (eds), *Politbiuro TsK RKP(b)-VKP(b) i Komintern, 1919–1943* (Moscow, 2004).
Bukharin, N. I., *Problemy teorii i praktiki sotsializma* (Moscow, 1989).

Chase, W. J., *Enemy within the Gates?: The Comintern and the Stalinist Repression, 1934–1939* (New Haven and London, 2001).

Dallin, A. and Firsov, F. I. (eds), *Dimitrov and Stalin, 1934–1943: Letters from the Soviet Archives* (New Haven and London, 2000).

Daniels, R. V. (ed.), *A Documentary History of Communism*, 2 vols (London, 1987).

Davies, R. W., Khlevniuk, O. V. and Rees, E. A. (eds), *The Stalin–Kaganovich Correspondence, 1931–36* (New Haven and London, 2003).

Getty, J. A. and Naumov, O. V., *The Road to Terror: Stalin and the Self-Destruction of the Bolsheviks, 1932–1939* (New Haven and London, 1999).

Khaustov, V. N. et al. (eds), *Lubianka. Stalin i VChK-GPU-OGPU-NKVD, ianvar' 1922–dekabr' 1936* (Moscow, 2003).

Khaustov, V. N., Naumov, V. P. and Plotnikova, N. S. (eds), *Lubianka. Stalin i glavnoe upravlenie gosbezopastnosti NKVD 1937–1938* (Moscow, 2004).

Khlevniuk, O. V. et al. (eds), *Stalinskoe Politbiuro v 30-e gody. Sbornik dokumentov* (Moscow, 1995).

Khlevniuk, O. V. et al. (eds), *Stalin i Kaganovich. Perepiska, 1931–1936 gg.* (Moscow, 2001).

Khlevniuk, O. V., *The History of the Gulag: From Collectivization to the Great Terror* (New Haven and London, 2004).

Koenker, D. P. and Bachman, R. D. (eds), *Revelations from the Russian Archives. Documents in English Translation* (Washington D.C., 1997).

Kvashonkin, A. V. et al. (eds), *Bolshevistskoe rukovodstvo. Perepiska, 1912–1927* (Moscow, 1996).

Kvashonkin, A. V. et al. (eds), *Sovetskoe rukovodstvo. Perepiska, 1928–1941* (Moscow, 1999).

Lenin, V. I., *Polnoe sobranie sochinenii*, 5th edn, vol. 49 (Moscow 1964).

Lenin, V. I., *Collected Works*, 4th edn, vols 35 and 36 (Moscow, 1966).

Lih, L. T., Naumov, O. V. and Khlevniuk, O. V. (eds), *Stalin's Letters to Molotov, 1925–1936* (New Haven and London, 1995).

McNeal, R. H. (ed.), *Resolutions and Decisions of the Communist Party of the Soviet Union, vol. 3: The Stalin Years, 1929–1953* (Toronto, 1974).

Murin, Iu. G. (ed.), *Iosif Stalin v ob"iatiiakh sem'i: Iz lichnogo arkhiva* (Moscow, 1993).

Reabilitatsiia. Politicheskie protsessy 30–50-kh godov (Moscow, 1991).

Rubinstein, J. and Naumov, V. P. (eds), *Stalin's Secret Pogrom: The Postwar Inquisition of the Soviet Jewish Anti-Fascist Committee* (New Haven and London, 2002).

Siegelbaum, L. and Sokolov, A. K. (eds), *Stalinism as a Way of Life: A Narrative in Documents* (New Haven and London, 2000).

Stalin, J., *Sochineniia,* vols 14–16, edited by R. H. McNeal (Stanford, 1967).

Stalin, J., *Marxism and the National and Colonial Question* (London, 1941).

Stalin, J., *Problems of Leninism* (Moscow, 1953).

Stalin, J., *The Great Patriotic War of the Soviet Union,* reprint edn (New York, 1969).

Stalin, J. V., *Works,* 13 vols (Moscow, 1952–5).

The Bolsheviks and the October Revolution: Central Committee Minutes of the Russian Social-Democratic Labour Party (bolsheviks) August 1917–February 1918 (London, 1974).

The Land of Socialism Today and Tomorrow: Reports and Speeches at the Eighteenth Congress of the Communist Party of the Soviet Union (Moscow, 1939).

Theses and Decisions: Thirteenth Plenum of the E.C.C.I. (New York, 1934).

Vilkova, V. P., *The Struggle for Power: Russia in 1923* (New York, 1996).

Memoirs and Diaries

Alliluyeva, S., *Twenty Letters to a Friend* (Harmondsworth, 1967).

Alliluyeva, S., *Only One Year* (London, 1969).

Banac, I. (ed.), *The Diary of Georgi Dimitrov, 1933–1949* (New Haven and London, 2003).

Bazhanov, B., *Bazhanov and the Damnation of Stalin* (Athens: Ohio, 1990).

Beria, S., *Beria: My Father. Inside Stalin's Kremlin* (London, 2001).

Chuev, F., *Tak govoril Kaganovich* (Moscow, 1992).

Djilas, M., *Conversations with Stalin* (Harmondsworth, 1969).

'Dnevnik Marii Anisimovny Svanidze' in Iu. G. Murin (ed.), *Iosif Stalin v ob"iatiiakh sem'i: Iz lichnogo arkhiva* (Moscow, 1993), pp. 155–96.

Dolot, M., *Execution by Hunger: The Hidden Holocaust* (New York, 1985).

Garros, V., Korenevskaya, N. and Lahusen, T. (eds), *Intimacy and Terror: Soviet Diaries of the 1930s* (New York, 1995).

Kopelev, L., *The Education of a True Believer* (London, 1981).

Kuusinen, A., *Before and After Stalin* (London, 1974).

Larina, A., *This I Cannot Forget: The Memoirs of Nikolai Bukharin's Widow* (New York, 1993).

Malyshev, V. A., 'Dnevnik narkoma', *Istochnik,* no. 5 (1997), pp. 103–47.

Mikoian, A., *Tak bylo. Razmyshleniia o minuvshem* (Moscow, 1999).

Resis, A. (ed.), *Molotov Remembers: Inside Kremlin Politics* (Chicago, 1993).

Rybin, A. T., *Next to Stalin: Notes of a Bodyguard* (Toronto, 1996).

Schecter, J. L. and Luchkov, V. V. (eds), *Khrushchev Remembers: The Glasnost Tapes* (Boston, 1990).

Shtemenko, S. M., *The Soviet General Staff at War, 1941–1945* (Moscow, 1975).
Simonov, K., *Glazami cheloveka moego pokoleniia: Razmyshleniia o I. V. Staline* (Moscow, 1990).
Sto sorok besed s Molotovym: Iz dnevnika F. Chueva (Moscow, 1991).
Talbott, S. (ed.), *Khrushchev Remembers* (Boston, 1971).

Biographical Studies

Amis, M., *Koba the Dread: Laughter and the Twenty Million* (London, 2002).
Antonov-Ovseyenko, A., *The Time of Stalin: Portrait of a Tyranny* (New York, 1983).
Brackman, R., *The Secret File of Joseph Stalin: A Hidden Life* (London, 2001).
Bullock, A., *Hitler and Stalin: Parallel Lives* (London, 1991).
Cohen, S. F., *Bukharin and the Bolshevik Revolution: A Political Biography, 1888–1938* (New York, 1975).
Conquest, R., *Stalin: Breaker of Nations* (London, 1993).
Deutscher, I., *Stalin: A Political Biography*, revised edn (Harmondsworth, 1976).
Graziosi, A., 'G. L. Piatakov: A Mirror of Soviet History', *Harvard Ukrainian Studies*, vol. 16 (1992), pp. 102–66.
Jansen, M. and Petrov, N., *Stalin's Loyal Executioner: People's Commissar Nikolai Ezhov, 1895–1940* (Stanford, 2002).
Khlevniuk, O. V., *In Stalin's Shadow: The Career of 'Sergo' Ordzhonikidze* (Armonk, 1995).
Knight, A., *Beria: Stalin's First Lieutenant* (Princeton, 1993).
Kun, M., *Stalin: An Unknown Portrait* (Budapest, 2003).
Laqueur, W., *Stalin: The Glasnost Revelations* (London, 1990).
Lewis, J. and Whitehead, P., *Stalin: Time for Judgement* (London, 1990).
McNeal, R. H., *Stalin: Man and Ruler* (London, 1989).
Medvedev, R., *All Stalin's Men* (Oxford, 1983).
Medvedev, Z. and Medvedev, R., *The Unknown Stalin* (London, 2003).
Merridale, C., 'The Making of a Moderate Bolshevik: an Introduction to L. B. Kamenev's Political Biography' in J. Cooper, M. Perrie and E. A. Rees (eds), *Soviet History, 1917–53: Essays in Honour of R. W. Davies* (Basingstoke, 1995), pp. 22–41.
Radzinsky, E., *Stalin* (London, 1997).
Rayfield, D., *Stalin and his Hangmen: An Authoritative Portrait of a Tyrant and Those Who Served Him* (London, 2004).
Read, C., *Lenin: A Revolutionary Life* (London, 2005).

Sebag Montefiore, S., *Stalin: The Court of the Red Tsar* (London, 2003).

Service, R., *Stalin: A Biography* (London, 2004).

Shukman, H., *Stalin* (London, 1999).

Smith, E. E., *The Young Stalin: The Early Years of an Elusive Revolutionary* (London, 1967).

Souvarine, B., *Stalin: A Critical Survey of Bolshevism* (London, n.d.).

Taubman, W., *Khrushchev: The Man and his Era* (London, 2002).

Thatcher, I. D., *Trotsky* (London, 2003).

Trotsky, L., *Stalin: An Appraisal of the Man and his Influence*, 2 vols (London, 1969).

Tucker, R. C., *Stalin as Revolutionary, 1879–1929: A Study in History and Personality* (New York, 1974).

Tucker, R. C., *Stalin in Power: The Revolution from Above, 1928–1941* (New York, 1990).

Ulam, A., *Stalin: The Man and his Era* (London, 1974).

Vasilieva, L., *Kremlin Wives* (London, 1994).

Volkogonov, D., *Stalin: Triumph and Tragedy* (London, 1991).

Yaroslavsky, E., *Landmarks in the Life of Stalin* (Moscow, 1940).

Selected Russian Secondary Sources

Balandin, R. K. and Mironov, S., *Zagovory i bor'ba za vlast' ot Lenina do Khrushcheva* (Moscow, 2003).

Bordiugov, G. A. (ed.), *Gotovil li Stalin nastupitel'nuiu voinu protiv Gitlera?* (Moscow, 1995).

Firsov, F. I., 'Stalin i Komintern' (part 1), *Voprosy istorii*, no. 8 (1989), pp. 3–23.

Firsov, F. I., 'Stalin i Komintern' (part 2), *Voprosy istorii*, no. 9 (1989), pp. 3–19.

Gimpel'son, E. G., *Novaia ekonomicheskaia politika Lenina i Stalina. Problemy i uroki (1920-e gody XX veka)* (Moscow, 2004).

Iunge (Junge), M. and Binner, R., *Kak terror stal "bol'shim": Sekretnyi prikaz no. 00447 i tekhnologiia ego ispolneniia* (Moscow, 2003).

Khlevniuk, O. V., *1937-i: Stalin, NKVD i sovetskoe obshchestvo* (Moscow, 1992).

Khlevniuk, O. V., *Politbiuro. Mekhanizmy politicheskoi vlasti v 1930-e gody* (Moscow, 1996).

Latyshev, A. G., 'Riadom so Stalinym', *Sovershenno sekretno*, no. 12 (1990), pp. 18–20.

Maksimenkov, L., 'Kul't. Zametki o slovakh-simvolakh v sovetskom politicheskom kul'ture', *Svobodnaia mysl'*, no. 11 (1993), pp. 26–43.

Nazarov, O. G., *Stalin i bor'ba za liderstvo v bol'shevistskoi partii v usloviiakh Nepa* (Moscow, 2000).
'O sud'be chlenov i kandidatov v chleny TsK VKP(b), izbrannogo XVII s"ezdom partii', *Izvestiia TsK KPSS*, no. 12 (1989), pp. 82–113.
Ostrovskii, A. V., *Kto stoial za spinoi Stalina?* (St. Petersburg, 2002).
Soima, V. M., *Zapreshchennyi Stalin* (Moscow, 2005).
Sokolov, B. V., *Stalin. Vlast' i krov'* (Moscow, 2004).
Suvenirov, O., *Tragediia RKKA 1937–1938* (Moscow, 1998).
Vatlin, A. Iu., 'Iosif Stalin na puti k absoliutnoi vlasti: novye dokumenty iz moskovskikh arkhivov' (unpublished ms).
Vatlin, A. Iu., 'Goriachaia osen' dvadtsat' vos'mogo. (K voprosu o stalinizatsii Kominterna)', in A. V. Afanas'ev (ed.), *Oni ne molchali* (Moscow, 1991), pp. 102–24.
Zhukov, Iu. N., *Stalin: tainy vlasti* (Moscow, 2005).

Monographs and Other Secondary Sources

Alexopoulos, G., *Stalin's Outcasts: Aliens, Citizens, and the Soviet State, 1926–1936* (Ithaca, 2003).
Andrew, C. and Elkner, J., 'Stalin and Foreign Intelligence', in H. Shukman (ed.), *Redefining Stalinism* (London, 2003), pp. 69–94.
Andrle, V., *A Social History of Twentieth-Century Russia* (London, 1994).
Apor, B., Behrends, J. C., Jones, P. and Rees, E. A. (eds), *The Leader Cult in Communist Dictatorships: Stalin and the Eastern Bloc* (Basingstoke, 2004).
Applebaum, A., *Gulag. A History of the Soviet Camps* (London, 2003).
Bacon, E., *The Gulag at War: Stalin's Forced Labour System in the Light of the Archives* (Basingstoke, 1994).
Barber, J., 'The Image of Stalin in Soviet Propaganda and Public Opinion during World War 2', in J. Garrard and C. Garrard (eds), *World War 2 and the Soviet People* (Basingstoke, 1993), pp. 38–49.
Barber, J. and Harrison, M., *The Soviet Home Front, 1941–1945: A Social and Economic History of the USSR in World War II* (London, 1991).
Beer, D., 'Origins, Modernity and Resistance in the Historiography of Stalinism', *Journal of Contemporary History*, vol. 40 (2005), pp. 363–79.
Boffa, G., *The Stalin Phenomenon* (Ithaca, 1992).
Bonwetsch, B., 'The Purge of the Military and the Red Army's Operational Capability during the "Great Patriotic War"', in B. Wegner (ed.), *From Peace to War: Germany, Soviet Russia and the World, 1939–1941* (Oxford, 1997), pp. 395–414.

Bonwetsch, B., 'Stalin, the Red Army, and the "Great Patriotic War"', in I. Kershaw and M. Lewin (eds), *Stalinism and Nazism: Dictatorships in Comparison* (Cambridge, 1997), pp. 185–207.

Boobbyer, P., *The Stalin Era* (London, 2000).

Borkenau, F., *World Communism. A History of the Communist International*, reprint edn (Ann Arbor, 1971).

Brandenberger, D., *National Bolshevism: Stalinist Mass Culture and the Formation of Modern Russian National Identity, 1931–1956* (Cambridge: MA, 2002).

Brandenberger, D., 'Stalin, the Leningrad Affair, and the Limits of Postwar Russocentrism', *Russian Review*, vol. 63 (2004), pp. 241–57.

Brent, J. and Naumov, V. P., *Stalin's Last Crime: The Plot against the Jewish Doctors, 1948–1953* (New York, 2003).

Brooke, C., 'Soviet Musicians and the Great Terror', *Europe-Asia Studies*, vol. 54 (2002), pp. 397–413.

Brooks, J., *Thank You, Comrade Stalin! Soviet Public Culture from Revolution to Cold War* (Princeton, 1999).

Buranov, Y., *Lenin's Will: Falsified and Forbidden* (New York, 1994).

Carr, E. H., *A History of Soviet Russia*, 13 vols (Basingstoke, 1950–78).

Carr, E. H., *The Twilight of Comintern, 1930–1935* (London, 1982).

Channon, J. (ed.), *Politics, Society and Stalinism in the USSR* (Basingstoke, 1998).

Cohen, S., *Rethinking the Soviet Experience: Politics and History since 1917* (New York, 1985).

Conquest, R., *The Great Terror: Stalin's Purges of the Thirties* (Harmondsworth, 1971), up-dated as *The Great Terror: A Reassessment* (London, 1990).

Conquest, R., *The Harvest of Sorrow: Soviet Collectivisation and the Terror-Famine*, reprint edn (London, 2002).

Courtois, S. et al., *The Black Book of Communism: Crimes, Terror, Repression* (Cambridge: MA, 1999).

Daniels, R. V., *The Conscience of the Revolution: Communist Opposition in Soviet Russia* (New York, 1969).

Daniels, R. V., *Trotsky, Stalin, and Socialism* (Boulder, 1991).

Daniels, R. V. (ed.), *The Stalin Revolution: Foundations of the Totalitarian Era*, 4th edn (New York, 1997).

Davies, R. W., *The Socialist Offensive: The Collectivisation of Soviet Agriculture, 1929–1930* (London, 1980).

Davies, R. W., *Soviet History in the Gorbachev Revolution* (Basingstoke, 1989).

Davies, R. W., *Soviet History in the Yeltsin Era* (Basingstoke, 1997).

Davies, R. W., *Soviet Economic Development from Lenin to Khrushchev* (Cambridge, 1998).

Davies, R. W., Harrison, M. and Wheatcroft, S. G. (eds), *The Economic Transformation of the Soviet Union, 1913–1945* (Cambridge, 1994).

Davies, R. W. and Wheatcroft, S. G., *The Years of Hunger: Soviet Agriculture, 1931–1933* (Basingstoke, 2004).

Davies, R. W., Ilič, M. and Khlevnyuk, O., 'The Politburo and Economic Policy-making', in E. A. Rees (ed.), *The Nature of Stalin's Dictatorship: The Politburo, 1924–1953* (Basingstoke, 2004), pp. 108–33.

Davies, S., *Popular Opinion in Stalin's Russia: Terror, Propaganda and Dissent, 1934–1941* (Cambridge, 1997).

Davies, S., 'The Crime of "Anti-Soviet Agitation" in the Soviet Union in the 1930s', *Cahiers du Monde russe*, vol. 39 (1998), pp. 149–68.

Davies, S., '"Us" against "Them": Social Identity in Soviet Russia, 1934–41', in S. Fitzpatrick (ed.), *Stalinism: New Directions* (London, 2000), pp. 47–70.

Davies, S., 'Stalin and the Making of the Leader Cult in the 1930s', in B. Apor et al. (eds), *The Leader Cult in Communist Dictatorships: Stalin and the Eastern Bloc* (Basingstoke, 2004), pp. 29–46.

Davies, S. and Harris, J. (eds), *Stalin: A New History* (forthcoming: Cambridge, 2005).

Dunham, V. S., *In Stalin's Time: Middleclass Values in Soviet Fiction*, enlarged edn (Durham and London, 1990).

Easter, G., *Reconstructing the State: Personal Networks and Elite Identity in Soviet Russia* (Cambridge, 2000).

Ellman, M., 'The Soviet 1937 Provincial Show Trials: Carnival or Terror?', *Europe-Asia Studies*, vol. 53 (2001), pp. 1221–33.

Ennker, B., 'The Stalin Cult, Bolshevik Rule and Kremlin Interaction in the 1930s', in B. Apor et al. (eds), *The Leader Cult in Communist Dictatorships: Stalin and the Eastern Bloc* (Basingstoke, 2004), pp. 83–101.

Erickson, J., *The Road to Stalingrad* (London, 1985).

Firsov, F., 'The VKP(b) and the Communist International', unpublished manuscript.

Fitzpatrick, S., 'Postwar Soviet Society: the "Return to Normalcy", 1945–1953' in S. J. Linz (ed.), *The Impact of World War II on the Soviet Union* (Totowa, 1985), pp. 129–56.

Fitzpatrick, S. et al., 'New Perspectives on Stalinism', *Russian Review*, vol. 45 (1986), pp. 357–73 and in *Russian Review*, vol. 46 (1987), pp. 375–431.

Fitzpatrick, S., *The Cultural Front: Power and Culture in Revolutionary Russia* (Ithaca, 1992).

Fitzpatrick, S., 'How the Mice Buried the Cat. Scenes from the Great Purges in the Russian Provinces', *Russian Review*, vol. 52 (1993), pp. 299–320.

Fitzpatrick, S., *The Russian Revolution*, 2nd edn (Oxford, 1994).

Fitzpatrick, S., *Stalin's Peasants: Resistance and Survival in the Russian Village after Collectivization* (Oxford, 1994).

Fitzpatrick, S., *Everyday Stalinism. Ordinary Life in Extraordinary Times: Soviet Russia in the 1930s* (New York, 1999).

Fitzpatrick, S. (ed.), *Stalinism: New Directions* (London, 2000).

Fitzpatrick, S., 'Politics as Practice: Thoughts on a New Soviet Political History', *Kritika*, vol. 5 (2004), pp. 27–54.

Fitzpatrick, S., Rabinowitch, A. and Stites, R. (eds), *Russia in the Era of NEP: Explorations in Soviet Society and Culture* (Bloomington, 1991).

Friedrich, C. J. and Brzezinski, Z. K., *Totalitarian Dictatorship and Autocracy*, 2nd edn (Cambridge: MA, 1965).

Gaddis, J. L., *We Now Know: Rethinking Cold War History* (Oxford, 1997).

Getty, J. A., *Origins of the Great Purges: The Soviet Communist Party Reconsidered, 1933–1938* (Cambridge, 1985).

Getty, J. A., 'Afraid of Their Shadows: The Bolshevik Recourse to Terror, 1932–1938', in M. Hildermeier with E. Müller-Luckner (eds), *Stalinismus vor dem Zweiten Weltkrieg: Neue Wege der Forschung* (Munich, 1998), pp. 169–91.

Getty, J. A., '*Samokritika* Rituals in the Stalinist Central Committee, 1933–1938', *Russian Review*, vol. 58 (1999), pp. 49–70.

Getty, J. A., '"Excesses are not permitted": Mass Terror and Stalinist Governance in the Late 1930s', *Russian Review*, vol. 61 (2002), pp. 113–38.

Getty, J. A., 'Stalin as Prime Minister: power and the Politburo', in S. Davies and J. Harris (eds), *Stalin: A New History* (forthcoming: Cambridge, 2005).

Getty, J. A. and Manning, R. T. (eds), *Stalinist Terror: New Perspectives* (Cambridge, 1993).

Getty, J. A., Rittersporn, G. T. and Zemskov, V. N., 'Victims of the Soviet Penal System in the Prewar Years: A First Approach on the Basis of Archival Evidence', *American Historical Review*, vol. 98 (1993), pp. 1017–49.

Gill, G., *The Origins of the Stalinist Political System* (Cambridge, 1990).

Gill, G., *Stalinism*, 2nd edn (Basingstoke, 1998).

Goldman, W. Z., *Women, the State and Revolution* (Cambridge, 1993).

Goldman. W. Z., *Women at the Gates: Gender and Industry in Stalin's Russia* (Cambridge, 2002).

Gorinov, M., 'Dynamics of the Mood of Muscovites, 22 June 1941–May 1942', in K. McDermott and J. Morison (eds), *Politics and Society under the Bolsheviks* (Basingstoke, 1999), pp. 199–244.

Gorlizki, Y. and Khlevniuk, O. V., *Cold Peace: Stalin and the Soviet Ruling Circle, 1945–1953* (Oxford, 2004).

Gorodetsky, G. (ed.), *Soviet Foreign Policy, 1917–1991: A Retrospective* (London, 1994).

Gorodetsky, G., *Grand Delusion: Stalin and the German Invasion of Russia* (New Haven and London, 1999).

Graziosi, A., *A New, Peculiar State: Explorations in Soviet History, 1917–1937* (Westport, 2000).

Gregory, P. R. (ed.), *Behind the Facade of Stalin's Command Economy: Evidence from the Soviet State and Party Archives* (Stanford, 2001).

Gronow, J., *Caviar with Champagne: Common Luxury and the Ideals of the Good Life in Stalin's Russia* (Oxford, 2003).

Gross, J. T., *Revolution from Abroad: The Soviet Conquest of Poland's Western Ukraine and Western Belorussia* (Princeton, 1988).

Gunther, H. (ed.), *The Culture of the Stalin Period* (Basingstoke, 1990).

Hahn, W., *Postwar Soviet Politics: The Fall of Zhdanov and the Defeat of Moderation, 1946–53* (Ithaca, 1982).

Hagenloh, P., '"Socially Harmful Elements" and the Great Terror', in S. Fitzpatrick (ed.), *Stalinism: New Directions* (London, 2000), pp. 286–308.

Hájek, M., *Jednotná fronta. K politické orientaci Komunistické internacionály v letech 1921–1935* (Prague, 1969).

Halfin, I., *Terror in My Soul: Communist Autobiographies on Trial* (Cambridge: MA, 2003).

Harris, J. R., *The Great Urals: Regionalism and the Evolution of the Soviet System* (Ithaca, 1999).

Harris, J. R., 'The Purging of Local Cliques in the Urals Region, 1936–7', in Fitzpatrick (ed.), *Stalinism*, pp. 262–85.

Harris, J. R., 'Was Stalin a Weak Dictator?', *Journal of Modern History*, vol. 75 (2003), pp. 375–86.

Harris, J., 'Stalin as General Secretary: the appointments process and the nature of Stalin's power' in S. Davies and J. Harris (eds), *Stalin: A New History* (forthcoming: Cambridge, 2005).

Harrison, M., '"Barbarossa": The Soviet Response, 1941', in B. Wegner (ed.), *From Peace to War: Germany, Soviet Russia and the World, 1939–1941* (Oxford, 1997), pp. 431–48.

Haslam, J., *The Soviet Union and the Struggle for Collective Security in Europe, 1933–39* (London, 1984).

Hatch, J., 'The "Lenin Levy" and the Social Origins of Stalinism: Workers and the Communist Party in Moscow, 1921–1928', *Slavic Review*, vol. 48 (1989), pp. 558–77.

Healey, D., *Homosexual Desire in Revolutionary Russia: The Regulation of Sexual and Gender Dissent* (Chicago, 2001).

Hellbeck, J., 'Fashioning the Stalinist Soul: The Diary of Stepan Podlubnyi (1931–1939)', *Jahrbücher für Geschichte Osteuropas*, vol. 44 (1996), pp. 344–73.

Hellbeck, J., 'Speaking Out: Languages of Affirmation and Dissent in Stalinist Russia', *Kritika*, vol. 1 (2000), pp. 71–96.

Himmer, R., 'The Transition from War Communism to the New Economic Policy: An Analysis of Stalin's Views', *Russian Review*, vol. 53 (1994), pp. 515–29.

Hlevnjuk, O., 'Les mécanismes de la "Grande Terreur" des années 1937–1938 au Turkménistan', *Cahiers du Monde russe*, vol. 39 (1998), pp. 197–208.

Hobsbawm, E., *Age of Extremes: The Short Twentieth Century, 1914–1991* (London, 1994).

Hobsbawm, E. and Ranger, T. (eds), *The Invention of Tradition* (Cambridge, 1983).

Hochschild, A., *The Unquiet Ghost: Russians Remember Stalin* (London, 1995).

Hoffmann, D. L., *Stalinist Values: The Cultural Norms of Soviet Modernity, 1917–1941* (Ithaca, 2003).

Hoffmann, D. L. (ed.), *Stalinism* (Oxford, 2003).

Hoffmann, D. L., 'European Modernity and Soviet Socialism', in D. L. Hoffmann and Y. Kotsonis (eds), *Russian Modernity: Politics, Knowledge, Practices* (Basingstoke, 2000), pp. 245–60.

Hoffmann, D. L. and Kotsonis, Y. (eds), *Russian Modernity: Politics, Knowledge, Practices* (Basingstoke, 2000).

Holloway, D., *Stalin and the Bomb: The Soviet Union and Atomic Energy, 1939–56* (New Haven and London, 1994).

Holquist, P., *Making War, Forging Revolution: Russia's Continuum of Crisis, 1914–1921* (Cambridge: MA, 2002).

Holquist, P., '"Information is the Alpha and Omega of Our Work": Bolshevik Surveillance in its Pan-European Context', *Journal of Modern History*, vol. 69 (1997), pp. 415–50.

Hosking, G., *A History of the Soviet Union* (London, 1992).

Hosking, G. and Service, R. (eds), *Russian Nationalism Past and Present* (Basingstoke, 1998).

Howlett, J., Khlevniuk, O., Kosheleva, L. and Rogovaia, L., *The CPSU's Top Bodies under Stalin: Their Operational Records and Structure of Command*, The Stalin Era Research and Archives Project, Working Paper No. 1 (Toronto, 1996).

Hudson, H. Jnr, *Blueprints and Blood: The Stalinization of Soviet Architecture, 1917–1937* (Princeton, 1994).

Hughes, J., *Stalin, Siberia and the Crisis of the New Economic Policy* (Cambridge, 1991).

Hughes, J., *Stalinism in a Russian Province: Collectivization and Dekulakization in Siberia* (Basingstoke, 1996).

Ilič, M., *Women Workers in the Soviet Interwar Economy: From 'Protection' to 'Equality'* (Basingstoke, 1999).

Ilič, M. (ed.), *Women in the Stalin Era* (Basingstoke, 2002).

Kennedy-Pipe, C., *Stalin's Cold War: Soviet Strategies in Europe, 1943 to 1956* (Manchester, 1995).

Kershaw, I. and Lewin, M. (eds), *Stalinism and Nazism: Dictatorships in Comparison* (Cambridge, 1997).

Kharkhordin, O., *The Collective and the Individual in Russia: A Study of Practices* (Berkeley, 1999).

Khlevniuk, O. V., 'The Reasons for the "Great Terror": The Foreign-Political Aspect', in S. Pons and A. Romano (eds), *Russia in the Age of Wars, 1914–1945* (Milan, 2000), pp. 159–69.

Khlevnyuk, O. V., 'The Objectives of the Great Terror, 1937–1938', in J. Cooper, M. Perrie and E. A. Rees (eds), *Soviet History, 1917–53: Essays in Honour of R. W. Davies* (Basingstoke, 1995), pp. 158–76.

Khlevnyuk, O. 'The Economy of the OGPU, NKVD, and MVD of the USSR, 1930–1953: The Scale, Structure, and Trends of Development' in P. R. Gregory and V. Lazarev (eds), *The Economics of Forced Labour: The Soviet Gulag* (Stanford, 2003), pp. 43–66.

King, D., *The Commissar Vanishes: The Falsification of Photographs and Art in Stalin's Russia* (Edinburgh, 1997).

Knight, A., *Who Killed Kirov? The Kremlin's Greatest Mystery* (New York, 1999).

Koenker, D. P., Rosenberg, W. G. and Suny, R. G. (eds), *Party, State, and Society in the Russian Civil War: Explorations in Social History* (Bloomington, 1989).

Kojevnikov, A., 'Games of Stalinist Democracy: Ideological discussions in Soviet sciences, 1947–52', in S. Fitzpatrick (ed.), *Stalinism: New Directions* (London, 2000), pp. 142–75.

Kostyrchenko, G., *Out of the Red Shadows: Anti-semitism in Stalin's Russia* (New York, 1995).

Kotkin, S., *Magnetic Mountain: Stalinism as a Civilization* (Berkeley, 1995).

Krementsov, N., *Stalinist Science* (Princeton, 1997).

Labin, S., *Stalin's Russia* (London, 1950).

Lampert, N. and Rittersporn, G. T. (eds), *Stalinism: Its Nature and Aftermath* (Basingstoke, 1992).

Lapidus, G. W., *Women in Soviet Society: Equality, Development, and Social Change* (Berkeley, 1978).

Lenoe, M., 'Did Stalin Kill Kirov and Does it Matter?', *Journal of Modern History*, vol. 74 (2002), pp. 352–80.

Lewin, M., *Lenin's Last Struggle* (London, 1973).

Lewin, M., *The Making of the Soviet System: Essays in the Social History of Interwar Russia* (London, 1985).

Lewin, M., *The Gorbachev Phenomenon: A Historical Interpretation* (London, 1988).

Lewin, M., *Russia/USSR/Russia: The Drive and Drift of a Superstate* (New York, 1995).

Lewin, M., 'Bureaucracy and the Stalinist State', in I. Kershaw and M. Lewin (eds), *Stalinism and Nazism* (Cambridge, 1997), pp. 53–74.

Lewin, M., 'Stalin in the Mirror of the Other', in I. Kershaw and M. Lewin (eds), *Stalinism and Nazism* (Cambridge, 1997), pp. 107–34.

Lewin, M., *The Soviet Century* (London, 2005).

Linz, S. J. (ed.), *The Impact of World War II on the Soviet Union* (Totowa, 1985).

Litvin, A. L., *Writing History in Twentieth-Century Russia: A View from Within* (Basingstoke, 2001).

Malia, M., *The Soviet Tragedy: A History of Socialism in Russia, 1917–1991* (New York, 1994).

Malia, M., *Russia Under Western Eyes: From the Bronze Horseman to the Lenin Mausoleum* (Cambridge: MA, 1999).

Mark, E., 'Revolution by Degrees: Stalin's National Front Strategy for Europe, 1941–1947', Cold War International History Project, *Working Paper No. 31* (Washington D. C., 2001).

Marsh, R., *Images of Dictatorship: Portraits of Stalin in Literature* (London, 1989).

Martin, T., 'The Origins of Soviet Ethnic Cleansing', *Journal of Modern History*, vol. 70 (1998), pp. 813–61.

Martin, T., 'Modernization or Neo-traditionalism? Ascribed Nationality and Soviet Primordialism', in D. L. Hoffmann and Y. Kotsonis (eds), *Russian Modernity: Politics, Knowledge, Practices* (Basingstoke, 2000), pp. 161–82.

Martin, T., *The Affirmative Action Empire: Nations and Nationalism in the Soviet Union, 1923–1939* (Ithaca, 2001).

Mastny, V., *The Cold War and Soviet Insecurity: The Stalin Years* (Oxford, 1996).

Mawdsley, E., *The Stalin Years: The Soviet Union, 1929–1953,* 2nd edn (Manchester, 2003).

Mawdsley, E., 'Crossing the Rubicon: Soviet Plans for Offensive War in 1940–1941', *The International History Review*, vol. 25 (2003), pp. 818–65.

McCagg, W. O., *Stalin Embattled, 1943–48* (Detroit, 1978).

McCauley, M., *Stalin and Stalinism*, 3rd edn (London, 2003).

McDaniel, T., *The Agony of the Russian Idea* (Princeton, 1996).

McDermott, K., 'Archives, Power and the "Cultural Turn": Reflections on Stalin and Stalinism', *Totalitarian Movements and Political Religions*, vol. 5 (2004), pp. 5–24.

McDermott, K. and Agnew, J., *The Comintern: A History of International Communism from Lenin to Stalin* (Basingstoke, 1996).

McDermott, K. and Morison, J. D. (eds), *Politics and Society under the Bolsheviks* (Basingstoke, 1999).

McLoughlin, B., 'Mass Operations of the NKVD, 1937–8: A Survey', in B. McLoughlin and K. McDermott (eds), *Stalin's Terror: High Politics and Mass Repression in the Soviet Union* (Basingstoke, 2003), pp. 118–52.

McLoughlin, B. and McDermott, K. (eds), *Stalin's Terror: High Politics and Mass Repression in the Soviet Union* (Basingstoke, 2003).

Medvedev, R., *On Stalin and Stalinism* (Oxford, 1979).

Medvedev, R., *Let History Judge: The Origins and Consequences of Stalinism*, revised edn (Oxford, 1989).

Merridale, C., *Night of Stone: Death and Memory in Russia* (London, 2000).

Millar, J. and Nove, A., 'Was Stalin Really Necessary? A Debate on Collectivization', *Problems of Communism*, vol. 25 (1976), pp. 49–62.

Morris, J., 'The Polish Terror: Spy Mania and Ethnic Cleansing in the Great Terror', *Europe-Asia Studies*, vol. 56 (2004), pp. 751–66.

Naimark, N. M., *Fires of Hatred: Ethnic Cleansing in Twentieth-Century Europe* (Cambridge: MA, 2001).

Naimark, N. M., 'Cold War Studies and New Archival Materials on Stalin', *Russian Review*, vol. 61 (2002), pp. 1–15.

Nove, A., *Stalinism and After*, 2nd edn (London, 1986).

Nove, A., *An Economic History of the USSR, 1917–1991*, 3rd edn (London, 1992).

Nove, A. (ed.), *The Stalin Phenomenon* (London, 1993).

Osokina, E., *Our Daily Bread: Socialist Distribution and the Art of Survival in Stalin's Russia, 1927–1941* (Armonk, 2001).

Osokina, E. A., 'Economic Disobedience under Stalin', in L. Viola (ed.), *Contending with Stalinism: Soviet Power and Popular Resistance in the 1930s* (Ithaca, 2002), pp. 170–200.

Overy, R., *Russia's War* (Harmondsworth, 1997).

Overy, R., *The Dictators: Hitler's Germany, Stalin's Russia* (London, 2004).

Parrish, M., *The Lesser Terror: Soviet State Security, 1939–1953* (Westport, 1996).

Petrov, N. and Roginskii, A., 'The "Polish Operation" of the NKVD, 1937–8', in B. McLoughlin and K. McDermott (eds), *Stalin's Terror: High Politics and Mass Repression in the Soviet Union* (Basingstoke, 2003), pp. 153–72.

Pohl, J., *Ethnic Cleansing in the USSR, 1937–49* (Westport, 1999).

Pollock, E., 'Stalin as the Coryphaeus of science: ideology and knowledge in the postwar years', in S. Davies and J. Harris (eds), *Stalin: A New History* (forthcoming: Cambridge, 2005).

Pomper, P., *Lenin, Trotsky, and Stalin: The Intelligentsia and Power* (New York, 1990).

Pomper, P., 'Historians and Individual Agency', *History and Theory*, vol. 35 (1996), pp. 281–308.

Pons, S., 'The Papers on Foreign and International Policy in the Russian Archives: The Stalin Years', *Cahiers du Monde russe*, vol. 40 (1999), pp. 235–49.

Pons, S., *Stalin and the Inevitable War, 1935–1941* (London, 2002).

Pons, S. and Romano, A. (eds), *Russia in the Age of Wars, 1914–1945* (Milan, 2000).

Popov, V. P., 'State Terror in Soviet Russia, 1923–1953', *Russian Social Science Review*, vol. 35 (1994), pp. 48–70.

Raack, R. C., *Stalin's Drive to the West, 1939–1945: The Origins of the Cold War* (Stanford, 1995).

Read, C., *The Making and Breaking of the Soviet System* (Basingstoke, 2001).

Read, C. (ed.), *The Stalin Years: A Reader* (Basingstoke, 2003).

Rees, E. A., *Stalinism and Soviet Rail Transport, 1928–1941* (Basingstoke, 1995).

Rees, E. A. (ed.), *Decision-making in the Stalinist Command Economy, 1932–37* (Basingstoke, 1997).

Rees, E. A., 'Stalin and Russian Nationalism', in G. Hosking and R. Service (eds), *Russian Nationalism Past and Present* (Basingstoke, 1998), pp. 77–106.

Rees, E. A. (ed.), *Centre-Local Relations in the Stalinist State, 1928–1941* (Basingstoke, 2002).

Rees, E. A. (ed.), *The Nature of Stalin's Dictatorship: The Politburo, 1928–1953* (Basingstoke, 2004).

Rees, E. A., *Political Thought from Machiavelli to Stalin: Revolutionary Machiavellism* (Basingstoke, 2004).

Rees, E. A., 'Leader Cults: Varieties, Preconditions and Functions' in B. Apor, J. C. Behrends, P. Jones and E. A. Rees (eds), *The Leader Cult in Communist Dictatorships: Stalin and the Eastern Bloc* (Basingstoke, 2004), pp. 3–26.

Reese, R., *Stalin's Reluctant Soldiers: A Social History of the Red Army, 1925–1941* (Lawrence, 1996).

Reid, S., 'All Stalin's Women: Gender and Power in Soviet Art of the 1930s', *Slavic Review*, vol. 57 (1998), pp. 133–73.

Reid, S., 'Socialist Realism in the Stalinist Terror: The *Industry of Socialism* Art Exhibition, 1935–41', *Russian Review*, vol. 60 (2001), pp. 153–84.

Reiman, M., *The Birth of Stalinism: The USSR on the Eve of the "Second Revolution"* (London, 1987).

Richardson, R., *The Long Shadow: Inside Stalin's Family* (London, 1993).

Rieber, A. J., 'The Marginality of Totalitarianism', in Lord Dahrendorf et al. (eds), *The Paradoxes of Unintended Consequences* (Budapest, 2000), pp. 265–84.

Rieber, A. J., 'Stalin, Man of the Borderlands', *American Historical Review*, vol. 106 (2001), pp. 1651–91.

Rieber, A. J., 'Stalin as Georgian: the formative years', in S. Davies and J. Harris (eds), *Stalin: A New History* (forthcoming: Cambridge, 2005).

Rigby, T. H. (ed.), *Stalin* (Englewood Cliffs, 1966).

Rigby, T. H., 'Early Provincial Cliques and the Rise of Stalin', *Soviet Studies*, vol. 33 (1981), pp. 3–28.

Rigby, T. H., 'Was Stalin a Disloyal Patron?', *Soviet Studies*, vol. 38 (1986), pp. 311–24.

Rigby, T. H., *Political Elites in the USSR: Central Leaders and Local Cadres from Lenin to Gorbachev* (Aldershot, 1990).

Rittersporn, G. T., *Stalinist Simplifications and Soviet Complications: Social Tensions and Political Conflicts in the USSR, 1933–1953* (Chur, 1991).

Rittersporn, G. T., 'The Omnipresent Conspiracy: On Soviet Imagery of Politics and Social Relations in the 1930s', in J. A. Getty and R. T. Manning (eds), *Stalinist Terror: New Perspectives* (Cambridge, 1993), pp. 99–115.

Roberts, G., *The Soviet Union and the Origins of the Second World War: Russo-German Relations and the Road to War, 1933–1941* (London, 1995).

Roberts, G., *Victory at Stalingrad* (London, 2002).

Rogovin, V. Z., *1937: Stalin's Year of Terror* (Oak Park, 1998).

Romano, A., 'Permanent War Scare: Mobilisation, Militarisation and the Peasant War', in S. Pons and A. Romano (eds), *Russia in the Age of Wars, 1914–1945* (Milan, 2000), pp. 103–19.

Romanovsky, N. V., *Russia (USSR) under High Stalinism. The Last Phase of Stalin's Rule, 1945–1953* (New Delhi, 1995).

Rosenfeldt, N. E., *Knowledge and Power: The Role of Stalin's Secret Chancellery in the Soviet System of Government* (Copenhagen, 1978).

Rosenfeldt, N. E., 'The Importance of the Secret Apparatus of the Soviet Communist Party during the Stalin Era', in N. E. Rosenfeldt, B. Jensen and E. Kulavig (eds), *Mechanisms of Power in the Soviet Union* (Basingstoke, 2000), pp. 40–70.

Rossman, J. J., 'The Teikovo Cotton Workers' Strike of April 1932: Class, Gender and Identity Politics in Stalin's Russia', *Russian Review*, vol. 56 (1997), pp. 44–69.

Samuelson, L., *Plans for Stalin's War Machine: Tukhachevskii and Military-Economic Planning, 1925–1941* (Basingstoke, 2000).

Sandle, M., *A Short History of Soviet Socialism* (London, 1998).

Sanford, G., *Katyn and the Soviet Massacre of 1940: Truth, Justice and Memory* (forthcoming: London, 2005).

Seaton, A., *Stalin as Warlord* (London, 1976).

Service, R., *A History of Twentieth-Century Russia* (Harmondsworth, 1998).

Service, R., 'Joseph Stalin: The Making of a Stalinist', in J. Channon (ed.), *Politics, Society and Stalinism in the USSR* (Basingstoke, 1998), pp. 15–33.

Shearer, D. R., 'Crime and Social Disorder in Stalin's Russia: A Reassessment of the Great Retreat and the Origins of Mass Repression', *Cahiers du Monde russe*, vol. 39 (1998), pp. 119–48.

Shearer, D., 'Social Disorder, Mass Repression and the NKVD during the 1930s', in B. McLoughlin and K. McDermott (eds), *Stalin's Terror: High Politics and Mass Repression in the Soviet Union* (Basingstoke, 2003), pp. 85–117.

Shukman, H. (ed.), *Redefining Stalinism* (London, 2003).

Siegelbaum, L. H., *Soviet State and Society between Revolutions, 1918–1929* (Cambridge, 1992).

Simon, G., *Nationalism and Policy Toward the Nationalities in the Soviet Union: From Totalitarian Dictatorship to Post-Stalinist Society* (Boulder, 1991).

Slusser, R. M., *Stalin in October: The Man who Missed the Revolution* (Baltimore, 1987).

Smith, J., *The Bolsheviks and the National Question, 1917–1923* (Basingstoke, 1999).

Smith, M. G., 'Stalin's Martyrs: The Tragic Romance of the Russian Revolution', in H. Shukman (ed.), *Redefining Stalinism* (London, 2003), pp. 95–126.

Solomon, P. H. Jr, *Soviet Criminal Justice under Stalin* (Cambridge, 1996).

Stites, R., *Russian Popular Culture: Entertainment and Society since 1900* (Cambridge, 1992).

Stites, R. (ed.), *Culture and Entertainment in Wartime Russia* (Bloomington, 1995).

Stone, D. R., *Hammer and Rifle: The Militarization of the Soviet Union, 1926–1933* (Lawrence, 2000).

Studer, B., Unfried, B. and Hermann, I. (eds), *Parler de Soi sous Staline: La Construction identitaire dans le communisme des années trente* (Paris, 2002).

Studer, B. and Haumann, H. (eds), *Stalinistische Subjekte/Stalinist Subjects/ Sujets staliniens: Individuum und System in der Sowjetunion und der Komintern, 1929–1953* (forthcoming: Zurich, 2005).

Suny, R. G., 'A Journeyman for the Revolution: Stalin and the Labour Movement in Baku, June 1907–May 1908', *Soviet Studies*, vol. 23 (1971–2), pp. 373–94.

Suny, R. G., 'Beyond Psychohistory: The Young Stalin in Georgia', *Slavic Review*, vol. 50 (1991), pp. 48–58.

Suny, R. G., *The Revenge of the Past: Nationalism, Revolution, and the Collapse of the Soviet Union* (Stanford, 1993).

Suny, R. G., 'Stalin and his Stalinism: power and authority in the Soviet Union, 1930–53', in I. Kershaw and M. Lewin (eds), *Stalinism and Nazism* (Cambridge, 1997), pp. 26–52.

Suny, R. G., *The Soviet Experiment: Russia, the USSR, and the Successor States* (New York, 1998).

Suny, R. G. (ed.), *The Structure of Soviet History: Essays and Documents* (New York, 2003).

Suny, R. G. and Martin, T. (eds), *A State of Nations: Empire and Nation-making in the Age of Lenin and Stalin* (New York, 2001).

Suvorov, V., *Icebreaker: Who Started the Second World War?* (London, 1990).

Thurston, R. W., *Life and Terror in Stalin's Russia, 1934–1941* (New Haven and London, 1996).

Thurston, R. W. and Bonwetsch, B. (eds), *The People's War: Responses to World War II in the Soviet Union* (Urbana, 2000).

Timasheff, N. S., *The Great Retreat: The Growth and Decline of Communism in Russia*, reprint edn (New York, 1972).

Todorov, T., 'Stalin Close Up', *Totalitarian Movements and Political Religions*, vol. 5 (2004), pp. 94–111.

Tolz, V., 'New Information about the Deportation of Ethnic Groups in the USSR during World War 2', in J. Garrard and C. Garrard (eds), *World War 2 and the Soviet People* (Basingstoke, 1993), pp. 161–79.

Topitsch, E., *Stalin's War: A Radical New Theory of the Origins of the Second World War* (London, 1987).

Trotsky, L., *The Revolution Betrayed* (New York, 1970).

Tucker, R. C., *The Soviet Political Mind: Stalinism and Post-Stalin Change* (London, 1972).

Tucker, R. C. (ed.), *Stalinism: Essays in Historical Interpretation* (New York, 1977).

Tucker, R. C., 'The Emergence of Stalin's Foreign Policy', *Slavic Review*, vol. 36 (1977), pp. 563–89.

Tucker, R. C., 'The Rise of Stalin's Personality Cult', *American Historical Review*, vol. 84 (1979), pp. 347–66.

Tucker, R. C., 'Stalin and Stalinism: Sources and Outcomes', in M. Hildermeier with E. Müller-Luckner (eds), *Stalinismus vor dem Zweiten Weltkrieg: Neue Wege der Forschung* (Munich, 1998), pp. 1–16.

Uldricks, T. J., 'Soviet Security Policy in the 1930s', in G. Gorodetsky (ed.), *Soviet Foreign Policy, 1917–1991: A Retrospective* (London, 1994), pp. 65–74.

Uldricks, T. J., 'The Icebreaker Controversy: Did Stalin Plan to Attack Hitler?', *Slavic Review*, vol. 58 (1999), pp. 626–43.

Urban, G. R. (ed.), *Stalinism: Its Impact on Russia and the World* (Cambridge: MA, 1986).

van Ree, E., 'Stalin's Organic Theory of the Party', *Russian Review*, vol. 52 (1993), pp. 43–57.

van Ree, E., 'Stalin's Bolshevism: The First Decade', *International Review of Social History*, vol. 39 (1994), pp. 361–81.

van Ree, E., 'Stalin's Bolshevism: The Year of the Revolution', *Revolutionary Russia*, vol. 13 (2000), pp. 29–54.

van Ree, E., *The Political Thought of Joseph Stalin. A Study in Twentieth-Century Revolutionary Patriotism* (London, 2002).

Viola, L., *The Best Sons of the Fatherland: Workers in the Vanguard of Soviet Collectivization* (New York, 1987).

Viola, L., *Peasant Rebels under Stalin: Collectivization and the Culture of Peasant Resistance* (New York, 1996).

Viola, L. (ed.), *Contending with Stalinism: Soviet Power and Popular Resistance in the 1930s* (Ithaca, 2002).

Volkogonov, D. A., 'Stalin As Supreme Commander', in B. Wegner (ed.), *From Peace to War: Germany, Soviet Russia and the World, 1939–1941* (Oxford, 1997), pp. 463–78.

Volkogonov, D., *The Rise and Fall of the Soviet Empire: Political Leaders from Lenin to Gorbachev* (London, 1998).

Volkov, V., 'The Concept of *Kul'turnost'*: Notes on the Stalinist Civilizing Process', in S. Fitzpatrick (ed.), *Stalinism: New Directions* (London, 2000), pp. 210–30.

von Laue, T., *Why Lenin? Why Stalin? A Reappraisal of the Russian Revolution, 1900–1930* (London, 1966).

Ward, C. (ed.), *The Stalinist Dictatorship* (London, 1998).

Ward, C., *Stalin's Russia*, 2nd edn (London, 1999).

Watson, D., *Molotov and Soviet Government: Sovnarkom, 1930–41* (Basingstoke, 1996).

Weeks, A. L., *Stalin's Other War: Soviet Grand Strategy, 1939–1941* (Lanham, 2002).

Wegner, B. (ed.), *From Peace to War: Germany, Soviet Russia and the World, 1939–1941* (Oxford, 1997).

Weiner, A., *Making Sense of War: The Second World War and the Fate of the Bolshevik Revolution* (Princeton, 2001).

Weiner, A., 'Nature and Nurture in a Socialist Utopia: Delineating the Soviet Socio-Ethnic Body in the Age of Socialism' in D. L. Hoffmann (ed.), *Stalinism* (Oxford, 2003), pp. 243–73.

Werth, N., 'A State against Its People: Violence, Repression, and Terror in the Soviet Union', in S. Courtois et al. (eds), *The Black Book of Communism: Crimes, Terror, Repression* (Cambridge: MA, 1999), pp. 33–268.

Wheatcroft, S. G. (ed.), *Challenging Traditional Views of Russian History* (Basingstoke, 2002).

Wheatcroft, S. G., 'From Team-Stalin to Degenerate Tyranny', in E. A. Rees (ed.), *The Nature of Stalin's Dictatorship: The Politburo, 1924–1953* (Basingstoke, 2004), pp. 79–107.

Wood, A., *Stalin and Stalinism*, 2nd edn (London, 2003).

Yakovlev, A. N., *A Century of Violence in Soviet Russia* (New Haven and London, 2002).

Zubkova, E., *Russia After the War: Hopes, Illusions, and Disappointments, 1945–1957* (Armonk, 1998).

Zubok, V. and Pleshakov, C., *Inside the Kremlin's Cold War: From Stalin to Khrushchev* (Cambridge: MA, 1996).

Index